Dangerous Curves

CRITICAL CULTURAL COMMUNICATION
General Editors: Sarah Banet-Weiser and Kent A. Ono

Dangerous Curves: Latina Bodies in the Media
Isabel Molina-Guzmán

Dangerous Curves

Latina Bodies in the Media

Isabel Molina-Guzmán

NEW YORK UNIVERSITY PRESS

New York and London

NEW YORK UNIVERSITY PRESS
New York and London
www.nyupress.org

Library of Congress Cataloging-in-Publication Data

Molina-Guzmán, Isabel.
Dangerous curves : Latina bodies in the media / Isabel Molina-Guzmán.
p. cm. — (Critical cultural communication)
Includes bibliographical references and index.
ISBN-13: 978-0-8147-5735-2 (cl : alk. paper)
ISBN-10: 0-8147-5735-9 (cl : alk. paper)
ISBN-13: 978-0-8147-5736-9 (pb : alk. paper)
ISBN-10: 0-8147-5736-7 (pb : alk. paper)
1. Hispanic American women in mass media. 2. Popular culture—United States.
3. Mass media and minorities—United States. I. Title.
P94.5.W652U665   2010
302.2308968'073—dc22   2009038448

New York University Press books are printed on acid-free paper,
and their binding materials are chosen for strength and durability.
We strive to use environmentally responsible suppliers and materials
to the greatest extent possible in publishing our books.

Manufactured in the United States of America

c 10 9 8 7 6 5 4 3 2 1
p 10 9 8 7 6 5 4 3 2 1

Contents

Acknowledgments

I want to take this moment to thank Larry Gross for showing me how to ask good questions, engage in methodical analysis, and always speak with clarity and passion. It was his belief in me that provided the opportunity to work with New York University Press, and for that I will always be grateful to him.

My deep thanks also go to Antonia Darder and Pat Gill. I would have held on to the manuscript for years before showing it to publishers without their strong encouragement and generous early feedback on the manuscript. I thank them for helping me push the book out the door.

However, I would not have had the space or time to complete this book without key institutional support from the University of Illinois' Program for Research in the Humanities, which provided me with a fellowship and course release time; the University of Illinois' Research Board, which provided me with research assistance funds; and the Latina/Latino Studies Program and Institute of Communications Research, which provided me with course release time and research assistance funds.

For their publishing and scholarly support, I am also indebted to Linda Steiner, former editor of *Critical Studies in Media Communication*; Suzanne Oboler, editor of *Latino Studies*; Félix Gutiérrez, special editor of *Journalism: Theory, Practice and Criticism*; and Myra Mendible, editor of *From Bananas to Buttocks: The Latina Body in Popular Film and Culture* (UT Press). The publication of earlier drafts of chapter 1 and chapter 3 in these outlets gave me the confidence to continue the project and provided me with significant feedback and provocative ideas about how to transform the publications for inclusion in this book.

Numerous colleagues read various chapters at different stages of their development. Paul Allatson, Eileen Diaz McConnell, Aisha Durham, Steve Hocker, Brett Kaplan, and Richard T. Rodríguez, your input was invaluable.

As colleagues and friends, Paul, Eileen, Steve, Ricky, your warmth and friendship is doubly special. *Mil gracias y abrazos.*

Emily Parks, then assistant editor at NYU Press, patiently guided me through the early stages of the project and reviews, and the excellent editorial team of Ciara McLaughlin and Eric Zinner worked to ensure the book's successful completion. Your gentle prodding worked. I thank the team at NYU Press and the excellent selection of anonymous outside reviewers who pushed me to write a more compelling and accessible book.

On a more personal note, moving from the big city to Champaign, Illinois, can make it a lonely, isolating Midwestern college town in which to live and work. Colleagues Fiona Ngo, Mimi Nguyen, and David Coyoca transformed it into an imagined urban oasis filled with culinary delights, smart conversation, and sophisticated humor. My longtime BFF Michelle Kinsman never let me forget my Philadelphia girl. Thank you for making it a more exciting, pleasurable, and bearable place to live and work throughout the past seven years. *Con ázucar y sabor, gracias.*

This particular book was shaped by my intellectual engagement with two *mujeres especial,* Lisa Cacho and Angharad Valdivia.

Anghy's scholarly footprints are all over this book. She is one of the pioneers of the Latino/o Communication Studies field, and my project literally would not exist without her unwavering commitment to feminist scholars of color. Many years ago she paid it forward to me as an awed Penn State undergraduate who did not know that graduate school existed. I hope this book pays it forward to other *mujers de color* striving to find their voice.

As she has done for so many of her colleagues, Lisa generously read through various drafts of this book, sharing her insights and providing me with key theoretical guidance. Our "check-in" meetings kept me on track and showed me the importance of rewarding myself for good work. During the most difficult moments of personal and intellectual frustration with the book, however, my conversations with Lisa about ethnic and race studies, citizenship, and body politics provided a comfortable space to think, work, and nourish myself.

Anghy and Lisa, *gracias* for believing in this book—even when I did not.

That said, this book would not exist in its current form without the efforts of Kevin Dolan. Throughout the six years he worked as my research assistant on this project, he remained intellectually engaged with the book. Ever the excellent journalist, Kevin forced me to unpack my words and write with clarity, and he tracked down every single reference and media citation to ensure the book's accuracy. Always the intellectual, he pushed me to define and refine my arguments, making the end product a better book. (He developed an EndNote style for NYU, watched *Maid in Manhattan,* and read through countless tabloids—need I say more.)

Finally, I end with *un gran abazo de amor para mi familia*—*mi madre* Isabel Luciana Molina, *mi padre* Rafael Antonio Molina, *mis hermanas* Michele Campos *y* Joana Sorrels, *mi sobrino* Brady Sorrels, and "my husband," Ian Sprandel. They not only put up with my long absences and deep silences throughout the writing of this book, they nurtured me with love and humor through my moments of sadness and kept me grounded with life's everyday triumphs and pleasures—*arroz con abichuelas*, Brady's first words, and the latest on J.Lo and *El Gordo y La Flaca*.

Every time I look at this book, I will be reminded that whenever I needed a plate of warm homemade food, a good glass of wine, and a moment away in the sun, Ian was there, regardless of how busy or hectic his own life was at the moment. Ian has been my partner through life for more than twenty years, so we have grown up together. I could not have finished this book without knowing that at the end of it all, he was going to be there waiting for me with a bowl of Puerto Rican spaghetti. Thank you, *mi amor*.

It takes a village to write a book, and my colleagues, friends, and family are that for me. Now that the book is finished, I take full responsibility for all its flaws, and I promise my extended family that, as long as I am not teaching, I will answer my cell phone and return my phone calls.

Introduction

Mapping the Place of Latinas in the U.S. Media

If the 1980s was, as media marketing professionals declared, the decade of the Hispanics, then Latinas have so far owned the new century.[1] Demographic shifts along with the globalization of deregulated media markets have dramatically increased the number of Latina/o media outlets, advertising dollars, and focus on Latina/o audiences.[2] For instance, while overall U.S. advertising revenue declined sharply after the September 11 terrorist attacks, spending on advertisements in Latina/o media has steadily increased, although it still remains a small segment of the overall market.[3] In particular, advertising and marketing professionals have increased their focus on 18- to 34-year-old Latinas, who are often portrayed by the media as avid consumers of everything from baby diapers to mascara.[4] I begin this book by reaffirming the claim that Latina performers, producers, and audiences are thus an essential part of global media culture.

Along with an increase in media and cultural visibility, there has emerged a vibrant field of scholarship, *Latina/o Communication Studies*, so named by Angharad Valdivia in her 2008 book by the same title.[5] I situate myself within both Latina/o studies and media studies to answer Valdivia's provocative questions: What are the contemporary politics of media representations about Latinas/os? And what are audiences asking the media to do in their representations? Throughout the book, I map out the symbolic value assigned to Latinas in a media landscape that remains simultaneously familiar and strangely new. Latina lives continue to be represented through media archetypes and tropes that have existed since the birth of popular film in the early 1900s, yet the new century also has opened more complex representational spaces. Latinas are political advocates, global figures, and producers of their own media stories. I unpack the representational stakes by turning to online audience discussions and blogs about mainstream media depictions of Latina bodies. Through online audience writings about Latina media representations, I chart the complex demands on ethnic women's bodies to stand in for their specific ethnic communities and serve the economic imperatives of globally integrated media industries.[6]

In particular, I document the lives, bodies, and voices of Latinas in the mediascape by engaging in a series of case studies. First, I examine newspaper and television news stories about the Elián González custody case (1999–2000) to understand the changing ethnic, racial, and gender roles that Cuban women played in the controversy. My focus then moves to analyzing celebrity tabloid coverage of Jennifer Lopez (2002–2004) to study Latina sexuality and identity and its surveillance in popular culture. The following two case studies shift attention to mainstream media produced by the iconic Latina celebrity Salma Hayek. I explore the production and reception of Mexican identity in the art-house movie *Frida* (2002) and the global production of Latina multiculturalism in the television series *Ugly Betty* (2006) to illustrate the powerful constraints surrounding representations of Latina lives. The book ends by turning attention to Hollywood depictions of and public discourses about domestic Latina labor and Latina immigration amid the anti-immigration backlash by analyzing Jennifer Lopez's *Maid in Manhattan* (2002) and Paz Vega's *Spanglish* (2004). Together the case studies provide a fertile terrain for charting the changing representational geography of U.S. and global media productions—a mediated terrain where racially ambiguous but ethnically marked feminine bodies sell everything from haute couture to tabloids, and where the lives of ethnic women are the focus of news, media gossip, movies, and online audience discussions. Ethnicity, and specifically minority female ethnic sexuality, can be savored, commodified, packaged, and safely distributed for the consumption of audiences throughout the world.

That said, I move away from a simplistic representational analysis of media stereotypes toward a more complicated discussion of the English- and Spanish-language media as global institutions that contribute to popular knowledge about ethnicity, race, and gender.[7] Underlying my study of the growing demand for multicultural women, their cultural labor, and their stories is recognition of the tumultuous context of a decade defined by increasing tensions about immigration and the associated changes in demographics, both of which are often perceived as threats to established definitions of U.S. citizenship and nation.[8] Examining the tension between the culture industry's demands for ethnic female sexuality and the continuing backlash against ethnic and racial minority women, *Dangerous Curves* positions Latina bodies in the media landscape as both culturally desirable and socially contested, as consumable and dangerous. Thus, the following questions guide the book:

What is desirable and consumable about these women? Under what representational conditions are Latinas depicted as socially acceptable, culturally dangerous, or politically transformative to specific audiences? What are the limits, possibilities, and consequences of Latinas' contemporary global marketability?

Defining the Cultural Dynamics of Latinidad

Studying the symbolic value and cultural reception of Latinas in the United States first demands a careful discussion of the term *Latinidad*. To carry out the goals of this book, I build on Frances Aparicio's work and my collaborative scholarship with Angharad Valdivia, both of which conceptualize Latinidad as a social construct that is shaped by external forces, such as marketing, advertising, popular culture, and the U.S. Census, and internally through the individual subjectivities and communal cultural expressions of people who identify as Latina/o.[9] For example, the advertising industry's consistent use of the traditional large family, the color red, heat metaphors, tropical settings, and salsa music to signify Latina/o identity and culture is an external force that shapes how Latinidad is understood by audiences. At the same time, in his book *Next of Kin,* Richard T. Rodríguez argues that the familiar trope of the close-knit patriarchal Latina/o family as a signifier of Latina/o identity is also an important representational tool for queer Chicana/o artists. Critiques of the Latina/o family through independent film and video allow queer[10] Chicana/o artists to reclaim Latinidad and reimagine their lives as central to the viability of the community. Latinidad thus becomes rearticulated internally through the experiences of queer Chicana/o cultural producers.[11]

While I contribute to the scholarship of Arlene Dávila and Charles Ramírez Berg by examining the signifiers of Latinidad that efficiently communicate stereotypical and archetypical gendered, racialized, and national identities to audiences, my study of Latinidad also focuses on the popular signifiers of Latinidad that may be equally embraced by Latina/o audiences as an opportunity to explore shared and divergent subjectivities.[12] As Aparicio contends, "This approach allows us to rethink the ways in which national categories of identity have limited and elided the new forms of identity formation emerging in Latina/o communities as a result of interlatino affinities, desires, and conflicts."[13] To acknowledge that desires and conflicts exist within and across Latina/o national groups recognizes there are actual and perceived differences and similarities among Latinas from various national, economic, and social backgrounds. The *Frida* case study, for instance, documents conflicts by audiences in the United States and Mexico engaged in competing constructions of Latina, Mexican, and Chicana identity. Thus, one of my objectives throughout the book is to explore audience sense-making about Latinidad through online discussions and blogs (Web logs) to understand emerging contemporary Latina identity positions and realities. Consequently, I analyze media depictions of and audience responses to Latinidad to study the cultural conditions that make Latina identity globally consumable and to interrogate the social and political consequences of increased media visibility for Latina/o communities.[14]

The Ethnoracial Dimensions of Latinidad

At this point, I want to recognize that my conceptualization of Latinidad assumes an ethnoracial Latina/o identity. In his discussion of contemporary Latina/o identity, Silvio Torres-Saillant argues that "in the current discursive atmosphere surrounding the debate on race and ethnicity no existing knowledge or truth claim commands such authority that it can categorically prohibit the fusion of race and ethnicity as a unit of analysis."[15] My work in this book suggests that the mainstream media fusion of ethnicity and race into a Latina/o ethnoracial identity is unstable with sometimes converging and competing definitions of ethnic and racial performances of Latinidad. That is, media signifiers of Latinidad rely on the production of familiar ethnic characteristics that communicate national origin through the use of language, dress, or music, such as the use of Spanish or salsa music to signal Latinidad. At the same time, media signifiers of Latinidad depend on phenotypic racial markers such as facial features, hair texture, and skin color. While at times the ethnic and racial signifiers of Latinidad may work in concert with one another, such as media representations of Salma Hayek as Mexican and brown, at other times they may contradict our commonsense assumptions about Latinidad, such as white Cameron Diaz's more recent identification as Latina.

Ethnicity and race are therefore slippery markers of Latinidad, and ethnoracial readings of identity may be transformed over time. For example, the Elián case study shows transformations in the ethnic and racial identity of Marisleysis González over a period of six months. While Marisleysis occupied the ethnic category of Cuban, she enjoyed the privileges of her assumed whiteness. However, as the media began portraying her as irrational and emotional, Marisleysis became associated with Latina brownness and was relegated to a marginalized identity more defined by the racialized discourse of the anti-immigration backlash toward Mexicans. The book's case studies thus demonstrate that the complex interplay between ethnicity and race in mainstream U.S. media representations of Latinidad must also be examined through the cultural, social, and political process of racialization. Regarding the relationship between racialization and the production of ethnoracial Latina/o identity, Torres-Saillant argues that:

> ethnoracial ontology lies firmly at the core of the construction of Americanness. In their foundational statements, the early ruling elites imagined the United States as a white, European-descended, monolingual nation, leaving outside the contours of Americanness those segments of the population that diverged from the imagined profile.[16]

Therefore, the process of racialization through which groups—regardless of physical appearance, ethnic identity, or national origin—are categorized as different or outside the dominant U.S. classification of social identities is significant for studying depictions of Latinidad, Latina/o identity, and U.S. national identity in the media.[17]

Given the history of Spanish and U.S. imperial conquest in Mexico, Latin America, and the Spanish Caribbean, contemporary mainstream media performances of Latina beauty and desirability—of marketability—enter a complex space. The Spanish colonizer's tolerance for interethnic marriage among the European colonizers, enslaved African, and indigenous populations resulted in social norms more tolerant of miscegenation.[18] Even as the ideology of racial mixture and democracy is celebrated among many Latinas/os, whiteness and white notions of beauty (*blanqueamiento*) still reign supreme, as most clearly exemplified in the representational privileging of lighter-skinned Latinas on television programs produced in Mexico, Puerto Rico, and Venezuela, among other countries.[19] Additionally, Arlene Dávila argues that contemporary U.S. media constructions of Latina identity, beauty, and desirability—often driven by U.S. Latina/o marketing and advertising firms—are also informed by colonial hierarchies of raced and gendered bodies that privilege whiteness over blackness.[20] Most often, mainstream media constructions of Latinidad racialize Latinas/os as brown in relation to whiteness and blackness. As a result, contemporary U.S. media often depict Latinas/os as not quite white but rarely black, instead occupying a panethnic identity space of racially ambiguous and commodifiable brownness. Through analyzing the ethnic and racial signifiers of Latinidad in relation to one another, I document how the media's production of Latinidad is racialized through the dominant Western ideology of racial binaries and racial hierarchies.

In doing so, the book contributes to the scholarship that recognizes Latinidad as an identity construct that always is only partially completed. Scholars such as Valdivia, María Lugones, and Néstor García Canclini have theorized Latinidad as a hybrid identity space.[21] In other words, Latinas/os may embody multiple and simultaneous ethnic and racial affiliations (American, Nuyorican, Afro-Puerto Rican, Chicana, and Latina). Latinas/os may also be ambiguously coded as ethnic and racial, providing for a more flexible performance of identity that does not always cohere to commonsense biological definitions of ethnicity or phenotypic definitions of race.[22] Indeed, according to the 2000 U.S. Census, many Latinas/os opted out of the binary U.S. race game by claiming a racialized otherness. Almost 48 percent of those who identified as Hispanic or Latina/o categorized themselves as white, even though many do not meet the dominant racial phenotypic notions of U.S. whiteness. More than 48 percent identified as "some other race" or "two or more races"— opting out of the Census's long-standing racial categories altogether.[23] The Census figures confirm previous studies that Latinas/os are engaged in an oppositional process of racialization by moving toward more racially flexible identities that are not overdetermined by phenotypic definitions of whiteness or stigmatized associations with blackness.[24] As Tomás Almaguer suggests, "In this regard, racialization is not simply a unilateral process imposed by the state but also reflects the Latino population's active engagement with its own culturally determined understanding of race."[25] Latina/o ethnoracial identity challenges dominant U.S. definitions of ethnicity and race. Thus, in this book I situate Latinas depicted in the mainstream media as women who constantly jostle one another for position within and against established U.S. racial formations that put whiteness at the top and foreground ethnic homogeneity over ethnic specificity.

Consequently, *Dangerous Curves* examines the ethnic and racial instability that surrounds media performances of Latinidad both as a symbol of potential transformations in identity and as an economic rationale for the global circulation of ethnically and racially ambiguous women. Mainstream media constructions of ethnically and racially ambiguous Latina bodies hold the potential to rupture commodified representations of Latina authenticity, hierarchical identity classifications, disciplining binary logic, and essentialist definitions of identity. Ethnic and racial ambiguity and sexualized Latina exoticness are equally central to media industry efforts to use multicultural accents to sell products and programming to global audiences.[26] Women are thus a key element of mediations about Latinidad going back to the nineteenth century. Although heteronormative black, Latino, and Asian masculinity remains threatening to the U.S. patriarchal and racial order, Latina, Asian, and multiracial women often perform a safe yet exotic sexualized femininity because of their racial and ethnic ambiguity.[27] Mainstream media constructions of Latinidad in the United States depend on this unstable ethnic and racial space—not white and not black but ambiguously and unsettlingly brown.

Gendering Latinidad in the Global Media Landscape

Shrinking national borders and an accompanying intolerance for ethnic and racial difference demand safe intellectual spaces to do, as Inderpal Grewal and Caren Kaplan call for, feminist work across cultural and academic borders.[28] The hypervisibility of ethnically and racially ambiguous Latina bodies in the media is illustrative of demographic shifts and global media transformations, but this celebration must be tempered. The speed and accessibility through which media images travel and are consumed demand that we thoughtfully question the media content we consume and consciously reflect on our expectations of the media. Given the anti-immigration context in which contemporary representations of Latinas are consumed in the United States, it is particularly important to think through the media's relationship to the public conversation about citizenship and national identity. One of my guiding arguments is the significance of the mainstream media's construction of Latinidad to affirming traditional notions of the United States as a white, Anglo-Saxon Protestant nation by setting up Latina/o identity and culture as inherently exotic, foreign, and consumable.[29]

I turn now to a more comprehensive discussion about the political, ethical, and theoretical implications regarding the media's ethnic and racial homogenization of Latinidad. First, I am ultimately concerned with the consequences surrounding the increased mainstream commodification and visibility of Latinas and Latina lives. This book focuses specifically on the mainstream media because they are the most widely circulated in the United States and abroad.[30] Even though the digital revolution has decreased production costs throughout the world, U.S.-based media conglomerates remain one of the primary producers and distributors of entertainment and news content.[31] Explaining the importance of the mainstream media in studying Latina/o popular culture, for instance, Michelle Habell-Pallán and Mary Romero argue it is "highly likely that heightened media visibility, counted with the growth of Latino populations throughout the nation, is contributing to the anxieties about who or what Latinas and Latinos are and their status within the nation."[32] It is precisely the "heightened media visibility" of Latinas in news and entertainment that I carefully interrogate by studying the media most audiences are likely to be exposed to inside and outside the United States.

Second, I conceptualize mainstream media as a set of social and institutional practices that produce ways of understanding social identities (race, ethnicity, gender, sexuality, and class). Throughout these case studies I think of mainstream media as a generally cohesive discourse about Latinidad. My application of the term *discourse*, as Alec McHoul and Wendy Grace explain it, is grounded in a Foucauldian approach. They note that "Among critical discourse theorists such as Foucault, the term 'discourse' refers not to language or social interaction but to relatively well-bounded areas of social knowledge."[33] The popular media, which are widely distributed and globally consumed, effectively work to create a discourse about Latinidad.

The media's role in the creation of a discourse about Latinidad and Latina/o identity and culture is particularly significant because most audiences live and play in highly racially segregated spaces. Nancy Signorielli and Larry Gross, members of the Cultural Indicators project, reported decades ago that most of what audiences learn about people who are different from them is through the popular media.[34] Audiences rely on the media to teach them about ethnic and racial communities with whom they do not regularly interact. Consequently, the media behave as a broad and accessible repository of cultural and social knowledge for audiences. For example, Sut Jhally and Justin Lewis's famous study of audience readings of *The Cosby Show* during the 1980s illustrated the significant role the television program played in reinforcing preexisting audience attitudes about race, affirmative action, and black poverty, particularly for white middle-class U.S. audiences with limited intercultural interactions.[35] Likewise, I argue the omnipresent circulation of media images about Latinas becomes part of the cultural ecology that influences general attitudes and beliefs about Latinas and, more importantly, their symbolic status within the nation.

Third, the symbolic values assigned to and associated with Latinas in news, film, and television are informative of preexisting hierarchical social relationships and in turn inform contemporary social and political realities. That is, popular media about Latinas cohere as a discursive regime that supports/colonizes *and* disrupts/ruptures particular ways of understanding the intersections of gender, sexuality, ethnicity, race, and class. In a Foucauldian sense, mainstream media discourses about Latinidad can therefore be explicitly and at times subversively pleasurable and simultaneously productive, albeit tenuously, of dominant power structures.[36] Indeed, Dávila argues:

> The challenge is thus not only to recognize the blurred nature of mass-mediated culture's genres and messages and to point to their variable and unintended modes of public consumption, but to recognize that in a context where nothing escapes commodification, commercial culture cannot be easily reduced to sheer pleasure or commercial manipulation, but must be considered as constitutive of contemporary identities and notions of belonging and entitlement.[37]

In sum, the guiding assumptions of this book call into question the embedded power relations in the media's privileging of particular performances of Latina identity while also highlighting moments of dissonance that contribute to the production of potentially transformative Latina/o social formations for audiences. To explore both sides of this dynamic, I employ two theoretical concepts: *symbolic colonization* and *symbolic rupture.*

Symbolic colonization is an ideological process that contributes to the manufacturing of ethnicity or race as a homogenized construct. It is the storytelling mechanism through which ethnic and racial differences are hegemonically tamed and incorporated through the media. What is of interest in my discussion of symbolic colonization is the ways in which media practices reproduce dominant norms, values, beliefs, and public understandings about Latinidad as gendered, racialized, foreign, exotic, and consumable. Racial formation theory suggests that the meanings assigned to race and racial groups are part of a historically unstable, continuous process intricately connected to political and social structures. Studying symbolically colonizing media documents the mainstream media's participation in the racial formation of Latinidad. Throughout this book I study the visuals, language, and narratives employed by the media to represent Latinidad as an ethnoracial construct located within dominant racial formations.

The second concept, symbolic rupture, turns attention to online audience reception of the mainstream media. Symbolic rupture points to the process of interpretation that allows audiences, including myself, as cultural readers to disrupt the process of symbolic colonization. To explore symbolic ruptures, I analyze audience discussions of the media in blogs and online discussion boards, paying close attention to points of agreement with or opposition to representations of Latinidad. My discussion of symbolic ruptures throughout the book ultimately documents how audiences negotiate uncomfortable transformations in the social and cultural terrain surrounding U.S. national identity, ethnicity, race, gender, and sexuality. For instance, blogs about Marisleysis illustrate how her racially ambiguous body comes to be coded as ethnic outsider and foreign threat while tabloid news stories about Jennifer Lopez code her as as sexually desirable, ethnically and racially ambiguous, and equally threatening to dominant ethnic and racial formations. Blogs about Lopez in turn speak to multiple audience readings that both reaffirm dominant racial formations and symbolically rupture dominant public understandings about gender, ethnicity, and race. The book therefore turns to journalistic and online audience discussions to grapple with the potential for symbolic ruptures within mainstream media depictions of Latinidad.

Symbolic Colonization and the Gendered Production of Latinidad

Media discourses that symbolically colonize Latinas as safe, homogenous, and globally consumable depend on a set of institutionalized media practices otherwise known as gendering or genderization.[38] Lucila Vargas's study of mainstream news practices and coverage of Latinas/os illustrated that Latinas/os are sexualized, feminized, and racialized through the gendered verbal and visual language of the mainstream media.

> This womanish construction of Latino news is achieved not only by downplaying strong masculine Latino voices, but also by relying on "common sense" associations and metaphors that link Latinos to woman as sign, and thus to qualities that a patriarchal capitalist culture regards as unworthy.[39]

The gendering of Latinidad presupposes that femininity and masculinity are interconnected with class, sexuality, race, and ethnicity as a system of social signification. Within the mainstream media Latinas are often gendered as feminine through language about their assumed fertility, sexuality, domesticity, and subservience, among other characteristics. The femininity of Elián's mother, Elisabet Brotons, is confirmed in the media through discussions of her self-sacrificial act to save him from communism.

Gendering is particularly interconnected with racialization as both work together to create a media discourse of Latinidad as Other. A white Latina, for example, may be read as nonwhite because of her national origin, as is Colombian-born Shakira, or because of her accent, as is Mexican-born Hayek. Both women, who are multiethnic and appear to be phenotypically white, are gendered and racialized outside whiteness by the media because of ethnic markers that are commonly associated with U.S. Latinas or Latin America as foreign and exotic. Women who can negotiate ethnic markers (national origin, language, or racial phenotypes) commonly associated with U.S. Latinas or Latin Americans, such as the European-born Penélope Cruz or the "all-American" blond, blue-eyed, California-born Cameron Diaz, may tenuously maintain their claims to whiteness. Together, gendering and racialization produce media discourses that racialize the feminine Other (Shakira and Salma Hayek) and genderize the racial and ethnic Other (Elisabet Brotons)—usually positioning Latinas as ethnic women who exist outside whiteness.

The gendering and racialization of Latinidad is central to symbolic colonization as it contributes to the dissemination of media discourses that present Latinas as homogenized docile bodies. By invoking the concept of "docile body," I am borrowing from Foucault's discussion of social bodies, such as the military or, in this instance, the media, that serve the interest of governance or maintaining governmental stability. For Foucault, the concept of governance is concerned with more than the state's civil institutions—schools, hospitals, prisons, and the military, among others.[40] Bratich, Packer, and McCarthy remind us of the important role culture and cultural institutions, as "a set of reflections, techniques, and practices that seek to regulate conduct," perform in maintaining governance.[41] With regard to the case studies in this book, I propose the corporate-owned mainstream media contribute to the governance of the state by circulating a disciplined and homogenized discourse of Latinidad. The media become, as Foucault suggests, a method for disciplining the ethnic, racial, and gendered body: "These methods, which made possible the meticulous control of the operations of the body, which assured the constant subjection of its forces and imposed on them a relation of docility-utility, might be called 'disciplines.'"[42] Through the media's commodification of gendered constructions of Latinidad—usually grounded in racialized representations of ethnicity—Latina bodies are disciplined into docility. The global media consumption of Latinas, made possible through the gendering and racialization of Latinidad, depends on the representation of Latinas from diverse national backgrounds as similar and familiar docile bodies.

However, as Susan Bordo reminds us, for Foucault "modern power (as opposed to sovereign power) is non-authoritarian, non-conspiratorial, indeed non-orchestrated; yet, it none the less produces and normalizes bodies to serve prevailing relations of dominance and subordination."[43]

Jennifer Lopez's beauty choices regarding her weight, hair color, and hair texture signal a conscious decision to work within dominant media practices about the performance of ethnicity, race, and gender. Nevertheless, as Valdivia points out in the case of Rosie Perez, an actor's decision not to or failure to participate in dominant media practices can be devastating. Perez has cited her accent and her weight as the key reasons for her marginalization within Hollywood.[44] Individuals participate willingly and unwillingly in the disciplining of selves. Latina celebrities' refusal or desire to lighten and straighten their hair or to transform their bodies to be more profitable, successful, and consumable illustrates the complex nature of docility and discipline.

Therefore, throughout this book I document how the media's gendering and interconnected racialization of Latinidad consistently draw upon Latina bodies and those signifiers (children, domesticity, fertility, powerlessness) associated with them. By doing so, I extend the work of Myra Mendible, who argues that cinematic representations of the Latina body have historically mandated docile subjection:

> Since the early nineteenth century, her racially marked sexuality signaled a threat to the body politic, a foreign other against whom the ideals of the domestic self, particularly its narratives of white femininity and moral virtue, could be defined. At the same time, the Latina body offered a tempting alter/narrative: an exotic object of imperial and sexual desire.[45]

Feminine nonwhite bodies are central to the biological, cultural, and social reproduction of the nation and as such must be disciplined in the interest of maintaining governance.[46] Within contemporary mainstream media, Latinas remain a key component of the nation-building project or, as Benedict Anderson so eloquently termed it, the "imagining of the nation."[47] Media discourses about Latinas inform the national imaginary about citizenship and the nation and are in turn defined by the imagined nation. News coverage of Latina immigrants coupled with depictions of Latina domestic workers in Hollywood movies point to ongoing cultural negotiations over the imagined nation brought on by demographic changes through immigration. Postcolonial media theorist Usha Zacharias writes that "cultural studies-related feminist scholarship on nationalism in many ways traces the uneven hegemonic signatures that write the symbolic bodies of women into the nation and the symbolic nation into women."[48] Within the context of the United States and its continuing involvement in regional imperialism and globalization, the mainstream media production of docile Latina bodies is essential to how the nation imagines itself.

For Latinas, it is the gendered media practices that surround sexual exoticness, racial flexibility, and ethnic ambiguity that position them as globally consumable docile bodies subject to the erotic and voracious gaze of the United States. Through dialect coaches, exercise, and dieting, among other bodily practices, Latina actors are expected to display a familiar hyperfemininity and exotic sexuality that always exists in relation to normative white heterosexuality. While some Latina performers such as Eva Longoria voluntarily subject themselves to some forms of bodily discipline, others such as Selena, who was rumored to have undergone liposuction, have been pressured to engage in dietary practices that are at best unhealthy and at worst deadly to attain mainstream success.[49] Each individual body has its symbolic value or worth relative to national discourses of beauty and desire, and some bodies are more vulnerable to discipline and more potentially valuable than others.[50] As such, Latinas embody the twenty-first-century project of discipline, productivity, and docility through the ways in which class, race, ethnicity, and gender intersect in media discourses about them.

Through strategies of surveillance and self-surveillance, the ethnic and racial differences between contemporary Latina public figures are blurred by media discourses that reinforce Western racial, ethnic, gender, and sexual normative standards of femininity, domesticity, beauty, and desirability—of global marketability. The contemporary media gendering of Latinidad maintains the relationship between women as nature and the Platonic binary ideal of masculine/mind over feminine/body.[51] Because the essential male body and the essential white body traditionally have held the most symbolic worth, representations of Latina beauty and desirability in the media translate into the privileging of Latina whiteness over Latina blackness and Latina femininity and heterosexuality over Latina masculinity and queerness. Within this schema, European Penélope Cruz is more beautiful, desirable, and consumable than Afro-Cuban Rosario Dawson, as Valdivia has documented in her work on the Europeanization of Latinidad.[52] Stories about the hyper-heterosexual Puerto Rican Jennifer Lopez are easier to tell and sell than those about queer Mexican artist Frida Kahlo, whose life story was reimagined in the movie *Frida* by emphasizing her heterosexuality. In other words, the gendering of Latinidad depends on the production of docile Latina bodies palatable to global capitalist demands for exotic sexuality, racial flexibility, and socially acceptable femininity while increasing the economic, social, and political subjugation of those same ethnic bodies. Ultimately, the gendering of Latinidad privileges a Latina sexuality that is heteronormative; a Latina ethnicity that is universal; and a performance of racial identity that is not quite white but never black. The gendering of Latinidad reproduces the dominant U.S. hierarchy of social identity that helps maintain the position of white male heterosexual elites who are the primary, but not exclusive, producers of mainstream news and entertainment.[53]

Although, as Anderson argues, the socially constructed borders of the imagined nation are malleable, I propose that its ability to accommodate ethnic and racial foreigners is limited. The symbolic colonization of Latinas and Latinidad within the mainstream media is therefore caught between two forces. On the one hand, Latinas are associated with desirable femininity, domesticity, and the heteronormative family. On the other hand, their ambiguity and sexuality are simultaneously constructed as racial and sexual threats to the national body. For instance, Elián's cousin Marisleysis is initially represented in news stories as appropriately feminine, domestic, and white ethnic, yet her hyper-emotional and defiant attitude along with images of her curvaceous femininity and consumable heterosexuality eventually push the socially acceptable boundaries of Latina ethnoracial identity. She is duly disciplined by the news coverage and audiences for her political, gender, and racial transgressions. The tensions regarding the disciplining and popularity of Latinas throughout the mainstream media weave together the empirical analysis of this book.

Hybrid Latina Bodies and the Production of Symbolic Rupture

But what happens when popular discourses about the nation and national identity are challenged by docile bodies that not only expand but redefine the very borders that contain and/or exclude them? As Foucault contends, power is both repressive and productive, and as such I propose that symbolic colonization depends on a double-edged sword of media practices. While the gendering of Latinidad disciplines the performance of Latina identity in the media, the difficult-to-categorize ethnoracial identity of some Latina bodies challenges dominant definitions of nation and citizenship. Depending on the situation, America Ferrera is American, Honduran, and Latina; Jennifer Lopez is white, black, and brown; and Salma Hayek is Mexican, Lebanese, and American. The contemporary popularity of Latina actors and characters on and off the screen is a testament to the marketability of Latinidad as well as a space of potential discomfort for audiences. Thus, through the case studies I explore the visibility of Latina characters, Latina actors, and Latina experiences in the mainstream media as creating moments of social and cultural dissonance. Indeed, Aihwa Ong suggests that it is the "struggles over representations that are part of the ideological work of citizen-making in the different domains of American life."[54] It is precisely the points of difference, disagreements, and incongruities between audiences that signal the process of imagining the nation.

Therefore, building on Ellen McCracken's arguments regarding the mainstream marketing of Latina authors, I call for an equally nuanced understanding of mainstream media production and reception:

> Crucial social antagonisms rupture the commodified surface of these minority women's narratives. . . . [R]ather than romanticizing ethnic groups as either autonomous or co-opted, a middle ground is necessary in which ethnic groups can be understood as an integral part of capitalist structures while at the same time producing cultural truths not consumed by these structures.[55]

As desirable and consumable subjects, Latinas perform/sell the authentic exotic Other for audiences of diverse linguistic, racial, ethnic, and national subjectivities. However, the fluid cultural, ethnic, and racial heritages of public figures such as Sonia Sotomayor are never quite assimilated or socially accepted, thereby threatening to rupture the dominance of historically established ethnic and racial categories pivotal to U.S. national identity and discourses of citizenship. Always on the margins of whiteness, Latinas also exist outside blackness. The racialized dimensions of Latina ambiguity mean they can never be fully incorporated into a nation obsessed with racial fixity.[56] Jennifer Lopez can be a Latina hip-hop diva or Boricua salsera but not Affleck's white lover. She can perform whiteness (*The Wedding Planner*) and blackness (the music video "Love Don't Cost a Thing"), but she must occupy an ambiguous racialized space between them in mainstream media discourses about her private life and in audience debates over her identity.

As a set of media practices that reproduce dominant norms, values, and beliefs about Latinidad as foreign, exotic, and consumable, symbolic colonization is not a direct, linear, or totalitarian ideological process. Audiences will not always read the gendering of Latinidad in negative or repressive ways. Rather, representations that depend on docile and disciplined depictions of Latinidad are continually negotiated by both media producers and their audiences. The same representations that are repressive are potentially productive of oppositional identity formations. Because media culture is never entirely homogenous and at times may contradict the demands of global capitalism, media discourses about Latinas may actually result in symbolic ruptures that destabilize dominant definitions of nation, citizenship, and ethnic, racial, and gender identity.[57] For example, some Latinas' ethnic and racial multiplicity can result in an undisciplined point of cultural resistance for the audiences who consume mainstream popular culture. Fans of *Ugly Betty* celebrate the universal message of ethnic assimilation and acculturation on the program as much as they cheer the potentially transformative queering of Latina identity and Latina families. They find their own complicated identities ultimately affirmed by the media. The range and diversity in audience responses to gendered media representations of Latinidad reaffirm the long-proved observation that we are social creatures for whom meaning-making is always informed by the social, political, and cultural context in which we live and not the intentions of the producers.[58]

The contemporary popularity of Latinas provides an opportunity for studying gendered and racialized constructions of Latinidad within cultural industries invested in reaching larger and more profitable multicultural and transnational audiences. Since it is precisely the multiracial and multiethnic backgrounds of global Latina figures that are particularly desirable or appealing to audiences, throughout this book I explore audience interpretations of Latinidad in the media. In claiming these multiracial and multiethnic women, some online audiences destabilize dominant U.S. ethnic and racial classifications of nationhood and citizenship. As María Lugones reminds us, maintaining governmental power does not depend on violence for its strength but instead draws on its ability to discipline and normalize through discourse.[59] Thus, the way some audiences make sense of the identity of the Latina figures in this book unsettles established categories of identity and offers potential moments of social, cultural, and political rupture. For instance, the *Frida* audience debate over the ethnic and national identity of Salma Hayek points to the difficulty in defining Latinidad, Latina identity, Mexican identity, ethnicity, and race. While some audiences read Hayek as Latina, Chicana, or Mexican, others did not. The visibility and positive reception of ethnically ambiguous and racially flexible Latina bodies contribute to rupturing binary and essentialist definitions of U.S. racial identity. Multinational media conglomerates can harness the performances of exotic Latina bodies to sell their programming to audiences across national borders, but they cannot control interpretations of the images and stories audiences consume. Paz Vega's whiteness and ethnically ambiguous look allowed her to perform a socially acceptable immigrant Mexican identity in *Spanglish*, but her "Spanish accent" became a source of conflict for some U.S. Latina/o audiences who read it as European and therefore inauthentic. Media industries unwittingly disseminate an unclassifiable difference that cannot be easily controlled, as audience negotiations often reveal.

Case Studies of the Latina Body in the U.S. Media

I explore the symbolic colonization and symbolic ruptures embedded in media discourses and audience readings about Latinas and Latinidad through a comparative media studies approach. The case studies in this book move through newspapers, television news broadcasts, ethnic and racial minority newspapers, tabloids, magazines, film, and television programs. To map out the Latina body in the U.S. media requires tracing it across the entire mediascape—fact and fiction, news and entertainment. My analysis of media representations looks across the page and screen to see how audiences interpret the depictions of Latinidad discussed in the book. I complement my contextual study of the media text by studying mediated audience receptions in such spaces as blogs, Web sites, online discussion boards, and letters to the editor. Finally, the full cultural, social, and political impact of symbolic colonization and symbolic ruptures cannot be evaluated when confined to one ethnic-specific U.S. Latina/o group. As such, the case studies weave together media depictions of Cuban, Mexican, and Puerto Rican women to think through the consequences of globally produced and consumed media that homogenize Latinidad through the practices of gendering and racialization.

I begin by looking at mainstream and ethnic news discourses of Latinidad through the record-setting coverage of the Elián González international custody battle. The first case study focuses on news stories about the lives, voices, and bodies of Cuban women, specifically those of Elián's mother (Elisabet Brotons), his cousin (Marisleysis González), and his grandmothers (Raquel Rodríguez and Mariela Quintana). The Elián case study documents the mainstream media storm surrounding his custody case through an analysis of how Cuban motherhood, womanhood, and femininity were used to convey a melodramatic and compelling story. By studying national English-language television news, English- and Spanish-language newspapers, and minority newspapers, the Elián case study examines the gendering of U.S. Cubans through stories focused on U.S. Cuban domesticity, religiosity, and irrationality. I explore transformations in U.S. Cuban claims to exceptionalist discourses of ethnic whiteness by illustrating their symbolic colonization into racialized brownness and ethnic foreignness. Through language that situated U.S. Cuban identity within popular Latina/o tropes of tropicality, emotionality, and irrationality, U.S. Cubans were symbolically colonized and positioned outside normative definitions of U.S. citizenship. Both the mainstream and ethnic media (not including U.S. Cuban media outlets such as *El Nuevo Herald*) participated in the symbolic colonization of U.S. Cuban identity or Cubanidad—demonstrating that symbolic colonization is not limited to the English-language mainstream media. Mainstream news outlets, African American newspapers, and Latina/o newspapers produced a gendered and racialized discourse about U.S. Cuban exiles that reaffirmed the changing racial status of exiled Cubans from privileged white ethnics to marginalized brown Latina/o immigrants.

Chapter 2 continues the focus on news by examining coverage of Jennifer Lopez's body, sexuality, and ethnic and racial identity in U.S. tabloids (*People, Us Weekly, Star, in Touch, National Enquirer*). In particular, it explores Lopez's performance as a racially flexible, sexually exotic, and ethnic docile body. Through careful discursive analysis, I document the tabloids' celebration of Lopez's marketable, ethnically ambiguous, and racially flexible body (not white but not black), as well as the turn against her for disrupting established U.S. ethnic and racial categories through her interethnic relationship with one-time fiancé Ben Affleck. Like the Elián case study, the Lopez saga shows that even as Latina bodies move across racial and ethnic categories, those categories are inevitably stabilized through symbolically colonizing media narratives. In both case studies, the ethnic and racial markers that exist outside whiteness and blackness create Latina bodies that are both economically productive/useful and culturally threatening. Given the complicated and tenuous position of Puerto Ricans within U.S. discourses about the imagined nation, I tease out the contemporary symbolic status of Puerto Ricans specifically and Latinas more generally in the tabloid coverage of Lopez. To do so, I contextualize the tabloids' gendering of Lopez against tabloid coverage of other celebrities such as Beyoncé Knowles, Jennifer Garner, and Julia Roberts. The case study concludes by analyzing audience readings of the tabloid coverage through celebrity gossip Web logs (blogs) and discussion threads responding to them. My analysis of blog postings and discussion boards indicates that some audiences reaffirm the tabloids' conservative racial ideologies while other audiences embrace Lopez as a multicultural symbol of ethnic pride. Rather than focusing on Lopez's cinematic and musical performances, I document how tabloid stories, as part of media discourses about Latinidad, symbolically colonize Lopez by producing a docile Latina/Puerto Rican body that is disciplined for her racial, sexual, and physical transgressions.

The next three case studies shift from news as entertainment to television and film as important elements of the public sphere. In the third case study, I focus attention on Salma Hayek and her production of *Frida*. I first discuss the movie's performance of ethnic authenticity through its symbolic colonization of Mexican identity and the gendering of Latinidad. The case study then turns to U.S. Latina/o and Mexican media audience negotiations over the movie's construction of Mexican ethnicity to further explore the limits of producing a consumable ethnic identity and the potential for symbolic ruptures over the mediation of Mexican and Latina identity. Audiences must negotiate the global demands for a consumable feminine Latinidad. Such was the case for U.S. Latina/o media, Mexican media, and online audience receptions of *Frida*. In particular, Mexican newspaper and IMDb (Internet Movie Database) audience discussions about Salma Hayek and *Frida* demonstrate the problematic nature of globally commodified media representations of gendered Latinidad and the limits of symbolic colonization by highlighting alternative constructions of ethnic and racial Latina/o identity. The *Frida* case study exemplifies the double-edged sword of symbolic colonization by analyzing the convergences and divergences among online audiences, Mexican newspapers, and mainstream English-language and U.S. Latina/o media discourses about Hayek and the movie.

The production of synergistic programming and use of cross-promotion strategies by media conglomerates encourage the development of shows and personalities that can easily move across multiple audience demographics. The fourth case study explores the cultural politics surrounding one such program, ABC's 2006 prime-time hit *Ugly Betty*. Mainstream entertainment coverage, audience blogs, and online discussion boards about the show provide insight into the hypervisibility of Latinidad as central to the future growth of global cultural industries. While the show's use of the personal and professional lives of two young second-generation Mexican women potentially disrupts popular conceptions of Latinas, their difference is ultimately contained through an emphasis on universal deracialized story lines dealing with love, family, beauty, and social acceptance. Thus, *Ugly Betty* illustrates the ways in which Latinas embody media industry efforts to use ethnic difference, racial ambiguity, and multicultural accents to sell products and programming to global audiences. However, the program's queer story lines and performance of working-class ethnic femininity symbolically ruptures the show's more homogenized construction of Latinidad. Readings of online audience and fan responses reveal nuanced negotiations surrounding the commodification of Latina panethnicity as a global multicultural product.

Representations of Latina work within the mainstream media serve the interest of a global state that economically benefits from the feminization of transnational migration and labor while also allowing media industries to tap into multiple ethnic, racial, and national audiences. The final case study examines the political dimensions of cinematic representations of Latina femininity and gendered Latina labor in the movies *Spanglish* and *Maid in Manhattan*. As cinematic constructions of Latina migration and labor grounded in the gendering of Latinidad, the movies erase the diverse, sometimes violent trajectories of transnational Latina immigrants and workers. Both movies depoliticize Latina work within the cultural sphere during a period of nativist backlash against immigration, pointing to the political consequences of symbolic colonization in media discourses about Latinidad. Mainstream media representations of Latina labor are cleansed of anti-immigration/imperialistic economic discourses and rearticulated through safer, historically familiar, and more comfortable representations of Latina domesticity and hyperfemininity. Such media omissions are significant because when the U.S. southern border is identified as a potential site of terrorism, the nostalgic imagery surrounding cinematic representations of Latina migration and labor contributes to the symbolic colonization of Latinidad by erasing the anti-immigration backlash that informs contemporary U.S. culture and politics.

Together the case studies map the media discourses about Latinas and Latinidad that circulate through a broad range of media genres (film, television, news, blogs, and Internet discussion boards) and media industries (mainstream, Latina/o, and ethnic non-Latina/o). Ethnic women have become the body of choice to inform and entertain multiple global audiences. As a result, it is critical to explore the role of the mainstream media and their audiences in disciplining, controlling, and contesting media discourses about Latinas and Latinidad. *Ugly Betty* and *Frida* illustrate the nuanced complexities of performing and selling an authentic Latina identity for global audiences. Representations dependent on the symbolic colonization of Latinidad through gendering are peppered throughout the media landscape in the news coverage of Elián, the publicity tour for *Frida*, the tabloid coverage of Jennifer Lopez's relationship with Ben Affleck, the entertainment news coverage of *Ugly Betty*, and the romantic comedy representations of Latina labor in Hollywood. Woven together, the case studies provide an intellectual space to think through the oppositions between the social, political, and cultural threat of Latinidad in the contemporary United States and the global demand for ethnically ambiguous and racially flexible yet authentic Latina bodies.

I also examine online audience readings of the representational politics surrounding Latinidad to disturb my potentially totalizing interpretations of symbolic colonization. As such, I recognize that audiences do not exclusively consume one medium in isolation from others, and in the virtual age of the Internet and multimedia technology, they often consume more than one medium simultaneously. Indeed, in the case of Latina/o audiences, the Pew Hispanic Center has found that Latina/o media consumption is multiversed, spanning across the English- and Spanish-language media.[60] Blogs and discussion boards allow audiences from diverse gender, class, ethnic, racial, and national backgrounds to collaboratively produce alternative ideological spaces to interpret and reaffirm oppositional identity formations.

Together the case studies point to the contemporary production of Latinidad as a mediated form of social, political, or economic capital. Mainstream media discourses about Latinas are indicative of the complex and complicated issues surrounding U.S. ethnic and racial classifications.[61] Lopez explicitly embraces her racial flexibility and Nuyorican (New York Puerto Rican) identity as a sellable marker of her panethnic Latina identity and the multicultural U.S.-Puerto Rican experience. Frida Kahlo, who existed before the label was created, is often treated as an iconic representative of Latinidad. And Salma Hayek, America Ferrera, and Paz Vega, all of whom once resisted identifying as Latinas, are benefitting from the media industry's fascination with Latinidad. Indeed, Hayek's and Ferrera's conflicted relationship with identifying as Latinas speaks to the vexed nature of the term much less its mediated representation. Throughout the early part of her career, Hayek privileged her Mexican and Latin American identity over associations with the racialized U.S. term *Latinas/os*. On the other hand, Ferrera, who grew up in a predominantly white Los Angeles community and school district, did not identify with or cultivate social or political relationships with Latinas/os or Chicanas/os until later in her adult life. Yet, both women have become contemporary media symbols of U.S. Latinidad. The case studies thus challenge and explore the efficacy and stability of Latinidad and Latina/o identity within media discourses of ethnicity and race. Rather than elide the cultural distinctions that exist among Jennifer Lopez, Salma Hayek, and Frida Kahlo or erase the problematic questions surrounding the ethnic and racial identification of Jessica Alba or America Ferrera as U.S. Latinas, this book engages media discourses about Latinidad through specific media case studies to explore the complex contemporary cultural terrain of Latina identity during a period of great public anxiety about changing definitions of citizenship in the United States and abroad.

1

Saving Elián

Cubana Motherhood, Latina Immigration, and the Nation

I begin this book by examining the journalistic production of Latinidad in the mainstream and ethnic U.S. news media.[1] Although media scholars often pay attention to the social or political role of news in influencing attitudes and behavior, little attention is given to the cultural function news performs. Within the media landscape, news is the privileged site of information for public sphere debates about immigration and citizenship. However, in this chapter I propose that news plays other equally essential roles. As Barbie Zelizer suggests, the news media are storytellers, and as storytellers they document and speak to contemporary anxieties about the nation and the changing status of marginalized groups within the national body.[2] Journalists are, however, unique storytellers. Film and television are categorized as fantastical fiction, news as "truth" or "fact."[3] Together, fiction and "fact," entertainment and news, comprise an integrated media terrain of discourses about gender, ethnicity, and race. To study contemporary journalistic accounts of Latina identity and Latinidad, I begin with the social and political implications of how the news media, as privileged storytellers, covered one of the biggest Latina/o news stories in the history of United States—the 1999–2000 Elián González transnational custody battle.

While the population of Latinas/os in the United States has dramatically increased throughout the past ten years, Latinas/os remain seriously underrepresented in print and television news. According to a report by the National Association of Hispanic Journalists, of all the news stories on ABC, CBS, CNN, and NBC in 2000, 0.53 percent were about Latinas/os, down from 1.3 percent in 1999. However, the 2000 figures did not include one major anomaly—news coverage of Elián González, a six-year-old Cuban boy rescued in international waters by U.S. fishermen on Thanksgiving Day in 1999.[4] Few stories in recent U.S. history captured the popular imagination and media's interest like the dramatic and sometimes surreal events regarding Elián's international custody battle—a photogenic Cuban boy sees his mother drown at sea as they travel on a rickety makeshift boat to the United States; the boy recovers in a Miami hospital as members of his exiled Cuban family, all of whom he has never met, claim legal custody of him; a heartbroken Cuban father and loyal communist party member involuntarily separated from his son challenges the legal rights of the Miami family; once-dormant Cold War tensions escalate as Cuba demands the return of the child; and a beautiful young second-generation Cuban American woman performs the role of nurturing mother for a grieving boy and a community in exile. The four major U.S. television news networks (ABC, CBS, NBC, and CNN) alone devoted 36.5 hours, or 5 percent of their overall programming time, to coverage of the Elián controversy. According to the Center for Media and Public Affairs, the Elián case received more television news coverage than the Columbine shootings, the death of Princess Diana, and the death of John F. Kennedy, Jr.[5] The only other nonelection story to receive more television news coverage was the first O. J. Simpson trial for the murder of his ex-wife. From the day of his rescue on November 23, 1999, until the day he departed with his Cuban father on June 28, 2000, the conflict among the Cuban government, the U.S. government, and the Miami Cuban exile community over Elián's immigration status captured the popular imagination and media interest in unprecedented fashion. By the spring of 2000, at the height of news coverage about Elián, 78 percent of the U.S. population was actively and regularly following the news surrounding the young boy and his family.[6]

Through this case study, I illustrate that underlying the Elián media coverage were cultural anxieties over globalization, immigration, and demographic increases in Latina/o populations. The Elián news coverage focused on Cuban immigrants during a time of increased domestic nativism and political backlash toward Latina/o immigration.[7] U.S. Cubans, one of the United States' most politically powerful and racially privileged Latina/o groups, found themselves in an unprecedented public storm critical of the exile community and U.S.-Cuban foreign policy.[8] Like the national polls, public opinion surveys in Florida, home to the largest population of Cubans in the United States, revealed stark ethnic and racial divisions.[9] While U.S. Cubans overwhelmingly supported the Miami relatives' right to file an asylum claim on Elián's behalf, Anglo American, African American, and non-Cuban Latina/o residents staunchly supported the father's bid for Elián's return to Cuba.[10] In an ethnographic study of contemporary ethnic and racial divisions in Miami, Stepick, Grenier, and colleagues argued that the Elián controversy "brought even the most peripheral citizens of the region face-to-face with profound issues of identity, power and prejudice."[11] The Elián case presents an opportunity for exploring the contested symbolic status of Cuban women in the cultural battle over U.S. definitions of nation and citizenship.[12] Below the story's surface brewed a noxious tempest against Latina/o immigration generally and U.S. Cuban exile privilege specifically. Columns, blogs, and letters to the editor in Miami's leading newspaper revealed a backlash against forty years of Cuban/Latina/o immigration. The ethnic news media, with the exception of *El Nuevo Herald*, similarly used the Elián case to point out policy disparities and racial inequities in U.S. immigration policy.

In the Elián news coverage, the media circulated a homogenizing construction of Latinidad that symbolically colonized the historically privileged immigration and racial status of Cubans, in turn reaffirming dominant U.S. racial formations. As discussed in the introduction, media discourses that symbolically colonize Latinas/os depend on a set of institutionalized practices otherwise known as genderization and the interconnected process of racialization.[13] Together, gendering and racialization, the process through which groups regardless of ethnic or national origin are assigned racial meaning, produce media discourses that symbolically colonize Latinas/os as marginalized and governable bodies. Because of the journalistic emphasis on young Elián, his Miami and Cuban families, and his Cuban American caretaker, studying the linkages between the gendering of Cuban identity and racialization of U.S. Cuban citizenship is central to making sense of the story. The Elián case illustrates how femininity, motherhood, and the Latina body are key sites for cultural and political conflicts over citizenship and immigration. In particular, both Elisabet (Elián's biological mother) and Marisleysis (Elián's surrogate mother) were integrated into the news coverage as contested stand-ins for national identity—one immigrant and the other "American." Both the mainstream and ethnic news media symbolically colonized Miami's exile community by feminizing exile Cuban identity through news stories grounded in irrationality, emotionality, domesticity, and religiosity, thereby racializing U.S. Cuban behavior as outside the norms of socially acceptable whiteness and blackness. The Elián story as infotainment provocatively signals the completion of U.S. Cubans' transformation from celebrated political, ethnic exiles to marginalized U.S. racial minorities.

As central figures (both living and dead) in the conflict, I pay particular attention to the journalistic rendering of the lives, voices, and bodies of Cuban women, specifically those of Elián's mother (Elisabet Brotons), cousin (Marisleysis González), and grandmothers (Raquel Rodríguez and Mariela Quintana).[14] The chapter's first section analyzes the symbolic politics of

Cuban motherhood. I situate news stories about Elisabet against stories about Mexican and Caribbean immigration, femininity, and motherhood to better understand the unique position she occupies in the U.S. national imaginary. The memory of Elián's dead mother, Elisabet, stands in for multiple competing national interests. That is, Elisabet becomes one of the primary vehicles evocative of the rights of a nation in exile. At the same time, her Cuban identity is recuperated through the voices of Elián's grandmothers, Mariela and Raquel. The romantic framing of Elisabet as self-sacrificing mother is counterbalanced in the media coverage through a competing frame focused on the extreme religiosity and suffocating familial ties of the exile Cuban community. I then explore how mainstream news stories about the unification of Juan Miguel González and his son Elián—five months after Elián's rescue at sea—work in contrast to *El Nuevo Herald's* emphasis on the exile community's rights to political asylum. By focusing on the importance of family reunification and paternal rights, the news coverage about Juan Miguel González affirms the symbolic status of fatherhood and the political power of the federal government in maintaining legal and political order over ethnic and racial minorities. The needs of the father and the nation outweigh the demands of Miami's Cuban exile community. Finally, the last two sections examine the gendering and racialization of Marisleysis as a stand-in for the exile Cuban community. News coverage critical of Marisleysis weakened the discourse of Cuban exceptionalism. As a family and community spokeswoman to the English-language media, Marisleysis' emotional instability and public threats of civil disobedience against the U.S. federal government contributed to her gendered marginalization and the racialization of the Cuban exile identity as nonwhite ethnics.

Contextualizing Cuban Immigration in the Contemporary U.S. Media

Until the 1980s, news stories framed Cubans and Cuban migration through the perspective of Cuban exceptionalism and U.S. Cold War foreign policy.[15] For example, news coverage of the 1960s Pedro Pan program, which allowed parents opposed to Castro's communist government to send their unaccompanied children to the United States, overwhelmingly framed Cubans as political rather than economic immigrants. María de los Angeles Torres's work on the Pedro Pan program documents how news images of these young children leaving their families in Cuba and entering the United States alone cultivated sympathy for the community as temporary political refugees rather than ethnic immigrants.[16] The emotionally laden visuals of child refugees signaled the repressive consequences of communism and bolstered popular Cold War rhetoric serving the United States' political, ideological, and symbolic goals.[17] Throughout the 1960s and 1970s, Cuban exiles were continually represented in the news as white, middle- to upper-class, educated, politically conservative, and unquestionably committed to U.S. capitalism and democracy.[18]

Popular conceptions of Cuban exiles throughout the 1960s and 1970s also differed radically from those surrounding the U.S.-Mexico Bracero Program (1942–1964) or the U.S.-Puerto Rico Operation Bootstrap program (1947–1965). Unlike Cuban émigrés, the hundreds of thousands of Mexican and Puerto Rican laborers who came to the United States under these programs faced media invisibility and distinct economic, racial, and linguistic discrimination. The United States provided exiled Cubans with special financial and educational programs to assist their transition, yet gave Mexicans and Puerto Ricans primarily working in labor-intensive agricultural, manufacturing, and domestic service jobs little access to federal assistance. Braceros toiled mostly under substandard working conditions in the agricultural fields of California, the Southwest, and the Midwest, while Puerto Ricans, especially women, were primarily expected to work in low-wage nonunion manufacturing and domestic service jobs in the Northeast and Midwest. Moreover, while Cubans and Puerto Ricans were encouraged to come to the United States as heteronormative family units, male Bracero workers were often forced to leave behind their families in Mexico.[19] Because Cubans were constructed as political refugees whose presence within the nation's imagined borders would be temporary, their depictions in the media benefited from a fragile protection against ethnic and racial discrimination.[20] On the other hand, Mexican immigrants, who were legally defined as temporary economic migrants, have historically faced negative news coverage accompanied by mass involuntary deportations during moments of economic crisis, such as the Great Depression.[21]

However, the continued and stable growth of the exiled Cuban community in the decades after their initial arrival—along with the economic recession of the 1980s and the waning importance of the Cold War—triggered an intense public backlash against Cuban immigration. Much of the news coverage focused negative attention on the 1980 Mariel boatlift that brought 125,000 Cubans to Miami. The negative coverage continued as thousands of Balseros began traveling to the United States in rickety makeshift boats. No longer celebrating the political courage and self-sacrifice of first-wave Cuban families, the mainstream media highlighted the racial and economic difference surrounding the "new" third wave of Cuban refugees.[22] Unlike the white middle-class professional Cubans of the 1960s and 1970s, the majority of recent Cuban exiles were black, single, and working-class laborers. The media drew attention to the race, gender, and sexuality of the Mariel and Balsero exiles (many were accused of being pedophiles and having sexually transmitted diseases), resulting in a competing news frame about Cuban exiles.[23] Given this new, more gendered and racialized construction of Cuban immigrants, recent Cuban immigrants have been welcomed by an increasingly hostile U.S. public, especially in Miami, where Cubans are the largest ethnic and racial minority group. In an attempt to deal with the backlash toward Cuban immigrants and normalize Cuban immigration, President Bill Clinton entered into the first formal immigration agreement with the Castro government in 1994. Contemporary media discourses about exiled Cubans are thus complicated. U.S. Cubans are defined both as ethnic and racial outsiders, such as in news accounts of the Marielitos and Balseros, and as "honorary white ethnics" through their Cold War position as political exiles.

Despite the negative framing of Cuban immigrants since the 1980s, the mainstream news media have traditionally excluded them from the anti-immigration discourse about Latina/o immigration. In other words, the backlash against Latina/o immigration has not generally included Cubans, until more recently that is. Indeed, a 1997 study of mainstream U.S. newspapers by Louis DeSipio and James Henson found that U.S. Cubans were more likely than Puerto Ricans and Mexicans to be covered by journalists through positive news stories focused on their political strength in Florida and their central role in U.S. foreign policymaking about Latin America.[24] U.S. Cubans were overrepresented in the mainstream news relative to their share of the U.S. Latina/o population and more likely to be depicted in stories about electoral politics and foreign policy rather than economic or social issues, such as immigration. As a point of contrast, news coverage about California's anti-immigration Proposition 187 in 1994 focused almost exclusively on the economic and social impact of Mexican immigration to the exclusion of other ethnic minority groups, even though Asians and Central Americans were and continue to be two of the state's fastest growing populations.[25]

Maternal Interventions and the Cultural Politics of Cuban Immigrant Motherhood

"Motherhood" is one of the central tropes associated with the politics of the family and the culture of domesticity in the United States. It is also one of the dominant storytelling devices associated with the gendering of

Latinidad. Within entertainment media, the self-sacrificing, almost virginal mother is a staple for most Hollywood dramas about Latinas/os, specifically Mexican women, such as Gregory Nava's movie *My Family, Mi Familia* (1995) or his PBS drama "American Family" (2002–2004).[26] Nonetheless, rarely are stories of self-sacrificing Latina mothers circulated in the news. When Latinas are discussed in the news, especially in the context of the anti-immigration politics sweeping through the United States and Europe, they are usually associated with undocumented immigration, hyperfertility, and demographic growth. More recently, in the wake of the 2006 U.S. immigration rights marches that swept the country, mainstream and Latina/o news organizations paid substantial attention to undocumented Latina immigrants as a way to humanize the issue through politically safer accounts of victimhood, transnational motherhood, and Latina/o family dynamics.[27] Whether constructed as criminals or as victims, Latina motherhood remains a central part of how the media make sense of Latinidad.

Romancing Elisabet

The absence of women and Cubans from the mainstream news coverage about immigration created the perception that Elisabet's journey from Cuba was special or unique. According to the 1994 Clinton-Castro agreement and the 1995 revision to the Cuban Adjustment Act, more than 17,000 Cuban immigrants to the United States are allowed to arrive safely and legally by airplane each year. (The United States can provide up to 20,000 visas per year but usually does not.) Nevertheless, it is the yearly life-and-death drama of the fewer than 2,000 Cubans who make the illegal journey by sea that provocatively captures the media's attention. The mundane, safe, and legal arrivals by Cuban émigrés lack drama and conflict. Elisabet's journey to the United States via an overloaded makeshift boat and her subsequent drowning in the shark-infested waters of the Florida Straits provided an emotionally dramatic backdrop for conservative anti-Castro politicians. Conservative U.S. Cuban politicians gain little from news coverage of the U.S.-Cuba visa program, viewed by some as the first step toward the normalization of U.S.-Cuban relations, and benefit greatly from the media storm regarding a boy whose mother died illegally fleeing the "tyranny of communism."

When compared with the virtual erasure of Arianna Horta, a mother on board Elián's boat who survived the fateful journey to Florida, we see how Elisabet's death as sacrificial mother was central to the journalistic storytelling.[28] Unlike Elisabet, Horta was a visible brown Cuban body who could testify to her own story and needs. Although she, too, was separated from her children—who remained in Cuba under their grandmother's care—her explicit desire to remain in Miami and be reunited with her two young girls was all but ignored by the mainstream and ethnic media. It was precisely Elisabet's bodily sacrifice, her death, that played a pivotal role in the political contestation over family, home, and nation. Elisabet's invisibility produced a provocative news peg through which journalists and competing social groups reimagine her life, needs, and desires to serve their interests.[29]

Elisabet functioned within the mainstream news stories as a type of disembodied Latina who subverts but does not erase women's voices and bodies from the dominant imaginary. She is thus a semiotic shadow casting a flickering shape on the public discourses about immigration without incorporating her body into the racialized politics of immigration in the United States. Unable to speak on her behalf, Elisabet's invisibility provides a contested space for narrating women's immigration experiences in the mainstream media. That is, the lack of an actual body or voice allows others to invoke her invisible body to celebrate or discipline the missing and the dead. Within the media, Elisabet's deceased body became a floating signifier—desexualized, gendered, and racialized. For Miami's mostly Cuban *El Nuevo Herald* staff, the gendered disembodiment of Elisabet created an opening for the circulation of sympathetic pro-Cuban exile stories, specifically that of the self-sacrificing mother. For the mainstream and other ethnic media, however, the self-sacrificing mother frame was questioned through stories about unequal immigration policies toward other Caribbean and Latin American immigrants.

Consequently, news coverage about Elisabet functioned in two ways: as emotional spectacle demanding discipline and as a contested but disciplined site of national ideologies. The figure of Elisabet was simultaneously central and peripheral to the news coverage. She was consistently nameless, subjectless, identified only through her biological relation to Elián. While doing research for this book, finding Elián's mother's name, much less its correct spelling, proved difficult. The mainstream and ethnic news coverage often referenced Elisabet only in relation to the child "whose mother died at sea as she was bringing him to Florida."[30] Her self-sacrificial life was mythologized through retellings in the mainstream media by exiled Cuban sources. As one survivor told the *Miami Herald*, "She (Elisabet) sacrificed until the end. . . . She gave him the remaining water and tied him to an inner tube until the last night, in the middle of the dark. Looking beyond at Miami's city lights she told me, 'Help me, help the boy get there.'"[31] Elisabet was the nameless mother who sacrificed herself to provide her son a better life in the United States.

The few visual images of Elisabet that circulated through the media reinforced her virginal maternal status. In two of the three family pictures released to the media, she is shown alone with Elián. In each of the photos, she looks into the camera, smiling softly while adoringly holding her young son. The third photograph shows Elisabet, Elián, and his biological father, Juan Miguel González. It is a classic family portrait, one that elides the more complicated sexual politics of her life. In her conservative attire, wearing little or no makeup, Elisabet presents in all three images simply as mother, not as worker, daughter, wife, or lover. Adding to Elisabet's maternal innocence is the scarcity of references to her personal, romantic, and sexual life, such as information about the man she was living with and possibly married to, Lazaro Muñero, one of the organizers of the illegal journey,[32] or the birth of Elián years after her official divorce from Juan Miguel González. Reducing her to a maternal descriptor, the news media positioned her within long-established popular archetypes of socially acceptable Latina femininity and domesticity, that of the self-sacrificing, almost virginal ethnic mother who gives up her happiness, in this instance her life, so that her child can obtain the "American Dream" of meritocracy and upward mobility.

The romanticized treatment of Elisabet as a "white ethnic" self-sacrificing mother in the mainstream news stands in stark opposition to the media reception surrounding other Latina immigrants. Six years after Elián's famous departure, another undocumented immigrant, Mexican citizen Elvira Arellano, fought to remain united with her son, Saul Arellano, a U.S. citizen.[33] Arellano, a single mother, initially was arrested in a 2002 immigration raid at Chicago's O'Hare International Airport, where she worked as a cleaning woman to take care of her disabled child. In 2006, after she failed to appear at a hearing for a Social Security fraud charge resulting from the initial arrest, the U.S. Department of Homeland Security issued a deportation order that led Arellano to become a vocal and visible national activist for families facing separation because of their mixed-citizenship status. She was ruled a fugitive in 2006 and spent a year living under the protection of a Chicago church. Arellano was arrested in 2007 during a trip to Los Angeles, where she was organizing immigration activists. At the height of the conflict, Arellano's supporters threatened "Elián-style" protests, and Saul, who was thrust into the media spotlight, came to be known as the "Mexican Elián."[34]

The differences in initial media coverage and public reception of the Elián and Arellano cases draw into view inequities in U.S. immigration law and the racially skewed perception surrounding Latina/o immigration. In the 1965 Hart-Cellar Act, family reunification became a cornerstone of U.S. immigration practices and policies. However, because immigration laws only provide for adult children, there is no consistent policy to deal with family reunification in the case of minor children. The Pew Hispanic Center estimates there are 1.8 million undocumented child migrants and 3.1 million children who are U.S. citizens living in households with at least one undocumented parent.[35] While the U.S federal government strongly argued for family reunification in the Elián case, it declined Arellano's bid for maintaining the family unification of her U.S.-born child. Juan Miguel González's paternal bid for custody of his child was privileged, and Arellano was left with an awful decision—leave her child in the only country he had ever known or take him to a country whose language he didn't speak.

Unlike the saintlike news stories about Elisabet, Arellano's integrity as a Mexican immigrant mother was often questioned by *Chicago Tribune* editorialists and letter writers who, using racially charged language, accused her of having a child only to "anchor" herself to the United States or of using her son to "shield" her from legal prosecution.[36] Arellano wanted to be known as a "simple mother, undocumented person, who fought" for the rights of the less powerful, but despite her son's status as a U.S. citizen and both the mother and child's stated wishes to remain in the United States, the sincerity and innocence of her maternal desires was often called into question.[37] The mixed, mostly negative, public reaction to Arellano occurred during a time of peak anti-immigration sentiment in the United States that led to speedy passage of restrictive immigration legislation in the U.S. House of Representatives.[38] Arellano was apprehended and repatriated quietly without the media spectacle that surrounded Elián, and few outside of Univisión audiences and the Latina/o community have heard of her case.

Speaking for the Dead

Because Arellano's body and voice could fight and speak for her rights and the rights of other undocumented immigrant mothers, she could not be invoked to serve the political interests of others. Public perception of Arellano's Mexican identity—shaped by the long history of U.S. anti-immigration policies and politics against Mexican communities—also irrevocably racialized her as nonwhite. Arellano's embodied visibility as a racialized undocumented Mexican woman made it safe for others to contest her. For Elisabet, her death and invisibility made her body docile. In other words, Elisabet became a social body that served multiple interests—the Cuban exile community in maintaining its political privilege; other ethnic and racial minority communities in contesting Cuban exceptionalism and unfair U.S. immigration policies; and the Cuban government in maintaining political stability in relationship to the United States.

Most mainstream coverage of women's immigration usually focuses on stories of victimization. Expectedly, U.S. Cuban sources often portrayed Elisabet as a self-sacrificing Cuban mother and victim of Cuban communism.[39] The mother's journey and death became evidence of her wishes,[40] and Fidel Castro was often singled out for blame, such as in this *Miami Herald* story discussing the Miami family's decision to file for asylum: "'We talked about how horrible it would be to make him a puppet for the government that sent his mother to her death,' [family lawyer Spencer] Eig said."[41] The mother and her actions stood in for the political interests of exiled Cubans. In another symbolic use of motherhood, soon after the Miami family's application for Elián's asylum, nearly 200 women and children took to the streets of downtown Miami wearing white ribbons and carrying white roses as symbols of Elisabet's purity and bodily sacrifice.[42] The framing of Elisabet as the innocent self-sacrificing mother and symbolic representative of the exile Cuban cause was repeated in national news, magazines, and television reports.[43]

Adding to the representation of Elisabet as virginal self-sacrificing mother, U.S. Cuban men and women interviewed by mainstream journalists often described the events surrounding Elisabet's death and Elián's rescue through gendered and religious imagery and language. In an early story aired on *CBS Evening News*, a segment taped outside Elián's hospital depicted an emotional Marisleysis saying, "The first thing that came to my mind: How did he survive by himself when he's only five? And I'm still thinking about it. And the only thing I can probably say is that it's just a miracle. God wanted him here for freedom." Elisabet's journey becomes a mythological tale of maternal love and bodily sacrifice.[44] A young mother places the son she struggled to give birth to after seven miscarriages[45] in the sole remaining inner tube with her only bottle of water. Unable to swim, she drowns during the night, but an exhausted and dehydrated Elián is guided to safety through shark-infested waters by dolphins sent to him by a guardian angel.

Associated Press (AP) photographs and television news coverage retold Elisabet's legend to audiences. One particularly interesting AP photograph was of a mural painted in Little Havana (see figure 1.1). In the center is Elián's inner tube, out of which arises a pleading black man (potentially a Balsero). Elián is guided by God's blessed hand, a trio of dolphins, and La Virgen de la Caridad del Cobre (Our Lady of Charity, Cuba's patron saint). The mural depicts the scales of justice with Pope John Paul II on the left and President

Bill Clinton on the right, both men hanging in balance. The Statue of Liberty, a pair of archangels, and Jesus Christ also appear in the background. In the mural's left corner, Elisabet gently smiles as she watches over Elián's "divine" rescue, and in the mural's right corner, Fidel Castro menacingly appears opposite her. The mural's use of race, skin color, and phenotypic shading is provocative. Elisabet and the Catholic religious figures all appear racially white. A slightly tanner Elián floats in the middle of the mural, and on its right side appear darker-skinned Cuban men. Whiteness and blackness, good and evil, left and right, battle over the fate of Elián. Photographs and news footage of the mural appeared in two ABC *World News Tonight* segments about the intermingling of religion and Cuban exile politics broadcast January 23 and March 30, 2000.[46] Given the AP's broad international circulation, it is difficult to determine how many other news organizations also circulated photographs of the mural.[47]

The religious tone of the images and the journalistic language gender the Elián news story by situating Elisabet and the Miami Cuban community within the signifiers of Catholic iconography most often associated with Latinas and Latinidad. Additionally, the journalistic emphasis on the melodrama surrounding Elián's rescue harkened back to older, more traditional coverage of the Cuban immigration experience as unique and exceptional. Elisabet's journey was romanticized by U.S. Cuban sources in the mainstream media as the ultimate maternal and political sacrifice inherently different from the journey of less sympathetic Latina immigrants.

Policing Cuban Motherhood and Immigration

In an article on the politics of race and ethnicity in contemporary immigration, Rubén G. Rumbaut argues that U.S. policy toward Cuban immigration has a historical racial bias.[48] Rumbaut observes that despite the economic exigency driving recent Cuban immigration, U.S. policies toward Cuban refugees over the past two decades continue to be informed by Cold War politics. The media's early framing of Elisabet and Elián as political exiles also carried with it an assumption of the racial privilege and social status still accorded to Cuban refugees despite the influx of working-class Afro-Cubans during the 1980s and 1990s. Although working-class Afro-Cubans qualify for similar asylum status, they have had a much tougher time integrating into Miami and its Cuban enclave. Reports by the Pew Hispanic Center indicate that Afro-Cubans are more likely to live in poverty and less likely to achieve the educational, social, and economic success of predominantly white first-wave Cuban refugees.[49]

Figure 1.1. This Associated Press photo of a Little Havana mural was widely circulated in newspapers and in television news footage. Its overtly religious tone affirmed the gendered discourse of Cubanidad in the Elián news story.

Eventually, Elisabet's and Elián's perceived race and ethnic identity as white Cubans and the preferential immigration treatment accorded to Cubans became contested in the media coverage of the controversy. Alongside news stories about the Elián case, journalists reported on stories about the differential legal treatment of immigrants from other parts of Latin America and the Caribbean. Contrasting the warm reception of Cuban children during Operation Pedro Pan in the 1960s to the contemporary reception of other Latina/o and Caribbean child refugees, the *Christian Science Monitor* reported on the impending deportation of a young Honduran boy with no living relatives in the United States or Honduras.[50] An earlier front-page story in the *New York Times* chronicled undocumented Haitian immigrants faced with deportation and the decision to take or leave their U.S.-born children.[51] Both stories discussed Elián in the context of the invisibility surrounding news coverage of other immigrants, in particular black Haitian immigrants, implicitly making the point that, had Elisabet and Elián not been Cuban and white, the U.S. public would never have learned of his story. Elisabet's and Elián's perceived racial identity as white ethnics insulated their story from the negative racialization of the Marielitos during the 1980s, the Balseros of the 1990s, and undocumented Mexican immigrants.

Moreover, for the ethnic media, Elisabet's and Elián's perceived racial identity also inadvertently produced an oppositional discourse of citizenship that questioned U.S. Cuban privilege. For example, the *Miami Times*, a black community newspaper, used Elián's story to draw attention to the unequal immigration treatment received by an undocumented Haitian mother rescued at sea whose children were repatriated to Haiti.[52] In another instance, U.S. Representative Charles Rangel, a New York City Democrat, wrote a column for the *New York Amsterdam News,* an African American newspaper, citing the unfair attention to the Elián case to ask for the equal treatment of all refugees.[53] Elisabet's identity and life story might have resonated with mainstream journalistic understandings of exile Cuban politics, but it riled black newspapers that saw Elisabet's status as a white Cuban insulating her from the racialized discourses of hyperfertility and poverty through which other Caribbean and Latina/o women and children who illegally journey to the United States are inscribed.[54]

An April 9, 2000, live segment of *CNN Late Edition with Wolf Blitzer* pitted Maxine Waters, an African American U.S. congresswoman who represents the south central Los Angeles area, against Ileana Ros-Lehtinen, a white U.S. Cuban who represents the southern Miami suburbs.

WATERS: Haitians are treated quite differently. I have not mentioned them, but since you brought it up, had that been a Haitian child, he would have been repatriated immediately, and you know that.

ROS-LEHTINEN: We have been very helpful to the Haitian community, when they have been seeking equality, and we will continue to do so. However, I think that people are correct when they say . . .

WATERS: Well, they don't receive the same treatment as Cubans. You know that, they don't.[55]

The unmasking of racial privilege accorded to Cuban refugees highlights the symbolic capital embedded in Elisabet's and Elián's whiteness.[56]

Stories about racial inequality and bias indicate a space of dissent within Miami's local media. The *Miami Herald* news and opinion coverage of Miami Cuban protests, disruptions, and political protests often characterized Miami Cubans as socially, politically, and economically disruptive—devaluing their symbolic status by situating them as racialized ethnic outsiders rather than white ethnic political insiders. Civil disobedience was acceptable, but only if performed appropriately by bodies normatively marked as citizens. Discussing the negative public reaction against Miami Cuban protests, one expert quoted in the *Miami Herald* argued, "A lot of people see the Cubans not as American citizens protesting. They see them as Cubans protesting America."[57] News stories, columns, and letters to the editor highlighted the extremist beliefs of conservative Cubans, often attributing Miami's inflamed racial tension to the exceptionalism of Cuban exile politics.[58] In the end, the U.S. Cuban community miscalculated the nostalgic power of exceptional anti-Castro/anti-communist rhetoric in a contemporary political environment defined less by defunct Cold War rhetoric and more by the racialized incorporation of Cubans into U.S. anti-immigration discourse.[59] Elisabet's power as symbolic mother was eventually weakened by oppositional news frames that foregrounded the racial inequality of U.S. immigration policies.

Speaking for the Father:
Patriarchal Restorations and the U.S. Rule of Law

News coverage about the grandmothers and women living in Cuba presented a second competing news frame for making sense of the Elián story. In January 2000, the grandmothers traveled to visit Elián and to lobby the U.S. government for his return. Although they could not speak fluent English, the grandmothers were used as a news source, usually to provide an opposing balance to the spokespeople of the exile Cuban community, such as in this January 31 *Newsweek* article:

> Rodríguez scoffed at the notion of her daughter as a political martyr. She suggested that Elisabet had been forced to make the risky journey by an abusive husband, and asked for help in securing her grandson's release "so that my daughter will rest in peace." For her part, Quintana fumed to reporters at the prospect of Elián becoming an American. "He is born in Cuba. He is Cuban," she said. "And nobody has the right, even Congress or the President, to change his status."[60]

Ironically, the grandmothers' account of Elisabet was recirculated and legitimized by usually hard-line anti-communist Republicans supportive of repatriating Elian. After meeting with the grandmothers during their January visit, Republican Senator Chuck Hagel of Nebraska was quoted as saying, "'It is obvious to me that [Elián's mother] was not a woman fleeing from a tyrannical regime.' Instead, he said, the women told him that Elián's mother 'was forced on that boat' by a violent, abusive boyfriend."[61] The image of Elisabet as a self-sacrificing single mother in search of political liberty and economic freedom proposed by U.S. Cuban sources was duly contradicted by the image of Elisabet as an abused woman under the coercive influence of her male partner and Elián as an unwilling political captive requiring "release." In the end, the grandmothers as news sources effectively used the Cuban birth of Elián and Elisabet as incontrovertible proof of the mother and child's authentic identity and national allegiance to Cuba.

One of the most complex issues regarding contemporary definitions of Cuban national identity is the social status of Cubans living on the island in relation to those who have left.[62] For the Cuban government and some Cubans, an authentically Cuban identity belongs only to those born and still living on the island. Thus, in mainstream news coverage, the grandmothers use their biological bonds to Elián and Elisabet to foreground their custodial claim to Elián as grandson and their ideological claim to Elián as Cuba's symbolic son. This competing account of nation and national identity grounded in the rhetoric of blood ties to Elián and unbroken ties to the country of birth presented a challenge to the political narrative of the U.S. Cuban community.[63]

Having never organized a march based on gender identity, the Cuban government also engaged in the symbolic politics of birth and motherhood to affirm notions of nationhood and sway U.S. public opinion. Weeks before the grandmothers' trip to the United States, the Cuban government organized the second largest march in support of Elián's return to Cuba, the "March of the Mothers." Led by a row of mostly pregnant women, an estimated 100,000 Cubans of all ages, races, and professions protested near the U.S. Interest Section in Havana. The women also symbolically adopted Elián at the protest and marched outside the U.S. diplomatic mission, reportedly shouting "Return our son!"[64] Not only was Elisabet recuperated as a lost daughter whose son should be returned to his biological family, but the Cuban nation itself was visually inserted into news stories as a mother figure with rights to her native son. Cubans no longer living on the island were marked as the outsiders lacking the moral and political authority to speak on behalf of the mother, child, or the motherland. Furthermore, the pregnant women at the march contributed to the power of the grandmothers' claim and provided a contrast to the U.S. Cuban claims about Elisabet, Cuba, and communism. The marchers' visual manifestation of their decision to have children in Cuba created empirical and symbolic evidence for U.S. audiences that Cuban women lovingly and willingly make the decision to live in Cuba with their families and to have children in contemporary Cuban society. It implicitly raised doubts in the news coverage about the credibility of U.S. Cuban sources, such as Marisleysis, who had neither lived in nor visited Cuba yet who publicly claimed that economic and political life in Cuba was so awful that any mother would risk her life to provide freedom for her child. More than 500,000 Cuban women participated in a second march held in June 2000—making it the largest protest march during the controversy. The Cuban government never organized a march exclusively for men or fathers.

"A Boy Belongs with His Father"

When the U.S. government pulled its support for Elián's asylum in early January, the grandmothers' testimony and the father's assertion of his custodial rights in the media added to the public shift against the U.S. Cuban exile community. Continuing the attack on U.S. Cuban exile privilege, the grandmothers and father maintained that Elián did not lack material needs and that only the family and father who had nurtured him since infancy could provide him with the necessary emotional support.[65] The Cuban government and Elián's Cuban family argued that the biological father's custodial claim should get primary consideration over all political concerns. Speaking on behalf of the U.S. government, then U.S. Attorney General Janet Reno affirmed the grandmothers' and father's claims in the news media. Juan

Miguel González's paternal claims to his son were sovereign, Reno argued, and would be upheld by the U.S. rule of law. Legal arguments about the rule of law are commonly couched as "race neutral." In debates regarding California's Proposition 187, for instance, it allowed supporters of the legislation to claim that the law was not about race or racism but about maintaining California's rule of law.[66] Using a rule-of-law argument provided Reno with an opportunity to claim that the legal decision to repatriate Elián was not about Latina/o immigration, Cuban exile rights, or Clinton foreign policy but about the state's "race neutral" interest in maintaining order through affirming the stability of the family.

By late January 2000, the assertion of paternal rights would gain traction in the mainstream and ethnic media coverage of the controversy. Acknowledging family reunification as the cornerstone of U.S. immigration law, Janet Reno argued that "the law recognizes the unique relationship between parent and child."[67] It is a conception of law and family that apparently is not applied equally, as was evident in the case of Arellano and her son. Moreover, lawyers and fathers' rights organizations in the United States also picked up the rule-of-law argument regarding the sanctity of the family.[68] Through news stories and guest columns in both the mainstream and ethnic media, fathers' rights activists used the case to draw attention to the unequal treatment of fathers in immigration custody disputes and the plight of U.S. fathers around the world. Within these texts, the Miami family's asylum claim and civil protests by the exile community were depicted as threats to the U.S. rule of law and the sanctity of the heteronormative patriarchal family.[69] Toward the final months of the Elián case, Elisabet was displaced by Juan Miguel González as the patriarchal, albeit temporary, symbol of the U.S. rule of law in the mainstream and ethnic media other than *El Nuevo Herald*.

The Miami family and exile Cuban community's refusal to acknowledge Juan Miguel González's paternal authority further contributed to the journalistic framing of the community as dangerous to the established legal, racial, and patriarchal order. "Not-so-veiled-threats," references to the anti-government violence of Waco, file footage of demonstrators burning tire fires and overturning police barricades—these images, selected quotes, and journalistic language characterized Miami and the U.S. Cuban community as boiling over with heat, hostility, and violence. Miami at the hands of exiled Cubans became a racialized south-of-the-border tropics teeming with restless natives ready to turn against the nation that helped them in their time of political need.[70]

Simultaneously, attempts by U.S. federal sources to speak on the father's behalf inadvertently (or perhaps consciously) infantilized and feminized the exile Cuban community in the mainstream news coverage. For example, an ABC *World News Tonight* report introduced a January story with the following sentence: "In language even a six-year-old might understand, the Justice Department made clear today what the law says about who controls the fate of Elián González."[71] The next day, *World News Tonight* led with "The attorney general is now telling everyone once again, 'Simmer down, this case belongs in the federal court.'"[72] The ABC telecast completed its coverage for the month with "It's already been an extraordinary two months, and this afternoon it took the U.S. government and a Catholic nun for the grandmothers of Elián González to sit down in private with their grandson, which means it took a stern warning from the Justice Department before Elián's Cuban American relatives backed off."[73] "Standing firm," "stern warnings," telling Miami's Cuban community "to simmer down"—the journalistic language affirmed the rights of the U.S. federal government as patriarchal authority and weakened the social, legal, and political status of the U.S. Cuban exile community. The U.S. federal mantra that "a boy belongs with his father" gained currency in the news media. News anchors such as ABC's Peter Jennings broke with standards of journalistic objectivity by expressing his incredulity at the Miami family's lack of respect for the relationship between father and son.[74] What type of community, the news reports suggested, would separate a son from the innate goodness of his father.

Increasing criticism of the Miami family and the U.S. Cuban exile community in the final months of the custodial standoff resulted in news accounts that reinforced the authority of the U.S. federal government and its courts by erasing the voice of U.S. Cuban sources even as they featured their civil disobedience. With the exception of a few news sources such as Pam Falk and Elena Freyre, most legal and psychological experts pooled from policy think tanks, institutions, or universities tended to be white men. Unlike the Miami demonstrators, who were almost always interviewed outdoors in street clothes and often wearing colorful paraphernalia, these experts were dressed in professional attire and predominately interviewed inside respectable private offices filled with academic and legal books or in conference rooms behind podiums with official government seals. Interestingly, although all of the government sources interviewed on air were white, most of them were women. Once again, it was the voices and bodies of women, specifically Reno, who became the mechanism through which the patriarchal rule of law was re-established by the forced return of a son to his father.

Recuperating the Nation: Marisleysis as La Llorona Cubana

An analysis of gender, ethnicity, and race in the Elián case cannot be complete without a discussion of one of its most polarizing and captivating media figures, Marisleysis González, the crying cousin (see figure 1.2). Equally as important as Elisabet and the Cuban grandmothers to the symbolic colonization of the U.S. Cuban community were the language and visuals that surrounded Elián's young, emotional, and sexually attractive maternal surrogate.[75] Marisleysis, the U.S.-born child of Cuban immigrant parents, came to symbolize the threat of the Latina Other—too emotional to be rational, too sexy to be an appropriate maternal figure, and too vociferous to be appropriately feminine. Often conflated with La Malinche, the indigenous Mexican woman constructed as betraying the Mexican people through her marriage and alliance with Hernán Cortés, La Llorona (the weeping woman) is also a cautionary tale that often features a U.S./Mexican border woman who is sexually seduced or sexually promiscuous and puts her self-interest before her children's welfare by drowning them. She is later condemned to tearfully search for the souls of her murdered children. Mainstream news discourses of Marisleysis constructed her in similar tones of gendered betrayal. Originally depicted as a strong and compelling spokeswoman, her physicality and emotional instability were eventually used to discipline the political excesses of Marisleysis and by association the Miami Cuban community.

News audiences were first introduced to Marisleysis at the bedside of a convalescing Elián. In evening television news coverage of the drama, she was perpetually by Elián's side as he left the hospital, navigated the throngs of cameras outside their Little Havana home, played in the yard, broke open a piñata, and opened hordes of birthday gifts. Equally prevalent were television news images of a young Marisleysis wearing makeup, heels, designer sweaters, or black suits—a carefully constructed appearance managed by the Cuban American National Foundation (CANF) to make Marisleysis appear more maternal, mature, and middle-class. She came to embody the dominant archetype of the working mother—juggling the care of Elián with the demands of a politically charged legal case. Marisleysis stood in politically, physically, and figuratively for the Miami family and the U.S. Cuban community. By the story's end, however, Marisleysis' behavior and physicality marked her as different and outside socially acceptable femininity. Her body is too youthful to be mature. Her sexual appeal is too overt to be maternal. Her full lips, light brown skin, dark eyes, and dark hair too ethnic to be white. Her voice is too loud and her nails are too long, too red, too artificial to be middle-class.

Figure 1.2. In one of the most popular images after the federal raid on the Gonzálezes' Little Havana home, the emotional toll on Marisleysis is visually apparent. Marisleysis became a flashpoint for anti–Cuban immigration discourses, eventually coming to visually symbolize the contemporary gendered and racialized position of the U.S. Cuban community.

Unlike Elisabet, who was always present in the news coverage through her absence, Marisleysis circulated in excess. It was this hyperbolized image of excess—often set in opposition to the grandmothers' more demure matronly image—that defines Marisleysis as culturally, socially, and politically threatening. Especially during the decline of U.S. political and popular support for the Miami family's asylum case, public perception of Marisleysis shifted from the politically protected voice of Elián's self-proclaimed surrogate mother to the hypervisible gendered and racialized spectacle of a community on the margins, a community no longer imagined as socially acceptable white ethnics but instead as unlawful brown ethnic immigrants.

Marisleysis was consequently rearticulated through the mainstream news media and blogs as a racialized and gendered Latina. In an ABC News Web site description of the various figures involved in the conflict, Marisleysis was characterized as "Often tearful, she has acted as a surrogate mother to Elián and has frequently appeared before the news media, pleading for the boy to be allowed to stay in the U.S. . . . But the struggle has affected her health, and has caused her to be hospitalized four times since the custody began."[76] Her emotional instability, indeed apparent neurosis, became the news story—effectively undercutting her symbolic power as surrogate mother and community spokeswoman. For instance, a news story on Salon.com drew attention to the fact that "The vision of [Marisleysis] González being taking out on a stretcher, oxygen mask to her face, has become a staple of TV news . . . one has to question what kind of emotional stability she can possibly provide for her 6-year-old charge."[77] Another feature article about Marisleysis concluded with this observation:

> But signs that the strain of the fight for Elián was getting to be too much for Marisleysis emerged recently, when she made a rambling, tearful speech at a congressional hearing in Washington. She spoke of how the child wants to stay here with her. "At night, when he wakes up scared, he says, 'I love you mucho, my cousin,' " Marisleysis told the politicians. Then she broke down and cried.[78]

Adding to the construction of Marisleysis as psychologically and emotionally defective, the *Miami Herald* published a report that before the Elián case she had experienced a series of stress-related disorders leading to three hospitalizations.[79]

Marisleysis' tearfulness, emotionally erratic behavior, and anxiety over Elián's asylum case were highlighted throughout the final months of news coverage. For example, a *CBS Evening News* segment updating the negotiations between the Miami family and U.S. government devoted significant time to a discussion of Marisleysis' most recent hospitalization alongside statements from her last news conference:

> "Last night, she spoke with defiance and fear," Byron Pitts reported. "If you send Elián back to Cuba," Marisleysis pauses and begins crying, "he's going to be tortured! Is that what the American people are going to allow?"[80]

The story could have paraphrased Marisleysis. However, like all broadcast media, it was precisely these exaggerated displays of emotion that were common to the coverage of Marisleysis. Because the audience was only privy to a few seconds of what was probably a lengthy news conference, the selected sound bite became significant. Implied in her statement was the suggestion that the exile Cuban community was not going to legally or physically allow Elián to be sent back to Cuba. Not only was her statement highly sensationalistic, exaggerated, and confrontational, it also subtly positioned Marisleysis and the U.S. Cuban community as separate, distinct, and dangerous to the imagined nation.

With dwindling support for the Miami family's asylum claim, the mainstream news coverage framed Marisleysis and the Miami Cuban community as hotheaded, lawless, and ethically questionable, signifiers that contradicted the traditional media discourses of Cuban exceptionalism and Cuban identity as white ethnics. A *USA Today* column about Marisleysis made the following observations:

> Marisleysis brought her mother act to Capital Hill. In an often rambling, seldom coherent news conference to a knot of journalists, she alternated between cheap shots at President Clinton and demands to see him. She also took a curious swipe at Reno. "You still don't know what being a mother is," Marisleysis, who like the attorney general is unmarried and childless, said of Reno. To say she is unstable is an understatement.[81]

Given that there have long been rumors about Reno's sexual orientation, one can read between the lines of Marisleysis' homophobic implication. However, by calling attention to the comments regarding Reno, the columnist also contested the legitimacy of Marisleysis' claims to motherhood.

Marisleysis stands in as a symbol of Miami as a racialized tropics inside the borders of the United States that threatens the imagined nation during a moment of demographic contestation. Not surprisingly, characterizations of Marisleysis and the Miami Cuban community as unstable and dangerous were inevitably circulated by U.S. audiences through Web sites and blogs. In writing about Marisleysis for his "Creep of the Week" Web site, John Montgomery wrote, "There's no one in the world more responsible for the 5 a.m. INS raid than Marisleysis. She and her father Lazaro have been intransigent and threatening with their refusal to turn Elián over to his father. . . . Defiant, dangerous and nuts."[82] U.S. Cubans, in this case second-generation Cuban American Marisleysis, became racialized outside the norms of whiteness and white social acceptability.

News stories and blog postings about Marisleysis produced a "consensus narrative" for dominant U.S. culture at a time when the mythologized borders of the imagined nation were being contested by increasing numbers of first- and second-generation immigrants from Mexico, the Caribbean, Latin America, and Asia. Through gendering Marisleysis and the Miami Cuban community within dominant characterizations of femininity such as emotionality and irrationality, national television news in particular circulated a symbolically colonizing narrative of Cuban identity. The gendering of the U.S. Cuban community erased the diversity of political, class, and racial trajectories within the community and marked U.S. Cubans for exclusion from the symbolic borders of the imagined nation as neither white nor black. In a widely circulated visual of Marisleysis' news conference after the federal raid on her family's Little Havana home where she demanded access to the child and accused the U.S. government of committing child abuse (see figure 1.2), Marisleysis is seen sobbing, wide-mouthed, at the loss of her surrogate child. Marisleysis publicly stands in as La Llorona, responsible for the loss of her child and the symbolic capital of her community. The weight she had gained throughout the ordeal is visible through her ill-fitting clothes. Also visible in the photograph are the markers of her working-class femininity: the heavy makeup and long false nails. Despite the respectable black suit she wears, she is no longer performing the signifiers of socially acceptable standards of middle-class U.S. Cuban femininity. Instead, Marisleysis is the uncontrollable Latina Other whose accusations of federal malfeasance now lack political credibility. She is tearfully condemned to search for her lost Elián and the lost political privilege of her community.

A Requiem for Marisleysis

Today, Marisleysis González quietly operates a hair salon in Miami. Interviewed for a story years after Elián's return to Cuba, a reporter wrote: "González was again before news cameras on Friday. She showed she hasn't forgotten the lessons gleaned from countless news conferences and talk show appearances, and gracefully, unemotionally, talked about life without Elián."[83] Marisleysis is rational and restrained, no longer tearful when discussing Elián. She is attractive and graceful. Having learned her lesson, she is once again respectful of her marginalized place and status within the imagined nation.

Nevertheless, the gendered and racialized symbolic colonization of Marisleysis and the U.S. Cuban community during the Elián case speaks to the shifting political and social status and racialization of U.S. Cubans from that of white ethnics to brown immigrants. Racial formation theory suggests that the meanings assigned to race and racial groups are part of a historically unstable, continuous process intricately connected to political and social structures.[84] Cubans who once occupied the position of privileged white ethnics within the U.S. imaginary found themselves outside the border of socially acceptable citizenship and within the problematic terrain of popular panethnic constructions of Latinidad.

In the wake of Elián's departure and Marisleysis' public breakdown, U.S. Cubans witnessed a decline in public support for the U.S.-Cuban embargo and increased support for the normalization of relations with Cuba.[85] Months after the political spectacle, a *New York Daily News* column by Roberto Santiago squarely blamed the exile Cuban community for exacerbating U.S. racial tensions. In his column, Santiago rallied support for a more moderate foreign policy toward Cuba, blaming the extremist politics of Miami Cubans and the Cuban American National Foundation (CANF), which financed the Miami family's legal and political battle, for historically alienating black Americans, Haitians, and non-Cuban Latinas/os.[86] Shortly after Marisleysis' tearful news conference, the head of the CANF in Washington, DC, José Cárdenas, a U.S. Colombian, explained to reporters why public sentiment turned against Marisleysis and her community:

> "The reality is that Washington is a conservative town and basically it doesn't really comprehend people that—" and here Cárdenas pauses, then squeezes his eyes shut as he rubs his temples with his fingers and casts about for a politic description of Marisleysis and her kin "—doesn't comprehend people that justifiably wear their emotions on their sleeves."[87]

For exiled Cubans, the post–Cold War politics of the federal government, along with demographic data documenting the permanent status of three generations of Cubans living in the United States, have moved them from an ethnic enclave associated with whiteness to unruly ethnic immigrants located within the racialized space of Latina/o brownness.

For performances of Latinidad in the United States, motherhood and its connections to race and nation are significant to understanding racial formations. Like women generally, Cuban women serve as symbols that always exist in relation to dominant constructions of their identity, femininity, and sexuality.[88] The contemporary signification of Cuban/U.S. Cuban women exists through and against Western constructions of Latina femininity, Latina sexuality, and white femininity. They also exist within U.S. colonial discourses that define them as dangerously impure racialized bodies with uncontrollable emotions and sexual desires.[89] Within U.S. media stories about family, home, and nation, such as those that surrounded the Elián coverage, women play a central role.

Elisabet embodied the politics of a nation and diaspora deeply divided from each other; the elision of the social, political, and historical context surrounding her journey opened a space for her to sign in as emotive spectacle, political subject, and disembodied Other. She became a floating signifier, part of the contested terrain of Latina signification.[90] Because Elisabet could not speak on her behalf, others, primarily women, were asked or compelled to speak for her. Subsequently, she was textually embodied in the coverage through the voice of women who were sometimes ideologically opposed to one another. In Elisabet's case, she was caught in the contradictory discourse between Cuban women who wanted to recuperate her as a lost daughter and U.S. Cuban women who wanted to symbolically locate her as the sacrificial mother of the contemporary anti-Castro exile movement.

Marisleysis' position in news stories was equally complex. Initially invited into the coverage as the family's unofficial spokeswoman, she occupied a space filled with the potential for political activism. However, when the U.S. public and government withdrew their support for Elián's asylum claim, so did the media, which increasingly presented the conservative Cuban exile community and its most entertaining representative, Marisleysis, as outside the boundaries of lawfulness, social acceptability, and whiteness, and as outside the borders of the United States as imagined nation. Marisleysis was defined by her willingness to fight for her political and personal beliefs, a role usually relegated to men within the exile Cuban community. Her entry into the political discourse of the public sphere was disempowered by the gendered and racialized signifiers of Latina femininity that came to define her in the media. Like Elisabet, Marisleysis became a floating signifier through which the representational politics of the conservative Cuban exile community were disciplined. Through her tears for Elián, she unwittingly disrupted the historical discourses of U.S. Cuban exceptionalism, exposed the nostalgic narrative of exiled Cubans as the model Latina/o minority, and contributed to the symbolic colonization of Cubans within contemporary news discourses of Latinidad.

Disciplining J.Lo:
Booty Politics in Tabloid News

The Elián controversy might be one of the most covered Latina/o news stories in U.S. history, but few Hollywood bodies are as anthologized in the academic and popular press as that of U.S.-born Puerto Rican actor/singer/designer/restaurateur Jennifer Lopez.[1] In 2004, the *New York Daily News* noted Jennifer Lopez could win an "Editors' Choice Award" for getting the most coverage that year in celebrity tabloids (*People, Us Weekly, Star, in Touch*). That year Lopez appeared on twenty-nine tabloid covers for a total of 14 percent of the issues, more than Jennifer Aniston and the Olsen twins.[2] The following year, *Forbes* magazine gave Lopez a power ranking of 24 based on her average movie salary, number of Web hits (more than 3 million), and news coverage (more than 15,000 stories), and in 2007, *Forbes* named her one of the world's Top 10 wealthiest women, outranking Latinas Cameron Diaz of Cuban descent and Christina Aguilera of Ecuadorian descent.[3] No other contemporary Latina-identified celebrity has captivated and frustrated the imagination of the U.S. public and popular news media more than Lopez. As one Chicago newspaper reporter humorously noted:

> It (Lopez's) is the first butt to earn a shout-out on the new "Hollywood Squares." The first to be publicly ogled by Mark Wahlberg, a k a Marky Mark, at the MTV Music Awards. The first to get a thumbs-up from *Elle*, that purveyor of fashionably diminutive derrieres, which declares in its November issue: "Eat something. From your lips to your hips. It's working for Jennifer Lopez."[4]

Lopez is a star, a U.S. star, a Puerto Rican star, a Latina star, and to be coded as a "star" by the media carries unique cultural significance.

Scholars such as Richard Dyer suggest that celebrity stars are a type of media sign that embody Western notions of individualism, wealth, desire, and social worth.[5] The star phenomenon consists of all available public texts about them—films, gossip columns, publicity news, and advertisements, among others. It is the mediated life of the performer, rather than the performance itself, that becomes the primary object of analysis.[6] Stroll by any checkout counter in U.S. grocery stores and you'll see evidence of the public fascination with celebrities on the covers of *Star*, *Us Weekly*, and *People*. Celebrity culture is everywhere, and it sells. Images of starving starlets in haute couture, club-hopping celebrity teens in drunken revelries, and dashing bachelors swinging through Hollywood soirées appear across the front pages of these magazines every week. Who is married? Divorced? Pregnant? "Enquiring" minds want to know, and few can resist a peek at the juicy tidbits of celebrity gossip available on the coffee table or at the dentist's office.

While news about celebrities clearly is a form of entertainment, Mary Beltrán proposes that public discourses about celebrity bodies also function as a space of cultural contestation, especially for marginalized ethnic, racial, and gendered groups. Building on the work of Richard Dyer, Beltrán writes, "Star images serve as definers of power and identity for a society. Nonwhite stars have a particular salience in this regard, given that social and racial hierarchies are both reflected and reinforced by a nation's system of stardom."[7] Indeed, social and racial anxieties are often worked out through the bodies of those who are most famous or infamous. For instance, at the height of HIV/AIDS activism in the United States in the 1980s, "outing," or revealing the sexual orientation of celebrities through the tabloids, was a key political strategy for gay, lesbian, bisexual, and transgendered activists literally fighting for their lives and cultural visibility.[8] Therefore, studying the tabloids is, as Elizabeth Bird suggests, significant precisely because their stories speak to broader social and cultural concerns.[9] Thus, if celebrity news as a form of public discourse helps define the boundaries of power and identity and delineates social hierarchies of race, ethnicity, gender, and class, this chapter explores what the tabloid discourse about Lopez, one of the most globally successful contemporary iconic figures, says about Latinidad and Latina identity.[10] The question this chapter asks is, what does the Lopez tabloid coverage tell us about Puerto Ricans, Latinas/os, and U.S. national identity during a moment of uncomfortable demographic transformation?[11]

Specifically, I examine U.S. celebrity tabloid discourses about Lopez's body, sexuality, and identity in the *National Enquirer, People, Star, Us Weekly*, and *in Touch* from 1999 to 2004. Additionally, I analyze audience readings of tabloid news about Lopez through a discussion of celebrity Web logs (blogs) on the Web site Blogcritics Magazine during the same period. I focus on tabloid coverage from 2002 to 2004 because this period documents the height of Lopez's cultural visibility in the music, film, and tabloid industries. It is during this period that Lopez launched her second restaurant and first clothing and perfume line and began her relationship with Ben Affleck. Similar to my study of Elisabet and Marisleysis in the Elián case, I trace the cultural and social conflicts surrounding the erasures and visibility of Lopez as a celebrity news figure. Tabloid news stories about Lopez illustrate how the Puerto Rican body functions as a sexually desirable, ethnically and racially ambiguous docile body that is financially productive within the realm of global popular culture and equally threatening to dominant ethnic and racial formations in the United States. The tension between global desire and domestic danger explains the gendering and racialization of Lopez as outside the boundaries of whiteness and middle-class respectability. Blogs about Lopez and reactions to them demonstrate how audiences negotiate the symbolic colonization of Lopez in ways that both reaffirm and symbolically rupture dominant public understandings about gender, ethnicity, and race.

'Enquiring Minds Want To Know'... the Significance of Tabloid News

Critical journalism scholars have long documented the blurring lines between the worlds of elite "mainstream" news media and popular tabloid journalism.[12] For instance, in her ethnographic study of tabloid journalists, Elizabeth Bird observed that tabloids such as the *National Enquirer, Star,* and *Us Weekly* often employ trained journalists who are burnt out from the low-pay, high-stress rigors of traditional publications such as *The Philadelphia Inquirer* and *Time* magazine.[13] Not surprisingly, many tabloid journalists report a commitment and adherence to the tenets of elite journalism: objectivity, credibility, and the related journalistic practices of research, fact verification, expert sources, interviews, and source triangulation. As Bird notes, "Tabloids are entertainment that also inform; newspapers are information, according to journalistic standards, but they must also entertain."[14] In other words, tabloids are a highly formulaic and predictable form of journalism explicitly motivated by the economic need to entertain. To tabloid journalists, their work is similar to that of elite reporting about soft news and human-interest stories that increasingly pervade the elite press.[15] In a recent example of the blurring of these distinctions, tabloid newspapers claimed to "break" important election news stories, such as the teenage pregnancy of Republican vice presidential candidate Sarah Palin's eldest daughter. Stuart Hall and others therefore define news more generally as "the end-product of a complex process which begins with a systematic sorting and selecting of events and topics according to a socially constructed set of categories."[16] Together both forms of journalism engage in routine storytelling conventions and practices that contribute to the production of social reality and collective identities.[17] Elite news journalists are concerned with providing information that audiences should know, a questionable proposition to some given elite press coverage of the Monica Lewinsky scandal and celebrity presidential endorsements, among others, while tabloid journalists pride themselves in openly giving audiences the information they want to know.[18]

Tabloid news about celebrities further troubles the distinctions between elite and popular news. In his study of the production and reception of celebrity culture, Joshua Gamson argues:

> The bulk of entertainment-media organizations are semiautonomous, and the most common resolution to conflicting pulls is a compromise. Entertainment journalism tends to shy away from criteria of truth and worth. Though not dismissed, they are limited to the pursuit of technical accuracy: facts are tirelessly checked, questions of legality carefully considered. But, faced with a need to deliver inside information where digging for it can threaten essential industry relationships, celebrity-based media work with entertainment criteria that bridge these interests.[19]

Like the elite media's coverage of political figures, celebrity tabloid journalists have a tense relationship with those they report on. Elite and tabloid journalists must carefully decide whom to write about and when to unearth and expose information about the public figures they cover. At the same time, those public figures are dependent on the media to gain attention and remain publicly salient.[20] Journalists and their sources (political or celebrity) engage in a complicated and precarious dance to control the stories told through the media.

Therefore, in this chapter and throughout the rest of this book I approach elite and tabloid news as forms of public discourse that speak to social formations of power and identity.[21] My previous discussion of the Elián case documents how coverage of the Cuban exile community was informed by the changing status of U.S. Cubans within Latina/o ethnic and racial formations. Growing anti-immigration sentiments contributed to the symbolic colonization of U.S. Cubans from exceptional white ethnics to racialized brown Latinas/os. Changes in tabloid coverage about Lopez over time similarly tell us something about the vexed interconnection between gender, race, sexuality, and Latina identity and the contemporary symbolic worth of Puerto Ricans within the national U.S. imaginary. Although U.S. citizens by law since the

Jones Act of 1917, Puerto Ricans remain constructed as racial and ethnic foreigners and therefore social threats to the U.S. imagined nation. In the context of the anti-immigration Latina/o backlash, the marginalized status of Puerto Ricans has only increased. Few know or understand the cultural and political differences between Puerto Ricans and other Latina/o groups. Puerto Ricans, especially Afro-Puerto Ricans, living in the United States also face racial, linguistic, and economic discrimination. Thus, the stories about Lopez told through the mainstream and tabloid news play a critical role in telling us about contemporary symbolic colonization of Latina and Puerto Rican identity. The social and political relevance of information circulated through the "news" is based not only on the "reality it produces" through its stories and audience interpretations of those stories, but it also tells us about the "social relations or identities it promotes" through its storytelling conventions.[22] In particular, the storytelling conventions of both the mainstream and tabloid media position journalists as powerful all-knowing, all-seeing transmitters of information about popular figures.

Having risen in popularity during the 1980s, weekly supermarket tabloids are a profitable multimillion-dollar business. In 2007, *Us Weekly, Star, in Touch*, and the *National Enquirer* had a combined total paid circulation of about 5.6 million, while *People* alone reached almost 3.7 million.[23] The tabloids' reach goes far beyond their circulation numbers as they get passed around among friends, family, and coworkers. The readers per copy estimates range from 5.8 for *in Touch* to 11.3 for *People*. With such large readerships, advertising in these publications is big business. In 2008, a full-page color advertisement cost as little as $87,000 for *in Touch* or as much as $309,800 in *People*'s year-end issue.[24] The readership and profitability of tabloids point to their continued but understudied importance in U.S. popular culture.

Tabloids are so popular precisely because they disseminate information the public *wants* to know—the personal and the intimate—and in doing so provide readers with brief moments of subversion from often negative economic and political news.[25] The 400-pound man imprisoned in his living room; the 45-year-old conjoined twins finally separated; alien visitors to planet Earth—with a focus on the personal, the unique, and the outrageous, tabloids provide a moment of escapist pleasure and resistance from the barrage of elite news content about a political system from which the public is increasingly alienated. John Fiske argues that tabloid news audiences are buoyed into a carnivalesque atmosphere of semiotic pleasure and ideological resistance. The ability to relate to the individual pleasure and pain of the heroines and villains staring back at them from the tabloid covers allows audiences to relate to them in ways they cannot relate to the political figures that grace the front pages of mainstream newspapers.

Celebrity tabloid news privileges the private rather than the public sphere.[26] As such, Gamson contends that the appearance of public access to the private lives of celebrities is at the cultural and economic heart of celebrity journalism:

> Indeed, the professional and commercial conflicts are resolved in . . . celebrity discourse: through the intimacy-stirring circulation of the personal details of love and pain and leisure, through gossip, through the cynic-flattering focus on image making and image management themselves, through the pragmatic mix of "man" and "myth," and the continual promise to sort out one from the other, to reveal the person behind the image.[27]

The emphasis on the "real" stories and bodies of celebrities, their personal achievements, and tragic failures function as an entertaining morality play for audiences. That is not to say that tabloid readers believe everything reported about celebrities; rather, Gamson argues tabloid readers carefully evaluate, interpret, critique, and sometimes identify with or contest the perceived authenticity of the stories they read.[28]

To study how tabloid readers interpret, identify, or critique the content they consume, we have to understand the ideological links between the content and its audiences. Elizabeth Bird's content analysis of tabloids concludes that most depict women and white celebrities alongside human-interest, rags-to-riches, how-to, and self-help stories. Bird concludes that the tabloids' ideological world is a conservative one through its reaffirmation of the political and social status quo. Thus, although audiences engage with the tabloids in multiple ways, Bird argues that one of the dominant reading strategies for tabloid audiences is through identifying with the stories of heteronormative whiteness and middle-class respectability. For instance, in her study of tabloid readers, Bird concluded:

> *Examiner* staff were clear in their perception that tabloid readers tend to be politically conservative, and this was generally borne out. I should stress, however, that this conservatism is not obviously party-affiliated; rather it is a tendency to be "traditional," "family-oriented," religious, and patriotic in a nostalgic, flag-waving sense.[29]

The education, economic, class, gender, and racial demographics of entertainment tabloids place emphasis on traditional notions of family, domesticity, and citizenship. According to the 2008 *Us Weekly* media kit, 73 percent of its readers are women; 53 percent make less than $75,000; 69 percent have attended some college; 45 percent are married; and 76 percent identify as white.[30] While other U.S.-based entertainment tabloids (*in Touch, Star, People*, and the *National Enquirer*) do not provide information on the racial demographics of their readers, similarities in the education, gender, and economic makeup imply a majority are white women.[31] I am not suggesting that ethnic and racial minorities do not read the tabloids or that ethnic and racial minorities do not also engage in conservative reading strategies. Indeed, I would posit, based on audience research conducted by Jillian Báez, that ethnic and racial minorities might be more invested in conservative notions of social respectability.[32] Regardless, the demographic makeup of tabloid audiences and the ideologically conservative messages of tabloid stories demand that we examine how the disciplining of femininity, domesticity, and sexuality holds specific consequences for ethnic and racial minority women, specifically Puerto Ricans and Latinas.

Booty(full) Desires . . .
and the Tabloid Consumption of the Latina Body

I begin my analysis by exploring Lopez's self-conscious negotiations with her ethnoracial identity. By self-conscious I recognize that, as Gamson illustrates in his study, celebrities are knowingly invested in tabloid attention about them:

> The aspirant or performer is on the one hand a *worker*, and what is developed and sold is the capacity to play a role and the actual work of playing the role. This is the entertainer's more "traditional" aspect: the aspirant's qualities and abilities (not necessarily talent, also often looks alone) are the basis for decision making. On the other hand, he or she is *celebrity*, and what is developed and sold is the capacity to command attention.[33]

In other words, celebrities and their agents and managers work together to produce a sellable image that resonates as interesting, authentic, or truthful to audiences.

Beltrán argues that for Lopez, the commodification of "celebrity-self" begins with her 1997 performance in the movie *Selena*, which earned her serious acting recognition and mainstream attention. Lopez's physical embodiment of Latinidad, in particular Selena's voice and look, catapulted her to cinematic stardom. Frances Aparicio suggests that the positive audience reception of the Puerto Rican actor's performance of a Mexican Tejana icon spoke to emerging Latina identity formations. Most Latina/o audiences are aware of the many similarities between both women. Both have similar body types, hair textures, skin color. Both were born in the United States to Latina/o parents, but neither learned Spanish until later in life. The movie provided unprecedented and celebrated visibility to both the Puerto Rican Lopez and the Tejana Selena. These similarities produced a bridge across the ethnic specific identities of Latina audiences and toward a more collective sense of ethnoracial Latina community.

By 2001, Lopez would go on to break records by becoming the third woman, and the first Latina, to hold the No. 1 album and movie spots simultaneously when her *J.Lo* album knocked a Beatles' rerelease album off the No. 1 Billboard spot and *The Wedding Planner* became the No. 1 grossing film in the United States.[34] Three years later, Lopez would be the most popular tabloid cover subject and highest paid Latina actor, receiving $20 million per film.[35] Hailed by the U.S. popular press as the "new face" of U.S. beauty— large(r) and curvaceous—Lopez herself has commented that the world knew her butt before the public knew her face, an association she carefully cultivated through her early career in interviews and music video performances. She remains one of the world's most popular and polarizing celebrities.[36]

The Early J.Lo Years

Media coverage during this period unequivocally emphasized her ethnically ambiguous, racially flexible, and desirable body. Because Lopez can personify multiple ethnic and racial identities, she is often coded as an ambiguously brown ethnic—rarely coded as either white or black. During her *In Living Color*/Sean Combs (Puff Daddy/P. Diddy) days, Lopez located her musical performances within the terrain of urban and black popular culture without consciously identifying as black. At the same time, Lopez's cinematic career depended on performances of ambiguously ethnic, racially undetermined characters, such as in *Out of Sight, The Cell,* and *Enough.* Her cinematic performances shifted her into almost-white but still ethnic territory. More recently, Lopez has settled into a more fixed ethnoracial identity through her marriage and creative collaborations with fellow Nuyorican Marc Anthony. Nevertheless, Lopez's ability to perform blackness, whiteness, and brownness throughout her career opened the representational spectrum through which her body and identity circulated within global popular culture.

Claiming that Lopez is racially flexible is not the same as stating that she is racially unmarked. Rather, I argue the opposite. Lopez consciously negotiates the ways in which she is racialized by shaping how she is coded in the media through transforming signifiers such as clothing, hair color, hair style, skin color, body weight, music and, of course, her paramours. These practices allow a racialized transformation into ambiguity that other Puerto Ricans and Afro-Cuban women, such as Rosie Perez and Rosario Dawson, have not been able to achieve. While Lopez's film career depends on her ability to perform an ethnically ambiguous whiteness, such as in *Out of Sight* (1998), *The Wedding Planner* (2001), and *Angel Eyes* (2001), her music career relies on the ability to marshal a more racially ambiguous ethnic identity. The strategy of racial flexibility and ethnic ambiguity has proved successful for Lopez's management team. To date her most globally successful movie, *Shall We Dance?* (2004), featured Lopez playing "Paulina," an ethnically ambiguous white character. On the other hand, Lopez's more successful music singles, "If You Had My Love" (1999) and "I'm Real" (2001), have been hip-hop tinged remixes featuring Lopez in African-style braided hair side by side with established rap artists Ja Rule and LL Cool J, among others. Together, her cinematic and musical performances illustrate Lopez's facile and deliberate moves across ethnic and racial identities. It is this facile border crossing through established U.S. racial categories, specifically whiteness, that the tabloids and bloggers respond to later in her career.

Throughout her career, Lopez has carefully managed her ethnoracial identity for the English-language mainstream media while celebrating a more fixed Puerto Rican and panethnic Latina identity in the Spanish-language media.[37] From the beginning, U.S. Latina/o print and television news often highlighted Lopez's second-generation heritage and her achievements as a New York-born Puerto Rican, a Nuyorican. For instance, a news story in New York City's *El Diario La Prensa* about dignitaries at the 1998 Puerto Rican Day Parade mentioned Lopez's participation.[38] Another story in Los Angeles' *La Opinión* drew attention to Lopez's nomination at the 1999 American Music Awards by emphasizing her Latina/o flavor ("Con Sabor Latino").[39] In both stories, which are representative of U.S. Latina/o media practices, Lopez is identified by her Puerto Rican ethnicity. Such identification practices affirm the star's Latina authenticity and membership in an imagined Latina/o community that is racially and ethnically distinct from dominant U.S. culture.

Lopez was also one of the first actors in contemporary Hollywood to embrace the Latina label and identification with the U.S. Latina/o popular culture boom of the 1990s, unlike Jessica Alba, Cameron Diaz, America Ferrera, and Salma Hayek, who initially resisted being identified as Latinas by the English- and Spanish-language media. In 1996, Lopez posed for the first cover of the bilingual magazine *Latina* and has appeared on the magazine's cover more than any other Latina public figure. Finally, Lopez used her physicality, dark hair, light-brown skin, and curvaceous body to establish her ethnoracial difference and communality with U.S. Latina/o media audiences. In an appearance on Univisión's *The Cristina Show*, Lopez responded to questions about the authenticity of her butt by happily twirling her body and exclaiming in less than proficient Spanish that indeed "it" was all hers by birthright. As Frances Negrón-Muntaner argues, Lopez successfully used the African resonances of her curvaceous body as empirical, irrefutable evidence of her Puerto Rican identity, her authentic self—proof that although she was born in New York and could not speak Spanish fluently, potential signifiers of ethnic inauthenticity, she was still a *real* Puerto Rican Latina.[40] Lopez has effectively promoted her perfectly round and larger-than-Hollywood-average backside—roughly a dress size 6—to cultivate her commitment to Puerto Rican and Latina pride in the U.S. Latina/o media.

However, for the English-language media, the early hyping of her butt focused on Lopez's exotic bodily difference, ethnic ambiguity, and racial flexibility. Warner Brothers' 1997 *Selena* specifically targeted Latin American audiences, U.S. Latina/o audiences, and young U.S. girls across all ethnic and racial categories.[41] Arenas Group, an advertising and talent management firm specializing in the U.S. Latina/o market, effectively designed *Selena*'s promotional campaign with the goal of broad ethnic and racial appeal. The Arenas Group was also brought in by ABC to promote *Ugly Betty*.[42] Part of Arenas's promotional strategy depended on Selena's all-American story as a working-class girl from Texas making it big and the ability of Lopez's ambiguous identity to captivate a broad range of audiences and crossover movie demographics. The low-production-cost movie achieved its goal, grossing a respectable $35.3 million.[43] *Selena*'s cross-cultural success demonstrated to mainstream media marketers that both Latinas/os and non-Latinas/os would pay to see Latina actors and characters. If packaged effectively, Latina panethnicity could be globally commodified.[44]

Subsequently, Lopez's cinematic success after *Selena* increasingly rested on her ability to land roles stripped of ethnic- and race-specific cinematic markers.[45] Before the critically acclaimed movie *Out of Sight* (1998), where she plays the ethnically and racially ambiguous character Karen Sisco opposite white leading man George Clooney, Lopez was confined to playing Latina characters, such as Rosie Romero in *Nurses on the Line: The Crash of Flight 7* (1993); a young María Sánchez in *My Family, Mi Familia* (1995); Grace Santiago in *Money Train* (1995); Miss Márquez in *Jack* (1996); Gabriela "Gabby" in *Blood and Wine* (1997); Terri Flores in *Anaconda* (1997); and perhaps her most famous ethnic role, Selena Quintanilla-Pérez in *Selena* (1997). *Out of Sight* allowed Lopez to showcase her body and acting abilities through a sexy and exotic character whose development was not informed by a particular ethnic or racial identity. The character never speaks Spanish, although she presumably understands the language, as evidenced in her interactions with Latina/o characters, and her last name "Sisco," which could be interpreted as a Latina/o name, is not spelled in the traditional Spanish way, "Cisco." Since her success in *Out of Sight*, Lopez has made a career of playing ethnically and racially ambiguous characters, such as the character in her most internationally profitable movie to date, the $170 million blockbuster *Shall We Dance?* co-starring Richard Gere.[46] It is only recently that Lopez has returned to cinematic roles with more specific Puerto Rican/Latina ethnic content, such as the poor-performing movie *El Cantante* (2006)[47] and the limited release *Bordertown* (2006), both movies that she produced through her company Nuyorican Productions. By successfully managing her identity in a Hollywood industry driven by ethnic and racial typecasting, Lopez has parlayed her ethnically ambiguous and racially flexible exotic beauty and body into a marketable global success.

By 2001, Lopez's celebrity status was beginning to climb. Her increased visibility provided a potential moment of symbolic rupture for Latina/o audiences. As defined in the introduction, symbolic ruptures point to the interpretive mechanism that allows audiences (including myself as a cultural reader) the opportunity to use their subjectivity to disrupt the process of cultural commodification. For many fans and audiences, Lopez's performance of Latinidad within global entertainment points to a potentially resistant moment of ethnic and racial transformation. Barrera, Beltrán, and Negrón-Muntaner argue that Lopez's self-conscious celebration of her posterior is a form of symbolic war on dominant racialized constructions of Puerto Ricans and Latinas as culturally, socially, and politically marginal. That Lopez embraced her booty as a marketable symbol of desirable beauty points to her ethnic pride in the face of ongoing racial discrimination toward Puerto Ricans and presents an open challenge to white cultural dominance. As Negrón-Muntaner notes, "A big *culo* upset hegemonic (white) notions of beauty and good taste because it is a sign of the dark incomprehensible excess of 'Latino' and other African diaspora cultures."[48] If, as Negrón-Muntaner suggests, a big booty is where racialized Puerto Rican identity is stored, then the hypermedia attention on Lopez's racially ambiguous and simultaneously racially marked bountiful derriere provides a rare moment of visibility for the second largest Latina/o group in the United States.[49]

In my own family, we regularly look out for Lopez's performances in the English- and Spanish-language media (for research purposes of course). Both my Puerto Rican mother and Dominican father, in particular, recognize Lopez's diva personality as excessive but find humor and pride in the media attention paid to the Boricua starlet and her infamous booty. In addition to celebrating Lopez's visibility as a "real" Puerto Rican woman, her ethnically ambiguous and racially flexible physicality reminds them of the women in their multiracial and multiethnic families. Through both her ethnic specificity and racial ambiguity, Lopez serves as a cultural symbol of Puerto Rican and Latina/o resilience in a nation that has antagonistically welcomed them. Lopez's media visibility creates an opening for cultural resistance because the unclassifiable nature of her identity vexes established representations of U.S. ethnic and racial identity.[50] Governmentality does not depend on violence for its power but instead draws on its ability to normalize classifications, and Lopez's conscious play with ethnic and racial classification potentially destabilized gender/race power hierarchies in the United States.[51] Flexible and ambiguous bodies that rupture classifications—in this instance black/white racial hierarchies of beauty—thereby expose binary logic and essentialist identity categories, inevitably problematizing the norm.

Moving "In" to Blackness

Having already caught the eye of Hollywood producers through her performances in *Selena* and *Out of Sight*, Lopez's ascendance into the realm of pop culture icon finally occurred in 2000, the year she presented her first Grammy music award wearing "The Dress," a green Versace gown strategically missing enough material to showcase her small perky breasts, flat tummy, shapely muscular legs, and, of course, her ubiquitous booty. A Google image search of the term "JLo's Versace Dress" quickly yields images of Lopez wearing the infamous piece of couture. In an article exclusively about the dress on the *Entertainment Weekly* Web site, the commentator described the moment in these terms: "She turned herself out as the fly girl hyperversion of postfeminist power, flaunting her control by toying with the threat of excess. In consequence, her star went supernova."[52] Employing the "threat of excess," her performance of sexuality and style drew unprecedented attention by breaking with normative notions of white femininity and social acceptability. The dress's overt sensuality and Lopez's inescapable celebration of her body and sexuality struck a nerve for tabloid journalists who both loved and hated it.[53] Lopez's choice of dress communicated a confident sexual femininity that one biographer described as a transformative moment:

> In the evening's highpoint, Latin beauty Jennifer Lopez wears an eye-popping Versace dress that looks like a pasted-on scarf. It barely conceals her body. The audience is visibly dumbfounded. Her co-presenter, the usually witty David Duchovny, is star-struck as he stutters his lines. A chiquita legend is born.[54]

The brightly colored translucent dress became a hypersexualized spectacle. Lopez is not just a legend. She is not any woman. Lopez is a consumable Latin "chiquita" legend, a legend commonly associated with the banana-wearing Brazilian Carmen Miranda's over-the-top tropical Hollywood legacy. To the biographer, Lopez's sexuality is situated in a panethnic performance of Latinidad. The Puerto Rican Lopez echoes the Carmen Miranda legacy and becomes the latest globally popular hypersexualized Latina chiquita.

However, to understand the ethnic, racial, and sexual linkages associated with the dress, it is essential to contextualize it within Lopez's relationship to blackness and the tabloid coverage of Lopez's life at the time. Lopez attended the Grammy event with her *beau du jour*, Sean Combs, who is often credited with the early success of her music career. As a producer in three of her most successful albums, *On the 6* (1999), *J.Lo* (2001), and *J to tha L-O!: The Remixes* (2002), Combs is credited with bringing hip-hop to Lopez's pop sound. The hip-hop tinged remixes and videos from these three albums proved highly popular and produced six of Lopez's nine musical hits. However, the popularity of the songs and music videos also produced a secondary effect in tabloid coverage of the celebrity. Alongside her romantic relationship with the hip-hop mogul, the videos visually situated the racially flexible Lopez within an urban Puerto Rican aesthetic, black popular culture, and racialized sexuality.

For example, the hip-hop video remix for her No. 1 Billboard hit "I'm Real" (2001) changed the original setting from a predominantly white rural countryside where Lopez is the innocent object of a young white male to a predominantly urban space where she becomes the sexualized object of

Ja Rule's black heterosexual desire. Other videos such as "Love Don't Cost a Thing" show Lopez sporting African braids, and all of them emphasize her booty through close-ups, low-cut jeans, short-shorts, and tight-fitting clothing. Black hip-hop artists, street hoops, bling, and Lopez's Puerto Rican booty work together to create an identity that is not-quite-black but clearly establishes her outside whiteness and within the domain of urban black and Puerto Rican culture.

Lopez's relationship with Combs, which spanned the release of her first and second music albums, moved her further toward "not-quite-black" blackness. She was further racialized through her implicit linkage to stereotypic associations between hip-hop culture and urban criminality when, three months before her Grammy appearance, Lopez and Combs were arrested—Lopez was eventually released without charges—on suspicion of involvement in a shooting outside a New York City nightclub. By the end of her relationship with Combs in 2001, Lopez, who began her entertainment career in 1991 as a brown-haired, curly-headed, hip-hop dancer on the black variety program *In Living Color*, was visually and musically situated within the domain of urban popular culture. The specific classed, raced, and gendered performance of identity associated with the marketing of her music and clothing line inevitably positioned Lopez as an ethnic Puerto Rican brown woman who was not white but not quite black.

Whatever else Lopez gained from her musical and romantic relationship with Combs, her association with him slowed her move toward whiteness. Lopez's conscious embrace of black popular culture and racialized class identity as an urban Latina (specifically a Puerto Rican from the Bronx) made it difficult to break from the typecasting that defined her cinematic career prior to 1997. For example, despite her critically successful performance as an ethnically ambiguous character in *Out of Sight*, director Adam Shankman resisted casting Lopez as the lead for *The Wedding Planner* because he wanted the character to be a second-generation European immigrant. Shankman thought Lopez was too ethnic and too racialized—and presumably nonwhite—to pull off a white ethnic character:

> In the film, the main character, Mary, was to be Armenian, because she had to be under strong and old-fashioned parental influence. After agreeing, in principle, that she could take the role, Shankman asked despairingly: "Are you going to make me order a rewrite to make Mary a Latina?" Lopez replied: "No—I'll get rid of all my friends and get new Armenian ones." The character was eventually changed to an Italian.[55]

Implicit in Shankman's assessment of Lopez's ability to play the role are two important assumptions about ethnic and racial identities: first, that Latinas are too ethnically and racially marked as brown to pass as Eastern Europeans; second, that Lopez is white enough to be Italian or that Italians are brown enough to be played by Latinas. Both assumptions recognize that Lopez is a sexualized and racialized body whose ambiguity and flexibility have limits.

Symbolic Colonization and the White Gaze

Despite the desirable transformative potential of Latina ethnic ambiguity and racial flexibility for audiences, coverage of Lopez in the celebrity tabloids points to its dangerous limits, especially about members of a Puerto Rican community historically constructed as social and political threats in the United States. Not surprisingly, as Lopez's celebrity power increased later in her career, the tabloid coverage surrounding her series of high-profile relationships became increasingly negative—first with black hip-hop mogul Sean Combs (P. Diddy), then with multiethnic (Filipino/white) backup dancer Cris Judd, and finally with one of Hollywood's most popular leading white men of Irish descent, Ben Affleck. Lopez's self-conscious celebration of her backside and careful movement from blackness toward whiteness resulted in tabloid stories and audience blogs increasingly critical of her moral values, personal behavior, and sexuality. In particular, I contend that tabloid stories from 2002 to 2004 framed Lopez through a gendered and racialized discourse of Puerto Rican hypersexuality. To define hypersexuality, I build on Celine Parreñas Shimizu's work on Asian American representations.[56] Parreñas Shimizu's study concludes that the sexualized representation of Asian American women in popular culture is informative of how the United States makes sense of race through sexuality. Discussions of media representations of ethnicity and race must therefore include an analysis of ethnicity and race as sexualized. With regard to Lopez, I argue the hypersexualization of Lopez and her body is intricately connected to how the celebrity tabloids and bloggers make sense of her ethnoracial Puerto Rican identity.

One key concept for explaining the limits of nonwhite bodies in popular culture, be it in the tabloids or the movies, is the notion of the "white gaze." Building on Laura Mulvey's definition of the male gaze, several scholars have used the term *white gaze* to describe "the power of whites to control or contain constructions of nonwhite ethnicity in U.S. popular culture."[57] In the context of Latinidad, the power of the white gaze is maintained through gendering and racialization that produces symbolically colonized media depictions.

The media practices that reproduce dominant norms, values, and beliefs about Latinidad as foreign, exotic, and consumable help "control or contain constructions" of Latinidad in the media. Tabloid stories about Lopez after her breakup with Combs illustrate how journalists' white gaze functions to symbolically colonize Lopez as an ethnically ambiguous and racially flexible body through the racialized framing of her sexuality.

The potential rupturing of ethnoracial U.S. identity caused by Lopez's global success demands ideological disciplining. The ethnic, class, and physical markers that define her are racialized outside whiteness and therefore open for tabloid journalistic surveillance and discipline. Pointing out the significance of the increased cultural surveillance surrounding Lopez, one British writer explained:

> She is seen by many in Hollywood as a little diva in a big hurry: the Puerto Rican girl from the wrong side of the tracks who speaks her mind. They say she is famous for her looks, her bottom, her ex-boyfriend. And her big mouth. Jennifer Lopez knows she is regarded with suspicion. But she also knows that, at 30, she has become the world's highest-paid Latina actress, with a successful singing career as well. She may be scorned, but she is fast turning herself into the next Madonna.[58]

As the writer suggests, Lopez's Puerto Rican ethnicity, working-class roots, and body are viewed as globally desirable and culturally dangerous. Lopez's symbolic currency as a consumable exotic ethnic and racially flexible Nuyorican star ruptures dominant U.S. racial formations, and those moments of instability must be ideologically contained.

Dangerous Flirtations with Whiteness

The end of Lopez's relationship with Combs in February 2001 introduced a new, more racialized story line about the celebrity—one that was much harder to control. Most of the coverage about the Combs romance focused on his broken heart and by implication Lopez's heartlessness. It is during this period that tabloid stories about Lopez as an extraordinarily beautiful, hardworking but excessively demanding diva began flooding the tabloids when she quickly rebounded with her marriage to Cris Judd. Tabloid journalists drew a subtle but poignant contrast between Lopez and her romantic partners. Emphasizing Lopez's difference from the "average" woman, a *People* story about her September 2001 wedding with Judd quoted an old acquaintance, "'Cris always dated straitlaced girls in high school,' says Melissa Dowd Roberts, who shared a locker with Judd at Niceville High, where he was known as a quiet but popular guy. 'It's a surprise that he ended up with Jennifer Lopez with her see-through dresses and all.'"[59] By using the quote, several telling associations are created within the story. Judd likes "straitlaced girls," and Lopez is the kind of hypersexualized woman that wears "see-through dresses." He's quiet, nice, and marrying for the first time. Lopez is a divorcée who married a guy she had dated on the rebound and had known for less than eight months. A cynical interpretation of the relationship might suggest that Lopez's marriage to the low-profile noncelebrity Judd was a conscious attempt, even celebrity stunt, to recuperate the star from her hypersexualized image. The same *People* story, which raised doubts about Lopez's marital intentions, also included "evidence" of Judd as the traditional, powerful male patriarch and Lopez, not as the diva, but as the appropriately feminine partner: "In Puerto Rico, where she performed two concerts last month, 'he was in full control,' says this source. 'He was the boss. He was the choreographer. She listened to him, and he was running the show.'"[60] The conflicting narratives of the relationship circulated in the story create doubts about the relationship, but, more importantly, they reinforce Lopez's difference from other women.

Questions about Lopez's motives and morality intensified when her marriage to Judd ended less than a year later under suspicions of a sexual affair with Ben Affleck. Covering the announcement of Lopez and Judd's split in June 2002, *People*'s story once again questioned Lopez's behavior by quoting from Lopez's interview with Oprah to promote her film at the time, *Enough*:

But Lopez herself hinted last month that, when it came to love, her approach is more c'est la vie than eternal monogamy. "You do what feels right at the time," she told Oprah. "And I've always been the type that follows my heart and my gut. I still go with those instincts, because I feel like they've never steered me wrong."[61]

Lopez used Oprah's forum to promote the movie while carefully managing information about her personal life that was vague at best. Although other tabloid sources insist on Lopez's commitment to monogamy and disavow the star's sexual relationship with Affleck during this period, contradictory tabloid reports of Lopez's actions and public statements create the public perception that she is untrustworthy, immoral, and sexually promiscuous.

Not surprisingly, Lopez's peak visibility from 2001 to 2004, with covers for *Cosmopolitan, Elle, FHM (For Him Magazine), GQ, Esquire, Stuff, Harper's*

Bazaar, and *Complete Woman,* among others, was also accompanied by an increase in tabloid stories about her as an excessively demanding diva. The Latina bad girl Lopez joined the likes of other racialized celebrity divas, such as model Naomi Campbell. "Besides an epic booty," wrote one entertainment reporter in 2001, "what Lopez brings to the table is the frisson of the most garish, multimedia, boldface fame imaginable. She's the perfect music star of our age: not a musician at all, in fact, but an 'image diva'—a high icon of notoriety, a singing/dancing triumph of context over content."[62] Like a modern-day Hottentot Venus, Lopez became an object to be gazed, poked, and prodded. Tabloid journalists reported on everything from Lopez's insistence on all-white hotel rooms to room-temperature Evian water.[63] She was no longer the universally appealing Latina who made it out of the Puerto Rican Bronx through merit and hard work. Lopez became framed by the tabloids as the Latina diva who had few characteristics in common with their average readers. In other words, the difference that made her a global commodity also marked her as exotic and suspicious—a difference that became even more culturally dangerous with her engagement to one of Hollywood's golden boys, Ben Affleck.

Consequently, Lopez's celebration of her Latina booty and her statements critical of monogamy, combined with the short turn-around time between her June 2002 split with Judd and November 2002 engagement with Affleck, contributed to hypersexualized tabloid coverage about the star. Unlike Cuban women who have been historically represented in Hollywood as chaste and conservative, Puerto Rican women are predominantly depicted as poor, uneducated, and sexually promiscuous. Lopez's serial monogamy and excessive performance of wealth tapped into preexisting media representations of Puerto Rican women. In the first months of 2002, Lopez was dogged by tabloid stories of an alleged "Lo-down and dirty" tape that depicted her having group sex with women and men.[64] The cover of *Star* claimed to have the latest on the "J-Lo Gay Sex Tape Scandal. Star Weeps Over Home Video Shocker" (see figure 2.1). The scantily clad celebrity is plastered across the cover textually and visually to draw attention to her hypersexualization. Bypassing stories of Princess Diana's alleged lover, Christopher Reeve's secret sex pact with his wife, Liza Minnelli's divorce, and Britney Spears' sexual slipup, the *Star* emphasizes Lopez's sexualized image and morally questionable behavior. Illustrating the enduring power of the story, a June 2002 *National Enquirer* story would return to the sex tapes to make sense of the breakup of Lopez's marriage with Judd: "An *Enquirer* investigation revealed that when Jennifer's hubby Cris Judd heard there was a steamy sex tape of his wife and Puffy, he exploded."[65] Reinforcing the depiction of Lopez as hypersexual and morally responsible for the

Figure 2.1. During her relationship with Ben Affleck, Jennifer Lopez's sexuality was the focus of much tabloid coverage. Lopez's revealing red dress is clearly the focal point of this *Star* issue. The emphasis on the lesbian content of the tape situates her sexuality as different and potentially aberrant.

destruction of her marriage, the *National Enquirer* also published file photos of Lopez and Combs kissing and Lopez wearing a teeny bikini.

Lopez's alleged infidelities were clearly being treated differently than those of other celebrities. In the same issue of the *National Enquirer*, a story about Julia Roberts' impromptu celebration of Daniel Moder's divorce decree—two years after they began their extramarital relationship—is buried within the inside pages. Although the story does construct Roberts' action as socially inappropriate—Moder's parents reportedly refused to attend the party— tabloid editors decided that interest in Roberts' infidelity did not supersede scrutiny of Lopez's relationships. The relationship between Lopez and Affleck was rumored but not confirmed in the early parts of 2002. When the February 2002 sex-tape story appeared, Lopez and Affleck were making the box-office flop *Gigli*.[66] Rumors of a blossoming relationship were widely circulating in the tabloids. Lopez's relationships and rumored infidelities present an opportunity to affirm the ideologically conservative notions of racial fixity by containing Lopez's ethnic, racial, and sexual transgressions.

The conservative moral ideology embedded in negative tabloid coverage of Lopez's alleged sex tapes, sexual relationships, and attitudes about sexual monogamy devalue her cultural capital as a racially and ethically flexible star by containing her within familiar narratives of Puerto Rican and Latina racialized hypersexualization. That is, the peak visibility of her success from 2001 to 2004—when she released two music albums, five films, and appeared on countless magazine and tabloid covers—resulted in tabloid coverage that contributed to the symbolic colonization of the Puerto Rican star. No longer interested in Lopez's glamorous wardrobe, beautiful voluptuous body, and Horatio Alger American dream success, the tabloids turned their white gaze on Lopez's exorbitant financial demands and uncontrollable sexuality. Coverage of Lopez's economic success as a "rags to riches" Latina from the Bronx was displaced by tabloid stories often questioning her social appropriateness. In particular, tabloid coverage of the alleged sex tapes tapped into dominant heterosexual fantasies about black studs and insatiable Latinas and positioned Lopez as outside normative white heterosexuality.[67]

Critical tabloid surveillance of Lopez reached its zenith throughout the publicity surrounding the relationship with Ben Affleck. The March 17, 2003, issue of *Us Weekly* published no fewer than four items on "La Lopez" and Affleck. Each tabloid item constructed Lopez as hot, spicy, and sexually voracious, especially in comparison to the socially acceptable black and white women also featured in magazines. For example, one story contrasted the Lopez-Affleck relationship to that of Gwyneth Paltrow and Chris Martin, suggesting that while Lopez-Affleck were highly sexual, emotional, and "tan," Paltrow-Martin were asexual, nonaffectionate, and "pale."[68] Not only did the tabloid language about Lopez call upon common Hollywood signifiers associated with Latina femininity as hot, spicy, and brown, it also circulated historically accepted notions of white femininity as restrained and frigid. Lopez might be the better looking, more passionate lover, but Paltrow was the "good girl" you bring home to mother.

The scrutiny of Lopez and her relationship became so intense that she referenced the public obsession in her music video "Jenny from the Block" (2002), a video which flaunted her wealth, lifestyle, body, and six-carat diamond engagement ring from Affleck. The video, shot in a spy-cam/paparazzi style, featured a series of misleadingly intimate moments between Lopez and Affleck. Among other scenes, the couple is shown eating at an outdoor café where Lopez is "seen" crying—only to reveal that she has dust in her eye—or through a window where Affleck appears to give Lopez a diamond ring—only to reveal that he was handing her an earring. The most memorable and talked about scene, however, revolved around a series of highly sexual images showing Affleck hovering over Lopez's body as he leans in to her buttocks to undo her bikini straps. The seemingly autobiographical video fanned the flames of tabloid speculation about the couple.

Tabloid stories detailing Lopez's alleged sexual relationships and exorbitant demands on Affleck for sex and gifts splashed across the covers of the supermarket tabloids. *Star* and *Us Weekly* featured Lopez's ex-husbands and their personal and intimate accounts of life with the star with headlines such as "Cris Judd: Life With and Without J.Lo" and "J.Lo and Me: The truth about our marriage: The proposal, the gifts, the wild times. J.Lo's ex-husband reveals the intimate details of their roller-coaster life together."[69] *Star* also published a cautionary first-person account by Lopez's first husband, Ojani Noa, "The Nasty Real J.Lo: Sex Crazed . . . Selfish . . . Cruel."[70] In both tabloids, Noa and Judd are characterized as victims of Lopez's aspirations, uncontrollable sexuality, and questionable morality. Lopez is framed as excessive and ultimately dangerous to the men in her life. For example, the *Star* story quoted Noa as saying, "Wedding vows mean nothing to her. . . . Ben Affleck should ask himself: 'If she climbed into it with you so easily, don't you think she'll do the same with someone else.'"[71] The framing of Lopez as a cheating, untrustworthy domestic partner became widely circulated in the entertainment media.

The tabloid framing of Lopez as sexually voracious, morally corrupt, and professionally duplicitous dominated the coverage throughout her relationship with Affleck. A November 2002 E! Online story about the Lopez-Affleck engagement reported:

> It is unclear exactly what "true Affleck fashion" is, but we hope, for their sake, that the upcoming marriage does not progress in "true J.Lo fashion."
>
> Lopez dispatched Hubby No. 1, then-waiter Ojani Noa, in a year. Hubby No. 2, dancer Cris Judd, got the boot after eight months.
>
> Legally, J.Lo is still Mrs. Judd. Their divorce won't be final until January 26, meaning the never-married Affleck must wait nearly three months before becoming "Hubby No. 3."[72]

Dispatching the first husband, booting the second husband, and becoming engaged to a third while still legally married, Lopez is constructed as sexually permissive rather than chaste, emotionally manipulative rather than sincere, and a self-serving partner rather than an appropriately feminine, selfless spouse.

If Lopez is the lying, cheating, bossy Latina dragon lady, then Affleck must occupy the position of the powerless white male held captive by her sexual allures. Publishing an exposé about the couple's alleged prenuptial agreement, *Star* continued the framing of Lopez as the Latina version of the dragon lady and Affleck as a white male dupe: "J.Lo Drops Pre-Nup Bombshell on Ben! Insiders Reveal . . . Her rules. Cheating; $5 million fine; Sex: at least 4 times a week; Kids: as many as she wants."[73] According to the tabloids, Lopez is the domineering, money-grubbing, hypersexual Puerto Rican woman who cannot wait to start overpopulating the earth with her multiracial offspring; whether Affleck agrees is immaterial. Affleck, like Noa and Judd before him, becomes another innocent male victim to Lopez's unrelenting drive for global entertainment domination.

Two narratives about Lopez thus circulated in the media throughout her relationship with Affleck. On the one hand, the traditional entertainment media, such as *People*, continued to report on Lopez's success as sexually desirable, marketable, and glamorous, thereby celebrating her global achievements. On the other hand, the celebrity tabloids focused on Lopez's questionable professional, emotional, and sexual motives, thus policing her access to dominant socially acceptable definitions of white femininity. The ideologically conservative tabloid content shifted Lopez to the bottom and other celebrities to the top of a racially informed moral hierarchy. Although both Julia Roberts and Angelina Jolie allegedly began relationships with married men during this same time frame, their white femininity, racially appropriate sexual relationships, and socially acceptable desire for motherhood insulated them from the more negative tabloid stories that surrounded Lopez. Tabloid headlines such as "Julia Roberts Bombshell! She's Visiting Fertility Clinic" or "Brad and Angelina Are Adopting! They're adopting: They just applied to adopt a baby in Ethiopia. How Brad and Angelina are more serious than you think" recuperated Jolie and Roberts as sympathetic and exemplary performers of white femininity and domesticity, thereby erasing the women's sexual transgressions.[74]

In the same issue as the sympathetic tabloid report of Roberts' visit to a fertility clinic, *Star* published a story on Lopez's feud with Affleck's best friend, Matt Damon:

"He told Ben that even though he thinks he's madly in love, he needs to hit the brakes because he couldn't possibly know the real J.Lo after less than a year with her," a source reveals. Insiders say Matt also reminded Ben that Jennifer was married when he fell in love with her and doesn't want him on the receiving end of a broken heart a year from now.[75]

Regardless of her original pursuit of the married Moder, Roberts is the doting wife who "has always loved kids." Lopez, however, is characterized as manipulative, domineering, and sexually unfaithful.[76]

Responding to the growing negative tabloid construction about her life, Lopez and Affleck sought to create positive publicity about their relationship. In a July 2003 *Dateline NBC* segment about the couple's engagement and everyday life, Lopez is depicted as the doting, affectionate, subservient fiancée who prepares Affleck's favorite foods, tends to the household chores, and devotes herself to creating a comfortable home for them.[77] Nevertheless, the tabloid coverage contined to hypersexualize Lopez, contributing to a gendered and racialized construction of the star that reaffirmed the inherent stability and goodness of whiteness through the framing of Latinidad and Puerto Rican identity as foreign, exotic, and sexually uncontrollable. Lopez's movement toward whiteness through her relationship with Affleck transgressed the boundaries of socially acceptable norms for ethnoracial minority women and mixed-race relationships in the United States. Beyoncé Knowles, whose black body/booty is also hyped in the tabloids, carefully cultivates her image to affirm upward class mobility and middle-class respectability within the sphere of blackness.[78] Despite the attention given to Knowles' body, tabloid stories about her often speak of her "regular" personality (i.e. non-diva-like behavior), Christian beliefs, and long-term stable relationship with black hip-hop artist Jay-Z.[79] Similarly, tabloid coverage of Demi Moore and Ashton Kutcher and Jennifer Aniston and Brad Pitt focus on the women's loyalty to friends and family, love of children, and normative heterosexuality.[80]

Further illustrating the double standard applied to same-race relationships, Affleck and his now-wife Jennifer Garner have not been dogged or plagued by rumors of infidelity, despite tabloid rumblings of a tryst on the set of *Daredevil* (2003). Furthermore, tabloid coverage of Affleck and Garner's engagement after a nine-month whirlwind romance on the rebound from long-term relationships avoided discussion of alleged infidelities. In the wake of their new relationship, Affleck's engagement with Lopez and Garner's marriage to Michael Vartan were all but forgotten by tabloid journalists. Instead, tabloid accounts focused on the celebrities' low-profile romance, a subtle repudiation of the media frenzy that surrounded Lopez and Affleck's engagement. The following tabloid account discusses the engagement, marriage, and Garner's pregnancy by depicting her as an average woman with down-home traditional values, not like Affleck's previous girlfriends:

> Ben, 32, is an A-List Hollywood star today, but he grew up in Cambridge, Mass., and comes from a decidedly non-Hollywood, glitz-free background. And one thing [his mother] Chris, a former schoolteacher, adores about Jen, 33, is the way she reflects that background. "Jennifer is a homebody; she likes to cook and knows how to make a happy home," says a friend of the Afflecks. "Chris finds Jennifer so natural and easy to talk to. There are no airs. She says Jennifer is totally genuine and a very nice person. Chris hasn't felt that way about all of Ben's girlfriends."[81]

Garner is genuine; Lopez is insincere. Garner is a homebody; Lopez is a diva. Garner is down-to-earth; Lopez is consumed by her wealth and fame.

Affleck and Garner's pregnancy announcement before their marriage is not coded as sexually aberrant but is instead discussed as an expression of their commitment to family values. For example, the *Star* quoted one source close to Affleck as saying, "As far as Ben's concerned, Jennifer can't get pregnant soon enough. . . . He's 100 percent sure he's found the person he wants to spend the rest of his life with."[82] Garner, who refused to share a bed with Affleck in her mother's home, is characterized as conservative and average. Affleck's mother, friends, and by the positive tone of the coverage, the tabloids, approve and accept Garner as a suitable romantic and sexual partner.[83] Garner's white femininity, normative sexuality, and low-key media visibility (Garner rarely graces the covers of fashion magazines or tabloids) were defined as socially appropriate and by implication different from Lopez. Despite an increase in multiracial relationships and U.S. residents who identify as multiracial, the symbolic world of the tabloids reaffirmed a racially fixed rather than racially flexible social order.

Lopez's construction of self as a star who personified complex characters across ethnic and racial categories was symbolically colonized through tabloid stories that reaffirmed a more fixed gendered, raced, and classed Latinidad. By the end of her relationship with Affleck, Lopez's gender, racial, and economic excesses were disciplined and contained, and Affleck's emasculated white masculinity was re-established. Even though early tabloid coverage of their relationship emphasized their working-class similarities, later coverage of their demise increasingly reported on their dissimilarities. One *Star* cover headline focused on Lopez's lack of class and cultural capital by claiming that "Ben orders J.Lo makeover . . . and she fires manager, agent and PR and puts Ben in charge: 'My woman needs class'" (see figure 2.2).[84] The color, print, and Chinese style of the dress along with the pan-Asian hairdo visually reinforces Lopez's association with Hollywood images of sexually domineering Asian dragon ladies. By publishing such a sexualized photo of Lopez to accompany the story, the *Star* was apparently judging Lopez's dress, hairstyle, makeup—even her bodily pose—as hypersexualized and classless. Affleck's demands that Lopez rehabilitate her "vixen" ways further indicate that the star needs to assimilate more effectively into the standards of white middle-class respectability.

Reports of Affleck's makeover demand also redefine him as masculine, powerful, and in control of the relationship and his Latina girlfriend. Tabloid reports of Affleck's takeover of the relationship depicted Lopez's sexualized and racialized diva image as inherently conflicting with Affleck's average "white" guy personality and identity, such as in this E! Online story about Lopez's dismissal of her manager, agent, and publicist:

It was a move that had gossip columnists speculating whether Lopez had completely lost it or was in fact engaging in a savvy act of spin control to keep her diva-like image in check.

"She obviously saw her image in crisis, and she is becoming known as the demanding diva. She wants to be recast as Jenny from the Block," said Jeannette Walls, gossip columnist for MSNBC.com.

Others pointed a finger at Lopez's beau, Ben Affleck, as the instigator of at least one of the controversial axings. Last Wednesday, the *New York Post* reported that Affleck demanded that J.Lo dump Medina because "Benny created this diva image of Jennifer."[85]

Figure 2.2. Ben Affleck's demands that Jennifer Lopez rehabilitate her "vixen" ways further indicate that the Latina star needs to assimilate more effectively into the standards of white middle-class respectability. Reports of Affleck's makeover demand also redefine him as masculine, powerful, and in control of the relationship and his Latina girlfriend.

Lopez's hypervisible image is in need of rehabilitation, and Affleck is in charge. The *Star* cover and the above story assume that Affleck's image is safe and normal. It is Lopez's excesses that need to be disciplined. Such stories contribute to the perception that an irreparable cultural and racial gap exists between the two stars. Foregrounding the cultural and racial differences between the two, an *Us Weekly* cover just after their final breakup in 2004 declared: "Why Ben won't marry her. They're still in love, so what's the problem—and why is she with P. Diddy? Inside the couple's new decision *not* to say 'I do.'"[86] Lopez might have demanded the prenup, but it's Affleck who dictates the end of the relationship. At issue, the article suggests, is Affleck's uncomfortable fit with the appearance-conscious Puerto Rican diva from the Bronx. Lopez's lavish spending, haute couture taste, and sexual disloyalty are presented as proof that she is not the "right" woman for Affleck.

Even though Affleck was the alleged adulterer in the relationship, tabloids blamed Lopez's sexually and financially demanding and controlling ways for the relationship's demise in January 2004. Tabloid reports of Affleck's alleged dalliance with a stripper were said to be the cause of the delay in the couple's 2003 nuptials,[87] but coverage of the final 2004 breakup often centered on Affleck's decision to "put his foot down" and take command of Lopez and the relationship.[88] Setting up tabloid expectations of Affleck's sincere discomfort with his engagement months before the cancellation of their planned 2003 wedding, an *in Touch* article reported that "Friends say Ben, who has long had his eye on a serious political career, is tired of living in Jen's shadow and fitting in with her relentless showbiz lifestyle, which has her choosing his clothes and sees him working out alongside her at the unthinkable time of 4:45 a.m.!"[89] Affleck is sincere in his personal ambitions; Lopez is aberrantly obsessed with the artificial and material. The publication of tabloid accounts a month after their 2004 breakup further recuperate Affleck's masculinity by providing evidence that he was the one who asserted his authority and control by ending the engagement.[90]

Five years after their breakup, the tabloids continued to frame Affleck as Lopez's unsuspecting victim and the one who finally determined his own fate. In a widely reported 2006 interview, Affleck was quoted as saying, "I should never have got engaged and never gone down that route. I thought I wanted certain things, but I didn't. I got lost and felt suffocated, miserable and gross. Being in the middle of a tabloid frenzy, it became so intense I had to stop and think, 'What am I doing with my life?'"[91] Affleck was always the normal one. His involvement with the Puerto Rican Lopez made him feel gross and, I would argue, made the nation feel uneasy. Lopez is the irrational part of his past that had to be excised, and now has to be rationally explained. Tabloid coverage of his presumably justified actions in ending the engagement do not afford Lopez access to the discourse of victimization and vulnerable femininity that have defined other women whose partners have cheated on them or left them, such as tabloid coverage of Jennifer Aniston after her 2005 split and divorce from Brad Pitt.[92]

Jenny from the Blogs

Elizabeth Bird argues that tabloid readers relish celebrity stories that privilege and culturally affirm their social roles and cultural status: "For women, tabloid stories, like soap operas, 'assert the legitimacy of feminine meanings and identity within and against the patriarchy.' . . . For men, the pleasure comes from obtaining 'information' that gives one an edge in resisting the dominance of mainstream culture and political attitudes."[93] An examination of tabloid celebrity blogs about Lopez and her relationship with Affleck illustrate a public unease with the Latina star's global success. Thus, the final section of this chapter turns to audience sense-making about tabloid coverage of Lopez and Affleck on the Blogcritics Magazine Web site. According to the Web site, founded in 2002 as a Web site for the online exchange of political and cultural ideas, "Blogcritics.org is a new kind of online magazine, an interactive community in which writers and readers from around the globe talk about stories, issues, and products."[94] A 2006 search of the Web site for the term "Jennifer Lopez" yielded 109 original blog postings. A search for the term "Bennifer," the tabloid moniker for Ben and Jennifer, resulted in nine original postings. Of the 109 blog postings about Jennifer Lopez, thirty-seven contained information critical of Lopez; thirty-seven contained information supportive of the celebrity; and the rest were informative in nature without language critical or supportive of the star. Because I am most interested in understanding how audiences negotiated tabloid coverage of the relationship, my analysis focuses only on the blogs and comments most relevant to studying audience reception of Lopez and her relationship with Affleck.

J.Lo the Sexual Freak

Writing about the 1990s backlash against multiculturalism in the United States, Cameron McCarthy argues that white populations left behind by globalization work out their economic anxieties by attacking educational programs and policies that benefit ethnic and racial minorities through a discourse of resentment.[95] The discourse of resentment mandates that difference (sexual, racial, or linguistic) must be managed to maintain hegemonic economic hierarchies that reaffirm the trope of U.S. liberalism and meritocracy, the belief that the United States is a "colorless" society that lets those with the best skills and desire move to the top of the democratic marketplace. Postings critical of Lopez and her relationship with Affleck engage in a similar discourse of resentment. Lopez's global success and commercial wealth are diminished by the bloggers and those commenting on the blogs through gendered and racialized readings of the star as nonwhite. For instance, a December 5, 2002, blog item quotes a *New York Post* Page Six item that recounts a warning sent to Ben Affleck:

> Arthur Gordon, author of "How to Get All the Girls You Want," has sent an open letter to Affleck informing the star his wife-to-be is a "Freak."
>
> "The bottom line for a Freak is the constant need to experience the new and exciting, usually sexual," Gordon writes. "This is the type of woman to whom boredom is the worst fate imaginable." Noting that J.Lo's track record suggests a short marriage, Gordon cautions, "There will always be one person she loves more than her husband du jour—herself."[96]

Eric Olsen, one of the founders of Blogcritics Magazine, then adds:

> Lopez totally rubs me the wrong way: I hate her music, dislike her split image of coy Cinderella and street-wise tit-flasher, and don't find her very attractive either. Within the (admittedly narrow) confines of sex goddessdom, could you have a worse body: no chest and huge ass (she does have a nice smile, though)? This woman has overstayed her 15 minutes tenfold. And now she has bewitched poor Ben.[97]

Building on the invocation of Rick James's famous use of the word *freak* to describe sexually assertive, adventurous, and promiscuous women, Eric Olsen equates Lopez with a "tit-flasher," someone who likes to expose herself in public. Lopez's body, a source of her economic success and cultural visibility, is constructed by Olsen as ugly ("no chest and huge ass") and manipulative ("she has bewitched poor Ben"). Olsen contests Lopez's visibility and her relationship with Affleck by drawing attention to Lopez's "no chest and huge ass," specifically pointing to Lopez's failure to embody the ideal of white femininity—thin women with bountiful breasts. Lopez's butt, the celebrated marker of her Puerto Rican identity and ethnic and racial difference, is devalued by Olsen. Negative tabloid audience readings of Lopez's body and popularity, in particular those that devalue her economic and cultural capital, exemplify the discourse of racial resentment in everyday life.

Drawing attention to Lopez as culturally, socially, ethnically, and racially different from her white fiancé reinforces fixed binary notions of U.S. ethnic and racial identity that privilege whiteness as the ideal of beauty and desire and racial fixity as the norm for romantic partners. The ideologically conservative context of tabloid news production and reception produced blogs and comments critical of Lopez's wealth and visibility. For instance, a December 2003 blog posting about a tabloid story alleging that Lopez engaged in theft exemplifies how the discourse of resentment is worked out through Lopez's Puerto Rican body:

> I read yesterday where Vuitton canned the princess because in the course of her ad photo shoots, she took off with tens of thousands of dollars worth of merchandise. You can take the girl off the street, but you can't take the street off the girl. You GO—and fast—J-Lo![98]

The blogger, bookofjoe, links Lopez's behavior at the shoot with racialized urban criminality and sexuality, an association that is reinforced through the blogger's original inclusion of a photograph purportedly showing Lopez without underwear as she gets out of a limousine. Lopez's theft, lack of underwear, and inability to keep her legs together affirm a construction of aberrance. She might be a millionaire, but her racialized working-class Latina background remains inscribed in her body and behavior.

The racial and sexual subtext of audience readings about Lopez is made even more explicit in some of the 114 responses to bookofjoe's original posting. While some posters questioned the credibility of the blog on the grounds that one of the world's wealthiest women wouldn't need to steal ("J.Lo is tooo rich 2 steal from anybody"),[99] others perceived it as proof of Lopez's lack of morality, with one noting: "That is one of the biggest reasons that we cant put people like you (latin) to work for major companies like ours because you people arent to be trusted do to your lack of backgound intellegence."[100] Circulating more explicit and virulently racist opinions grounded in negative stereotypes about Puerto Ricans, several posters argued the blog posting and photograph were proof that Lopez was stupid, lazy, criminal, sexually immoral, and just "not a nice person."

Hey, she is Puerto Rican . . . let her steal, surpirsed she doesn't have 6 kids by now. If all she does is steal here and there she is a shinning light for her people to look up to. So did she try to sell this stuff from the back of a limo or something—I don't see whats the big deal.[101]

For the poster, Lopez's identity as Puerto Rican explains her actions. Puerto Rican women are stereotyped as untrustworthy and hypersexual criminals, a negative racial and sexual stereotype of Puerto Ricans and Lopez. Other posters described the celebrity as "spoiled" and "entitled," a star whose economic and professional success put her out of touch with a presumably more humble and authentic Latina reality.[102] Underlying many of the postings about this blog, even those more supportive of Lopez, is a critique of the excessive display of economic capital by an ethnoracial minority woman. The cultural disciplining of Lopez in the tabloids speaks to the economic and racial anxieties of some celebrity news consumers.

"Our Long National Nightmare Is Over"

Blogs and Internet discussions specifically about Lopez and Affleck's relationship likewise reproduced conservative narratives about sexuality and race. The end of their relationship was celebrated by a majority of bloggers and posters in Blogcritics. These audiences viewed Lopez as transgressing sexual and racial norms and in turn used dominant U.S. ideologies about ethnicity and race to discipline the Puerto Rican celebrity. For instance, a January 23, 2004, blog by Eric Olsen welcomed tabloid news of the demise of Lopez and Affleck's relationship:

But Ben Affleck and Jennifer Lopez were poison. Her crass hyper-ambition and diva airs made him look desperate and needy and lacking in self-confidence, as if he were under some kind of love spell. And rather than emphasizing her best self: the plucky Puerto Rican kid who rose from the barrio on talent, hard work, and determination, their relationship made her look like a manipulative, greedy bitch. Plus, they never looked right as a physical match: he kind of soft and lumpy, she with the Aztec face, no chest and crazy wide ass.[103]

The manipulative and greedy Puerto Rican Lopez is blamed for making the white Affleck needy, desperate, and insecure. Eric Olsen conflates Puerto Rican, Aztec, and Mexican physicality and positions them against and outside whiteness, an ethnic blurring that at least one poster responding to the blog found troubling:

> Regarding your comments about Jennifer Lopez (a Puerto Rican) and her "Aztec" face: There are no Aztecs in Puerto Rico. Aztecs are Native Americans only found in Mexico. Also, I don't see why someone who is part Native American (as Jennifer probably is, but not Aztec) can't be attractive. Are you racist?[104]

Because Lopez is not Mexican, the poster calls into question Olsen's misreading of the star's identity and critiques the use of homogenous signifiers of Latinidad. Rather than signing in for Puerto Rican beauty and identity, to Olsen her butt signals her exotic Latina difference. Lopez's supposedly "indigenous Mexican" face, lack of breasts, and large butt are characterized as not fitting in with white standards of feminine beauty and middle-class respectability—standards ultimately critiqued by this poster.

A majority of the nineteen comments responding to Olsen's January blog, however, similarly engaged in the policing of Lopez's foray into whiteness. One poster directly addressed Affleck, saying: "Ben you wrote 'Good Will Hunting' and dated Gwenyth Paltrow. Now you have made a nightmare known as Gigli and dated a girl from 'the block.'"[105] The poster calls the relationship "wrong and immoral," encourages Lopez to reunite with Sean Combs, and makes a derogatory reference to Lopez's promiscuity. Through comparing Paltrow, the right kind of woman, with Lopez, the wrong type of woman, a "girl from the block," Lopez is defined as aberrant, nonwhite, hypersexual, and once again associated with the racialized space and excesses of the urban city. Declaring the relationship a "national nightmare,"[106] blog postings regarding the tabloid coverage of the relationship reinforce the belief that Lopez devalued Affleck's racial and gendered symbolic worth.[107] The discomfort with Lopez and Affleck symbolized a more general discomfort with ethnoracial minority identity, mixed-race relationships, and the changing face of the United States.

However, not all of the online comments about Lopez and her relationship with Affleck were negative. Several posters commenting on the Louis Vuitton article attacked the discourse of racial resentment and discomfort embedded in the initial posting and subsequent responses: "All these comments are made because white people cant stand a hispanic like J.LO is making it in the bizz and making good money just as any of the white actors and actresses."[108] Other posters used Lopez's achievements and work ethic to question the veracity of the blog and recuperate her respectability: "I think that people are just sooooo jealous of her because she is a latino singer who made it big. And all these white people are tryin to hate on her, but in the end those crackers are just losers."[109] Lopez's body becomes a contested site of the status of ethnic and racial minorities in the imagined nation. Audience research on Latina reception of Lopez documents the complicated vectors of identity through which her body is read. Jillian Báez's study concludes that positive readings of the multihyphenate Latina entrepreneur are influenced both by ethnic affiliation and class status, with middle-class Puerto Rican women more likely to celebrate Lopez's hypervisibility and media success. Although working-class Puerto Rican and Mexican women often object to Lopez's hypersexualization, she remains a powerful icon of Latina independence and success, particularly for Puerto Rican women who are more likely to identify with her.[110]

Together the blogs and comments illustrate how Latina bodies as historically contingent artifacts are informed by specific social and political contexts. Tabloid stories unabashedly take an ideologically conservative point of view. The Puerto Rican Lopez as U.S. celebrity is celebrated for her Horatio Alger success yet disciplined for her racial transgressions into white heteronormative domesticity. Latinas can stand in for the globally exotic and symbolize ongoing changes within the U.S. nation, but they cannot represent or reproduce the nation itself. The African resonances located within her bountiful body/booty are too large a threat for a nation still invested in notions of binary racial purity as either black or white.

Tabloid news about Lopez as one of the most profitable and visible Latina celebrities is constrained by the disciplining discourse of racial resentment—a complex backlash against Puerto Rican cultural visibility and economic success in the United States. In particular, the tabloid coverage and blogs signal ongoing public anxieties regarding the changing status of ethnic, racial, and gender identities. As one poster on the Louis Vuitton discussion thread stated, the conversation turned into "race baiting."[111] The ethnic ambiguity and racially flexible visibility of some Latina stars heralds a transformation in cultural labor by rupturing the dominant black-white racial binary that has long defined U.S. culture. Consequently, tabloids titillate their audiences by highlighting Latina celebrities' desirable attributes (clothes, achievements, bodies) and simultaneously contribute to the symbolic colonization of Latinidad by circulating stories that punish them for their flexible identity and economic privilege.[112]

Returning to U.S. Latinidad

The tabloid coverage about Lopez symbolically colonizes Puerto Rican and Latina identity by recuperating the social position of white identity through reaffirming cultural boundaries that cannot be transgressed without penalty. Lopez's potentially rupturing performance of ethnic, racial, sexual, and class identity resulted in the need for gendering and racializing the celebrity. Unlike her contemporaries, such as Halle Berry, Beyoncé Knowles, Jennifer Garner, Angelina Jolie, or Julia Roberts, Lopez's uncategorizable racial body, panethnic identity, overt sexuality, and conspicuous wealth are codified as hot, spicy, excessive, and aberrant. Garner, Jolie, and Roberts maintain their white respectability despite reports of sexual infidelities in the tabloids. Berry and Knowles are multiracial women, but their normative performance of black identity maintains the dominant racial ideology of hypodescent (one drop of black blood makes one black). Lopez's seemingly shifting performance of whiteness, blackness, and brownness, however, adds to a cultural discomfort with the changing formations of ethnoracial identity in the United States. Latinas' place in tabloid celebrity culture and the United States is thus profoundly unstable and contradictory. Visibility in a media environment historically characterized by the erasure of Latina/o actors, characters, writers, and producers is often viewed as progress. It is, however, a story of progress and visibility fraught with cultural perils for ethnoracial minority communities.

Writing about the sociological function of celebrity culture, Christine Gledhill argues that coverage of Hollywood stars is representative of the ideological conflicts in contemporary popular culture.[113] Tabloid coverage and blogs about Lopez and her relationship with Affleck document the limits of Latinidad, ethnic ambiguity, and racial flexibility. Initial tabloid constructions of Lopez's beauty/booty as globally desirable become contested as she embodies whiteness by losing weight (in particular her booty), straightening and lightening her hair, flaunting her wealth, and starting a relationship with Affleck. Tabloid coverage about the American dream—about a Puerto Rican woman who beats the odds to make it in a field where few Latinas have succeeded—was replaced by a more gendered and racialized story of Latinidad. Coverage of Lopez's relationship with Affleck focused on her not as exotic, desirable, and marketable but as disruptive to white heteronormative masculinity. That a brown-haired, brown-eyed *trigueña* Puerto Rican from the Bronx could captivate the heart of an all-American white boy from the Boston suburbs disturbed conservative notions of white heterosexuality and the established U.S. racial order that places Puerto Rican identity outside of whiteness. Tabloid coverage unequivocally marked Lopez as nonwhite and outside middle-class respectability.

The tabloid and audience policing of her body is evocative of the continued legal, economic, and political policing of Puerto Rican emigrants to the United States. During the 1950s, Puerto Rican Operation Bootstrap emigrants were encouraged to migrate as agricultural workers, garment manufacturers, and domestic laborers. Their ethnoracial difference and limited English skills made them desirable workers who could be more easily controlled through low wages, unsafe work environments, and unfair labor practices. However, when their numbers swelled and they embraced a racialized political identity in the 1970s, Puerto Ricans became associated with blackness, poverty, and criminality. Such marginalization resulted in Puerto Rican militant social movements on the island and in New York, Chicago, and other major urban centers. Because Puerto Ricans existed outside whiteness and blackness they were constructed as socially and politically threatening to the racial, social, and political order. Their laboring bodies required spatial, cultural, and racial containment from other ethnic and racial minorities.[114]

Similarly Lopez entered the lucrative stream of global popular culture as a docile, exotic, desirable, commodifiable body, yet she was forbidden to partake in the full rights and economic privileges of whiteness. The anti-climatic end of her relationship with Affleck signaled the restoration of white patriarchal order and racial fixity. Affleck eventually set the rules and terms of their relationship, and Lopez was coded as too different to be associated with whiteness or blackness. Richard Dyer argues that Hollywood stars are their bodies and meanings about their bodies are ultimately created through the complex interactions between artistic performance, media institutions, and public discourse.[115] Key physical characteristics—race, ethnicity, gender, sexuality, and class—become particularly important in making sense of the public conversations that surround star bodies. In other words, understanding the bodily discourses that surround ethnoracial women tells something not only about the stars but also about our contemporary racial social structures, norms, and conflicts. Within the world of tabloid celebrity news, the "all-American" boy became the victim during a period when U.S. control of Puerto Rico was being violently contested in Vieques and anti-Latina/o and anti-immigration sentiments were proliferating throughout the United States.

Since her marriage to salsa artist and fellow Nuyorican Marc Anthony in 2005, the tabloid stories about Lopez as a demanding, excessive, and hypersexual diva have been relatively silenced. The birth of her twins has been unilaterally celebrated by the tabloids and entertainment media. No longer the sexualized Latina diva, she has been constructed as a good Puerto Rican wife and mother—so much so that Lopez lost her tabloid title of best Hollywood booty in 2006 to white, although part American Indian, celebrity Jessica Biel.[116] Lopez's "kiss my brown booty" moment of Boricua subversion has been safely contained through a return to a more sexually conservative performance of Latina femininity. In 2007, the cover of *Us Weekly* exclaimed "J.Lo's Dream Comes True. Yes, She's Pregnant! After struggling to conceive, the former diva is 'over the moon,' craving Doritos and pickles and hoping for a girl."[117] The "former diva" is once again a beautiful and socially desirable Puerto Rican woman. Other examples of Lopez's image transformation include *Self* magazine featuring Lopez on the cover of its "2008 Inspiring Women Special" and a 2008 issue of *People* that celebrated the star's athletic achievement, "J.Lo did it! Triathlon After Twins."[118] No longer obsessed with expensive gifts and publicizing her booty, Lopez is framed as a loving and adoring mother and wife. Her 2007 Spanish-language album, *Como Ama Una Mujer,* and related Univisión miniseries finally cemented her safe and welcomed return to a socially acceptable Latina femininity.[119]

Tabloid coverage and Internet discussions about Lopez and her romantic relationships illustrate how ethnic women function in symbolically important ways as constitutive of national identity discourses. The cultural status of Latinas is always mediated by the project of U.S. empire-building. Lopez's currency as an ideal commodity that is symbolic of the changing ethnic and racial face of the United States was devalued for its sexual and racial transgressions and was ultimately disciplined. Her relationship with Affleck changed the public discourse about Lopez's body and sexuality, which moved Lopez outside the boundaries of social acceptability. Tensions surrounding Lopez reveal a cultural discomfort with the incorporations of Latinidad, Latinas, and Puerto Ricans as nonwhite bodies that challenge the U.S. national imaginary and dominant notions of citizenship and racial identity.

3

Becoming Frida

Latinidad and the Production of Latina Authenticity

Central to mainstream media representations of Latinidad is the production of ethnic authenticity, of an authentic ethnic or panethnic identity often grounded in familiar and marketable characteristics. Furthermore, media produced by U.S. ethnic and racial minorities equally depend on a mode of "strategic essentialism" to produce authenticity. In the next two chapters, I build on Juana María Rodríguez's discussion of strategic essentialism as the reduction of "identity categories to the most readily decipherable marker around which to mobilize" to map out the discourse of Latinidad in global film and television shows produced by Latinas.[1] While the notion of strategic essentialism was initially coined by Gayatri Spivak[2] and has most readily been used by postcolonial scholars interested in studying how identity is used by activists to disrupt Western ethnic, racial, and gender hierarchies, I engage contemporary media to think through the uneasy deployment of strategic essentialism by Latina mainstream media producers, such as Mexican actor Salma Hayek, to manufacture ethnic authenticity as a representational intervention in to the mainstream.

In the case of the movie *Frida*, I examine Hayek's use of strategic essentialism to mobilize Mexican ethnic authenticity, which must then be negotiated by U.S. and Mexican media and audiences that foreground their identity discourses. That is to say, the movie itself, publicity about the movie, and Salma Hayek's role as lead actor and producer were all invested in promoting a definition of Mexican authenticity that situated the movie and Hayek's performance as unique and different from traditional Hollywood fare about Latinas and Latinidad. Nevertheless, analysis of English- and Spanish-language media coverage and Internet discussion boards about the movie illustrates a more complex reading of Latina identity and Mexican authenticity.

The reduction of complexity embedded in the "myth of authenticity," to borrow Gareth Griffiths' words, is a problematic but integral signifying practice in the effective global commodification of Latinidad.[3] Media stories grounded in authenticity inevitably rely on constructions of identity based on reductive assumptions that homogenize cultural practices and reify racial differences. Thus, media practices that define one Latina as more "real" or "legitimate" than another inevitably participate in symbolic colonization by reproducing dominant norms, values, and beliefs about Latinidad. Consequently, global media produced by Latinas based on mainstream signifying practices of ethnic authenticity are especially scrutinized by audiences. Because of an environment in which Latinas remain generally underrepresented in the media, there are perpetual conflicts over what iconic Latina figures may be represented, by which ethnic and racial groups, and under what cultural conditions.[4] Such was the case for *Frida*. Mexican newspaper and online audience discussions about Hayek and *Frida* challenged the cinematic and publicity constructions of Mexican authenticity by circulating competing definitions of ethnic identity. Therefore, I begin the chapter with a discussion of how Frida Kahlo scholars imagine the artist's identity to contextualize Hayek's publicity campaign and the movie's representation of ethnic authenticity. The complex public response to Hayek and *Frida*'s production of ethnic authenticity is explored in the last half of the chapter, which turns to an online discussion board and the U.S. Latina/o and Mexican media coverage about Hayek and the movie.

The chapter analyzes interviews with Hayek and director Julie Taymor in the mainstream and U.S. Latina/o media. Specifically, I collected movie reviews, stories about the movie, and personality profiles through the Ethnic NewsWatch (ENW) database. Of the twenty-six Latina/o newspapers available on ENW, some are independently owned and geared to a specific ethnic audience, such as San Diego's *La Prensa*, which is primarily aimed at U.S. Mexicans and is owned by a Mexican American family. Others are owned by English-language chains, such as Miami's *El Nuevo Herald*, a former Knight Ridder (now McClatchy) property primarily aimed at U.S. Cubans. To further trouble the movie's representation of authenticity, I also examined 2002 news and editorial coverage about the film from two Mexico City newspapers, *Reforma* and *La Crónica de Hoy*.[5] Together these U.S. Latina/o and Mexico City news, reviews, and opinion stories are part of the pre- and postproduction machinery that influence a film's domestic and global success or failure. Lastly, included in the analysis is one discussion thread from the Internet Movie Database Web site (www.IMDb.com). Of the eighty-eight discussion threads on the IMDb *Frida* Web page, this chapter's analysis focuses on the longest-running and most relevant discussion thread, "Another case of the 'prostitution of mexican culture' " (sic).[6] Unlike the other discussion threads that were short in duration (from two to fifteen postings) and covered such mundane topics as the soundtrack or nudity in the film, the postings in "Another case" remained active for more than a year and dealt explicitly with authenticity and the commodification of ethnic identity in the film. The discussion thread provides access, albeit problematically, to how audiences interpreted, negotiated, or contested the film's production of ethnic identity through their individual constructions of self.[7] Examining the process through which Kahlo's life story is translated through the global media and negotiated by audiences provides insight into the representational complexities surrounding representations of ethnicity, gender, and national identity.

Imagining Frida Kahlo

Born Magdalena Carmen Frida Kahlo y Calderón in 1907 to a middle-class Catholic mother of Mexican descent and a bourgeois Jewish father of German descent, Kahlo attended elite private schools until she was eighteen, when a bus accident left her crippled and critically wounded. During her convalescence, she began painting portraits of her family and herself (a majority of Kahlo's paintings are self-portraits). Kahlo's folkloric *retablo*-style surrealist paintings became the first by a Mexican woman to be exhibited in New York, Paris, and Mexico. When Kahlo died in 1954 (there is disagreement over whether she died from natural causes or an intentional morphine overdose), she was such a revered Mexican cultural and political figure that her coffin was wrapped in the communist flag and lay in state in Mexico City's Palacio de Bellas Artes, the same theater where *Frida* premiered in November 2002. Despite her national fame in Mexico, it was Hayden Herrera's 1983 biography that brought Kahlo's introspective paintings—often dealing with life-altering events such as miscarriages, abortions, sexual infidelities, and the near-fatal bus accident—to the international arena.[8]

According to Herrera, Kahlo liked to play with notions of identity, making up bits about her life or replacing older accounts with more novel and interesting versions. Herrera argues that Kahlo often responded to questions about her age, ethnicity, gender, and sexuality with answers that differed depending on her reading of the interviewer's identity. Kahlo was also consciously self-aware of her selection of clothing and performance of beauty, Herrera suggests. For example, Kahlo often wore men's clothing during the periods when she was disenchanted with her husband and famous muralist, Diego Rivera, and mostly wore indigenous clothing and jewelry when she was interacting with non-Mexicans or traveling outside Mexico. Both practices, Herrera claims, allowed Kahlo to emotionally and politically distance herself from others through a visual and symbolic othering that could not be ignored by those around her.

Therefore, because of the fluidity with which Kahlo approached her life and identity, the lack of consensus about the details of her life is not surprising.[9] The most popular account of Kahlo's life is based on Herrera's biography, which maintains the authentic Kahlo was a woman obsessed with a desire for children, her husband, and his artistic and political work. However, feminist art critics and Chicana/o scholars present an alternative reading of Kahlo's life, sexuality, and femininity. Instead of emphasizing Kahlo's devotion to Rivera, contemporary Kahlo scholars focus on her individual work within Mexico's Communist Party in support of land redistribution; her political support for the nationalization of private industries; and her personal involvement in the United Front for Women's Rights group, one of Mexico's earliest feminist organizations.[10] Additionally, feminist art scholars suggest that a closer analysis of Kahlo's art and personal documents actually reveal a more ambivalent sexuality and desire for children.[11] Interestingly, Emma Hurtado, Rivera's last spouse and longtime administrator of Rivera's and Kahlo's estates, maintained strict control of Kahlo's personal documents—perhaps in an attempt to carefully manage Kahlo's life story. Regardless, most feminist art historians and cultural critics agree that Kahlo's life and art challenge normative constructions of gender, sexuality, and national identity.[12]

I begin this chapter by pointing out the disagreement over Kahlo's life story to show that, despite the lack of consensus about the artist's authentic life or identity, the characterization of Kahlo as an anti-establishment, defiant rule-breaker remains consistently romanticized within global popular culture—making her an alluring and profitable multicultural and political icon for contemporary audiences invested in multicultural identity politics.[13] Kahlo is often invoked as a strategic essentializing symbol of difference for multiple identity communities (feminist, queer, Chicana/o, among others) precisely because she vexed stable notions of identity through her art and life. To early Chicana/o activists, Kahlo's Mexican identity, anti-imperialist/capitalist politics, and performance of indigenous Mexican culture affirmed the movement's politics based on recuperating Mexico's mythologized indigenous empire and celebrating the indigenous racial heritage of U.S.-born or incorporated Mexicans. Similarly, in the 1970s, feminist and queer activists also laid claim to Kahlo by emphasizing her bisexuality, gender-bending behavior, and the personal themes of her paintings as symbols of female strength and early feminist consciousness. Kahlo's body and art become markers of a collective ethnic, gender, and sexual difference that can be used to create cultural and political communities. They function as symbols of Chicana, Latina, postcolonial feminist resistance to patriarchal oppression, U.S. imperialism and, more recently, Western-led globalization. As a stand-in for the nation and national desires, in the words of Norma Alarcón, Caren Kaplan, and Minoo Moallen, Kahlo is an "iconic signifier for the material, the passive, and the corporeal, to be worshipped, protected, and controlled by those with the power to remember and to forget, to guard, to define and redefine."[14] She stands in for and against the nation. The question becomes: In a global media environment, who has the power to imagine Kahlo's place within the nation?

Performing 'Frida'

I answer the question of who has the power to imagine Kahlo by first analyzing the work of producer and star Hayek and director Julie Taymor in depicting a profitable and particular narrative of ethnic, specifically Mexican, authenticity grounded in the signifying practices of strategic essentialism.[15] Frida is Taymor's most profitable cinematic directorial project and Hayek's most acclaimed cinematic role, culminating in Hayek's 2003 Oscar nomination for best actress. Before Frida, Taymor's most successful directorial project was the 1997 Broadway production of The Lion King. Throughout the past twenty years, several high-profile entertainment figures (Madonna, Jennifer Lopez) explored the possibility of producing a film about Kahlo. Hayek and her U.S.-based production company, Ventanarosa Productions, won the race to produce Kahlo's story in 2002 by bringing the English-language movie to the silver screen. Since its U.S. premiere in November 2002, the $12 million low-budget art-house movie has earned almost $26 million in U.S. box office receipts and another $30 million in worldwide receipts.[16] Hayek's and Taymor's production of the film, which is largely based on Herrera's work,[17] is central to understanding the global performance of ethnic authenticity by Latina producers working in the mainstream media.

To better understand the cultural and political economic context surrounding Frida's production, it must be situated within the global production of culture.[18] Rather than positioning Hollywood at the center of cinematic production, most movies today are produced by a transnational industry. Therefore, Hollywood plays a central but not exclusive role in the production and consumption of cultural work. The transnational flow of people, audiences, labor, and capital requires that cinematic productions sell tickets and DVDs not only in their home country but also in other markets. Among others, one of the key markets central to the success of Hollywood-based productions is Mexico and Latin America. Media analysts predict that Latin American audiences will eventually produce more than $1.6 billion in revenue, with Mexico, Brazil, and Argentina accounting for more than 88 percent of that market.[19] Thus, the flow of people, images, labor, and capital through the movie industry does not move exclusively from west to east or north to south. With the profitable rise of the Asian, Indian, and Latin American movie markets and industries, it is starting to move in the opposite direction, from south to north and east to west.

Movies in particular are created through global production teams and sites and marketed with an eye toward worldwide distribution. As such, movie profits increasingly depend on international creative labor and ticket sales from global audiences. The production, marketing, and reception of *Frida* are then no different from other films. Most of *Frida* was filmed in Mexico by award-winning Mexican cinematographer Rodrigo Prieto (*Brokeback Mountain*, *Babel*, *21 Grams*); the much-touted animation effects were produced in a German studio by two German computer graphic artists; and the movie itself was edited at a Hollywood studio and directed by a white U.S. woman. A multinational media conglomerate, Walt Disney Corporation, financed, distributed, and marketed the art-house film through its subsidiaries Miramax International Films and Buena Vista International Films. The movie's top grossing markets were the United States, Mexico, and Germany.

The context that surrounds today's cinematic movie production and reception is what makes *Frida* especially interesting for this book. Hayek and Taymor strategically produced a very particular construction of Mexican identity as authentic to attain the broadest global commercial and artistic success. By highlighting the connections between Kahlo and Mexico's indigenous culture as well as Hayek's Mexican nationality, *Frida*'s director and producers strategically essentialize both Hayek's and Kahlo's identities to tell the story and promote the movie. The next two sections examine Hayek's deployment of her physicality and nationality to authenticate her performance of Kahlo, while Taymor called upon established Hollywood signifying practices for performing Latinidad to produce a recognizable representation of an authentic Mexican identity.

Salma's Frida

Without *Frida*, Salma Hayek's career might have been relegated to the unidimensional terrain of Latina stereotypes—one more emotionally unpredictable, sexually voluptuous, thickly accented Latina appearing in Hollywood movies such as *Desperado* (1995), *From Dusk Till Dawn* (1996), *Fools Rush In* (1997), *54* (1998), and *Wild Wild West* (1999). In these movies, which are similar to other movies that incorporate secondary ambiguously coded Latina characters, Hayek's career exemplifies the enduring legacy of the cinematic gendering and racialization of Latinidad. Depictions of Latinas with olive skin, long dark hair, brown eyes, and Spanish accents call upon familiar visual and linguistic signifiers of Latina identity—what Arlene Dávila termed the "Latin look."[20] Hayek acknowledges that before *Frida*, she was often typecast as the "bikini girl," a modern version of the Latina spitfire. Hayek reprised the Latina "bikini girl" role in at least three of her more successful films: *54*, *Desperado*, and *Wild Wild West*.[21] In each of these films, Hayek portrays a sexually attractive, emotionally temperamental Latina who speaks Spanish at the angry drop of a hat. As such, these roles depend on the use of cinematic practices that symbolically colonize Latinidad through a gendering and racialization that subverts the economic, religious, and cultural multiplicity among Latina and Mexican American communities in the United States.

I argue that Hayek's national origin, national identity, and Spanish-accented English situate her within the Latin look yet keep her outside whiteness. Unlike Jennifer Lopez, Hayek's ability to move between cinematic representations of ethnic or racial specificity, such as in *Fools Rush In* where she plays a U.S. Mexican, and representations of ethnic or racial ambiguity, such as *54* where she plays a panethnic Latina, is constrained by the issue of language or, more specifically, linguistic accent. Hayek's Spanish-accented English and Mexican identity racialize her as nonwhite within U.S. racial formations. Her Mexican ethnicity marks her as brown, calling forth her Otherness, and bringing to bear upon her body a history of dominant Western signifiers about Latinidad. Together with Hayek's archetypical Latin look, her accent taps into popular cinematic representations of Mexicans from south of the border as hot, spicy, and exotic.

Indeed, English-language entertainment news coverage about Hayek often characterizes her through familiar media signifiers of Latinidad—such as the teaser for Hayek's February 2003 *Vanity Fair* interview, "The Fire and Passion of Salma Hayek" (*Salma* is spelled in bold red letters); the October 2002 *Cleveland Call and Post* footer, "Showtime goes to the canvas with the spicy superstar"; the July 1999 *in Style* headline "Salma likes it hot"; or the July 1999 *George* headline, "Mexican firecracker." Hayek's accented English is such a primary sign of her exotic otherness that when profiling her, journalists often emphasize her accent as much as they do other personality characteristics. For example, in a September 2002 *Premiere* story about *Frida*, the reporter wrote out Hayek's accented pronunciations: "She starts to speak in her sing-songy voice—vowels are stretching, R's are rolling. 'We work in the *gaaarden*. We have Chai *teeeas* when we were on the phone or working on a script. We have lunch *outsiiiide*, with *sangriiia*'."[22] Together with the reporter's descriptions of Hayek's curvaceous body and exotic looks, journalistic discussions of her accent contribute to the racialized hypersexualization of Latina identity.

Because Hayek cannot erase the linguistic accent that defines her as a racialized ethnic Other in the United States, the roles offered to her by Hollywood producers have been limited. Commenting on the sexualized typecasting that dominated her early roles, Hayek once said:

> That sexual side is a very small part of me. But those characters were more a reflection of how other people saw me—it's more about who they are. I used to whine and complain about it. And then I said, no more. I was done sitting around complaining that I am the victim of a society that doesn't like my accent because it reminds them of their service people.[23]

Without explicitly saying so, Hayek links the hypersexualization of her early roles with industry perceptions of her accent. She acknowledges that in California her accent is associated with Mexican domestic workers, an ethnoracial group that is racialized as nonwhite. Not only does her accent racialize her identity, but it also sexualizes it. In a profile of the actor, *Latina* magazine summarized Hayek's career in this way: "When she arrived in Hollywood, the industry didn't take her seriously: to them she was just a Mexican soap opera star with a heavy accent who could never play anything but a caricature."[24] Hayek's accent and body limited her to one-dimensional roles, the article goes on to suggest.

Although most audiences would categorize Hayek as phenotypically white—and so theoretically capable of performing the same range of roles as Jennifer Lopez—Hayek's accented English and Mexican origin reinforce ethnoracial hierarchies of identity in the United States. Even Hayek recognizes that her accent situates her as foreign, specifically as Mexican. Hayek, like other Mexican and Puerto Rican female actors with linguistic accents, is ultimately constrained by Hollywood's conservative typecasting culture regarding language.[25] Angharad Valdivia argues that linguistic accents, more so than any other racial signifier, have limited the Hollywood careers of stars such as Hayek and Rosie Perez.[26] The accents mark their ethnicity as "non-American" and code them as racially nonwhite. As Puerto Rican and Mexican women, their identities are already racialized as exotic and nonwhite in ways that, for instance, Penélope Cruz's accent and identity as a European is not. Hayek's and Perez's accents, alongside their national origins as Mexican and Puerto Rican, reinforce their status as outside the U.S. imagined nation, especially in the contemporary anti-immigration context.

Language and nationalistic ethnic discourses are precisely at the core of Hayek's effort to transform her Hollywood image. Through her performance of Kahlo, Hayek attempts a move away from the "bikini girl" by redefining Latina cinematic archetypes and opening a more diverse representational space for Latina/o actors. Part of the driving force behind Hayek's production company, Ventanarosa, which translates into "rose-colored window," is a desire to provide an outlet for more nuanced Latina images and stories. Discussing her motivation for producing *Frida*, Hayek explained:

> As an actor, I would like to be able to have a voice in order to talk about what interests me. [*Frida*] is a conviction, an extraordinary woman with an extraordinary story. It was worth telling this story, which develops during a Mexican era in which my country was a very interesting place. Actually it still is, but this is a part of Mexico that few people know about. So I was very passionate about telling the story of the heroes that I grew up with. I wanted the world to know that.[27]

Since *Frida*, Hayek has engaged in a variety of Latina/o-themed productions. She directed Showtime's *The Maldonado Miracle* (2003), a coming-of-age story about a young Mexican boy, and she starred in as well as co-produced *In the Time of the Butterflies* (2001), a cinematic version of Julia Alvarez's highly acclaimed historical novel about three feminist Dominican revolutionaries. Most recently, she co-produced and acted in ABC's *Ugly Betty*. Regardless, it is the role of Frida Kahlo that Hayek claimed as hers and worked for more than eight years to bring to fruition. Hayek's motivations for producing the film are not all political. The movie provided the actor with an opportunity to establish her credentials as a serious actor and producer.

Evidenced in Hayek's publicity campaign for the movie is the actor's ambivalent relationship to Latinidad—wanting to claim her place within Latinidad and simultaneously resisting its U.S. ethnoracial connotations. Indeed, Hayek has traditionally rejected the ethnoracial U.S. label "Latina" in favor of the more Europeanized identity "Latin." Hayek, whose father is of Lebanese descent, often unequivocally defines her heritage as Mexican.

She wields her accent and Spanish fluency as privileged signs of her Mexican or "Latin" authenticity. Nevertheless, Hayek often seeks to distinguish herself as different from other Latina actors, actors such as Jennifer Lopez and Rosie Perez, by marketing herself and her production company as authentically Latin. Because Lopez and Perez were born in the United States and cannot speak Spanish fluently, Hayek argues they are not Latin. Ignoring Lopez's and Perez's self-identification as Nuyoricans, Latinas or Hispanics, Hayek conflates the ethnoracial label *Latina* with the label *Latin* and then calls into question their right to claim or be claimed as Latin. In a July 2001 article in *el Andar* magazine, for instance, Hayek employs the politics of language to define her Latina authenticity and devalue Jennifer Lopez's: "'Her [Jennifer Lopez's] Spanish is very bad,' Hayek said, even though both films were in English, and 'now it's very convenient, because when she has to be Latin, she's Latin.'"[28] Throughout Hayek's publicity tour for *Frida*, she consistently engaged in nationalistic arguments based on language to differentiate between real and fake Latins (Latinas). Engaging language as a tool for marketing her identity in relationship to U.S. Latinas, Hayek claimed her right to perform the role of *Frida*. Thus, she turns her linguistic accent, a racialized marker of ethnic Otherness in the United States, into a marketable cinematic signifier of authenticity, particularly important for the biopic genre usually evaluated on its reproduction of realism. Hayek reframes her Spanish accent as desirable and indeed necessary for the realism of the film. In fact, all of the movie's actors speak Spanish-accented English to establish the movie's Mexican or ethnic mise-en-scène as well as make the movie more accessible for English-speaking audiences—an imperative of global Hollywood.

In combination with language, Hayek foregrounds her national origin as Mexican and her physical similarity to Kahlo as further evidence of her and the movie's authenticity. In an interview with *Vanity Fair* about her version of the biopic, Hayek explains why she was able to embody the famous artist with so much skill and authenticity: "She was very graceful and feminine. We have the same bone structure, and she was my size. I put on her clothes—maybe I am a half-inch taller."[29] Hayek's emphasis on her physical likeness to Kahlo allows her to claim that she is the authentic spiritual descendant and biological embodiment of the artist. For Hayek, her Mexican identity, Spanish fluency, and physical resemblance to Kahlo reinforce her ethnic authenticity. Not surprisingly, Hayek routinely called attention to her nationality and resemblance to Kahlo in publicity for the movie, such as this story in *Hispanic* magazine:

Hayek, who fought for nearly a decade to get the movie made (beating out rival projects led by Jennifer Lopez and Madonna), obviously feels a personal connection to her subject: Her magnetic performance is not so much an impersonation of Kahlo as it is top-to-bottom inhabitation, channeling the artist's pride, determination, sexuality and brash, defiant spirit.[30]

Picking up on arguments by the movie's lead actor, director, and producers, ethnic authenticity cannot be performed by any actor (Latina or not), it must be performed through a "personal connection" facilitated through the "real" body of another Mexican woman. Hayek, not Madonna or Jennifer Lopez, is the authentic ethnic or, more specifically, the biologically authentic Mexican woman.

Frida's promotional campaign is grounded in strategic essentialist arguments about authenticity based on unsustainable biological definitions of race and nation. Hayek's performance of ethnic authenticity ultimately elides the complexity of identities in Mexico, Latin America, the United States, and elsewhere.[31] In other words, Hayek's construction of identity suggests that only someone who is born in the correct country, who speaks the correct language, and who looks like the actual person or character is authentic enough to perform the role. Hayek's definition of ethnic authenticity erases her own mixed heritage as the daughter of a first-generation Lebanese father whose family immigrated to Mexico. She draws attention to her childhood in Mexico, knowledge of Mexican history, early acting career in Mexico, and continued relationship with her country of origin to establish her right to the role over other actors, such as Jennifer Lopez and Madonna.

Taymor's Mexico

Stories featuring Latinas that counter the traditional cinematic narratives of Latinidad are generally not economically viable. Latina stories can be told, but only within expected and socially acceptable parameters. Speaking about her experiences after the global hit *Real Women Have Curves* (2002), Josefina López said, "After *Real Women* I got mad. I thought that this opened doors for me, but it's still very hard. So much of the industry is about tits and ass and the exploitation of women, and it's very hard to change that. Women are the window dressing for a story."[32] The predominantly male-dominated cinematic industry, Josefina López suggests, demands beautiful heterosexual bodies and makes it difficult to produce complex stories about any women, much less Latinas. As a result, women screenwriters and directors are forced to compromise. In the case of *Frida*, Kahlo's anti-imperialist politics, her nonconformist performance of self, and her defiance of Western notions of femininity do not fit within accepted cinematic representations of Latinidad. Such elements of Kahlo's life are therefore erased through a more conventional telling of her life in Taymor's *Frida*.

In addition to dealing with industry constraints regarding depictions of Latinas, Taymor also had to negotiate the constraints of the biopic genre itself, a cinematic mode of storytelling that rewards authenticity as a tool for approximating some objective definition of reality. Not surprisingly, Taymor's directorial decisions produce a Latinidad familiar to audiences. In particular, the movie's uses of dress, color, music, and Hayek are informed by the media's traditional representation of Latina identity.[33] Cinematic marketing relies on syncretic identity constructions that yield more stable, long-term, and economically viable demographic categories through suppressing differences and highlighting cultural similarities within an ethnic group.[34] As noted in the book's introduction, the key media signifiers of Latina identity are "the Latin look," Spanish language, conservative values, and Latin American cultural practices. Therefore, successful cinematic marketing and depictions are dependent on a syncretic ethnic identity that homogenizes rather than emphasizes the group's multiplicity.[35]

Working within a media industry that depends on syncretic constructions of ethnic identity, *Frida*'s biographical adaptation elides the complexity of Kahlo's life and Mexican culture, choosing instead to simplify the cinematic story line by featuring the heterosexual love story between the artist and her husband. The movie shifts the anti-capitalist and feminist themes of Kahlo's life and artwork to the cinematic background, instead portraying Kahlo/Hayek as an ethnically gendered body that is culturally accessible, biologically natural, and sexually exotic.[36] Taymor portrays Kahlo's life story by employing familiar signifiers of Mexican identity and depoliticizing Kahlo—in particular her involvement in the nationalist politics of *indigenismo*, an ongoing cultural and political movement grounded in the recuperation of Mexico's indigenous culture.[37] By reimagining Kahlo's life through standard Western cinematic signifying practices and familiar story lines, Taymor produces a cinematic aura of authenticity that contributes to the symbolic colonization of Latinidad.

First, signifying practices such as the use of accented English, primitive colors, folkloric dress, and music present a seemingly authentic global Latina/o identity dependent on writing out differences within Mexico and

Mexican identity. For example, with regard to the purposeful use of primitive primary colors, during an interview at the American Film Institute Taymor commented:

> We talked about the color of Mexico. It's the first thing we said. The color of Mexico in the '20s is unpolluted color, meaning that if you shoot in Mexico City now you can't get that color. So the exterior of Mexico City, when they are running from the bus and the schools, is shot in San Luis, which really is a small town and probably still looks the way that Mexico City did in the 1920s. . . . At E-Films we did a lot of work with true color . . . but a lot of those Tehuanas, that's the color, so it is the color of Mexico. It is the color of Mexico at the time and still Mexico if you go to Oaxaca or you go to Puebla. You still see that kind of rich vital color, and we really wanted that.[38]

The ultravibrant terra cotta reds and primary blues and yellows are characterized as more important cinematic signifiers of an authentic Mexican identity than the Spanish language. Moreover, the bright colors—along with scene props such as junglelike foliage, tropical-looking flowers, and pet monkeys—are part of a signifying schema that creates an image of a safe and acceptable Latin America by defining it as a primitive, exotic, and historical space. Color was so central to the movie's production of Mexican authenticity that Taymor worked with E-Films to digitally filter and cleanse the vestiges of industrialization polluting the landscape of today's Mexico into an imagined construction of the untouched, pure colors of Mexico's less industrialized past.

Folkloric dress, indigenous artifacts, and Hayek's physicality are equally integral to producing an authentic Mexican identity devoid of politics (see figure 3.1). Indeed, the movie continually emphasizes the most popular signifiers associated with Kahlo—her unibrow, braided hair, and colorful indigenous clothing. Colorful dresses, bright red flowers, and indigenous jewelry further define Kahlo and Hayek as authentically Mexican and universally exotic without referencing the political intent embedded in the artist's motivations for wearing these particular clothes. In Kahlo's biography, Herrera notes:

> In the costumes flaunted by Kahlo . . . she embodies the two main goals of postrevolutionary Mexican leaders: She exalts contemporary manifestations of Mexico's pre-Hispanic past (the Aztec jewelry and her achievement of a "native look" with her simple coiffure) and simultaneously directs

attention to the rich diversity in Mexican culture (the different types of *rebozo,* her dress, pose, and props).[39]

Frida's signifying practices privilege Kahlo's "native look" but do so by eliding the artist's political critique of imperialism. As discussed earlier in the chapter, Hayek's ability to wear Kahlo's actual clothing is touted as central to her performance of the artist and the movie's aura of authenticity.[40] The aesthetic celebration of indigenous cultural forms within *Frida* co-opts indigenous Mexican culture as signifiers of an authentic Kahlo and Mexico at the cost of erasing the continued economic and political marginalization of indigenous Mexicans at the heart of Kahlo's political work. Frida Kahlo and Diego Rivera were both active proponents of the Mexicanidad movement, which called for the nationalization of Mexico's major industries, redistribution of wealth and property, and establishment of land rights for Mexico's indigenous and peasant populations. Culturally, the movement called for the privileging of *lo indigena* or *indigenismo,* Mexico's indigenous and folkloric culture and heritage, as the site of authentic Mexican identity.[41] To Kahlo, wearing indigenous clothing and jewelry was a sign of her political allegiance to indigenous communities. Yet Taymor's decision to predominantly feature Hayek in Kahlo's folkloric style without referring to its political intent contributes to the production of authenticity and the movie's marketability. In other words, the movie's production of an authentic Mexican identity that is commercially viable and globally consumable depends on stripping the political content of Kahlo's life by depicting more popular symbols of Mexican culture.

Closely drawing upon Herrera's biography, the movie's script further depoliticizes Kahlo's identity by focusing on her obsessive desire to please her husband, the famous Mexican muralist Diego Rivera. The decision to background Kahlo's political identity and complicated sexuality shifts the art-house movie story to more popular and familiar Latina narratives of ethnic femininity, sexuality, and domesticity. Like other Hollywood films, it is Kahlo's love story and not the political story that carries the cinematic story forward. Kahlo's complicated sexuality and politics are not central components to the audience's understanding of the artist's life. Responding to questions about the erasure of Kahlo's politics and queer sexuality, Taymor suggested:

Frida adored her husband, Diego. As monstrous as he was with his infidelity, they really loved and supported each other as artists, and she really wanted to be with him. . . . She was political, but that was not her essence.

Figure 3.1. As many mainstream and U.S. Latina/o media claimed, Salma Hayek did not depict Frida Kahlo, she personified her. In this image from the movie, Hayek is costumed in many of the signifiers of "authentic" Mexican identity used to signal Latinidad—tropical flowers, bright colors, and folkloric clothing.

Her essence was herself. Who is Frida without Diego? You don't have to be faithful to be loyal. Where do you draw the line? In our culture that's very difficult. If you show her sleeping with this person or this person, then how do you believe that she loved Diego?[42]

To Taymor, the important relationship, the one with emotional and cinematic significance, is Kahlo's heteronormative relationship with her husband. Depicting Kahlo's numerous and meaningful nonmonogamous long-term relationships with women and men violates the cinematic rules of Latina/o heterosexual love upon which the movie and Hollywood's general treatment of ethnic women relies.[43]

Although I recognize and celebrate queer readings of the film (it earned a GLAAD nomination for outstanding film), Taymor downplays the emotional significance of Kahlo's lesbian relationships in favor of the heterosexual love story. Any *meaningful* lesbian relationship is relegated to the background and subtext and between-the-lines readings. For instance, the movie incorporates the music, vocals, and images of the great Mexican singer Chavela Vargas, but any mention of Vargas's long-term lesbian relationship with Kahlo is tragically relegated to the DVD's special features. Furthermore, while one of the most circulated images from the movie is the sexually charged tango/kissing sequence between Kahlo/Hayek and Tina Modotti, played by Ashley Judd (see figure 3.2), the scene and kiss are not integral to the plot or character development. Regardless, the tango sequence was featured on a movie poster, screened on programs such as *The Oprah Winfrey Show*, and published in newspapers and magazines. However, the interesting platonic friendship and one-time romantic relationship between the women is erased from the movie's story. Instead, the dance sequence, similar to the movie's other references about Kahlo's bisexuality, serves to titillate audiences while further defining Kahlo's life through common signifiers of Latinidad, particularly the tango as a popular symbol of Latin America, Latinidad, and Latina/o sexuality.[44]

Finally, Hayek's performance of Kahlo is itself integral to maintaining the dominant heteronormative gaze of the movie and contributing to the marketable production of authenticity. I cannot ignore that in this rendition of her life, Kahlo's non-normative beauty, body, and sexuality are cinematically reinterpreted through the body of the glamorous Hayek. Prior to *Frida*, Hayek appeared in countless movies, magazine covers, and advertisements for Revlon cosmetics and Lincoln cars. Hayek's global visibility, history of highly sexualized roles, and familiar beauty are impossible to erase from the screen. She might look like Kahlo, but she is still the beautiful Salma

Figure 3.2. The tango sequence between Salma Hayek and Ashley Judd was one of the most widely circulated scenes. Featuring a scene that amounted to less than five minutes of total screen time allowed the movie's director to feature Hayek's body and sexuality as ethnic spectacle.

Hayek. The movie's cinematography takes advantage of Hayek's iconic face and voluptuous body. It is difficult to imagine that a "realistic" depiction of Kahlo, who was severely injured and crippled, would have been much fun to watch. Even with cosmetic enhancements to re-create Kahlo's hairy eyebrows and light facial mustache, Hayek's beauty cannot be hidden. Nor, I contend, is there any real intent to do so by the actor or director. Together the cinematic focus on Hayek's body and face along with the visual representation of indigenous culture and emphasis on Kahlo's relationship with Rivera produce a consumable albeit homogenous representation of Latina and Mexican authenticity.[45]

To highlight the conscious production and directorial decisions of the *Frida* project, I draw attention to the first but little-known biopic about Kahlo, *Frida, Naturaleza Viva* (1984), directed by Paul Leduc. Leduc's film was shot in Spanish with English subtitles, used a nonlinear narrative script, had minimalistic dialogue/sound, and highlighted Kahlo's Marxist commitment over her personal relationships. Ofelia Medina, the popular Mexican actor who played Kahlo in Leduc's movie, de-emphasized her natural physical beauty by wearing minimal stage makeup and drab, loose-fitting laborers' clothing. Medina actually spoke out in the Mexican press against Hayek's hypersexualized performance of Kahlo.[46] Like *Frida*, Leduc also marginalizes Kahlo's lesbian relationships by associating it with her alcohol and drug problems. However, his script rarely focuses on the relationship between Kahlo and Rivera, choosing instead to foreground her political activism in Mexico's Communist Party and personal struggles with her physical injuries. I raise the contrast between the two movies not to say one is better than the other, although *Frida* was the clear commercial success, but rather as an illustration of how both films are shaped by different directorial and screenwriting decisions—what one director/screenwriter omits, another emphasizes. The deletions and selections in turn have implications for the ideological articulations and success of each movie.

Reinforcing Hollywood's historical constructions of authentic Latina femininity, Taymor's decision to minimize Kahlo's leftist politics and emphasize Hayek's body, beauty, and sex appeal inevitably makes the radical Mexican artist a more consumable cinematic figure for global audiences. Speaking about the use of Kahlo to promote a 1990 exhibit of Mexican artists, Jean Franco observed, "The private had not only become public, as feminists once claimed, but had become publicity."[47] Likewise, Taymor's *Frida* privileges Kahlo's private life, not her public political life, as the focus of the cinematic story. An interesting paradox is produced. On the one hand, *Frida* provides unprecedented and celebratory visibility to an actor, woman, and nation generally erased within mainstream visual culture. However, the economic imperatives of global cinema shape the movie's construction of authenticity by locating Kahlo's Mexican identity within a symbolically colonizing discourse of Latinidad. The actors' use of accented English and the director's decision to use colorful scenery and costumes, indigenous cultural artifacts, folkloric Mexican music, and Hayek's eroticized body call forth dominant syncretic constructions of Latina identity. Displacing the anti-capitalist and feminist themes of Kahlo's art and life provides a more familiar rendition of Mexican gendered identity as passionate, festive, and heterosexual and racialized ethnic women as culturally accessible and consumable.

Making Sense of 'Frida'

Despite the constraints the movie faced, my analysis of the media and audience reception regarding the film points to its complicated reception. In this section, I treat journalists writing about the movie as a specialized type of media audience, and I look to one online discussion about the movie as a unique form of media reception. I begin this section by exploring the response of the U.S. Latina/o media and one IMDb discussion thread about the movie. While the majority of Latina/o media outlets and IMDb posters in the discussion thread unequivocally celebrate the film, how they make sense of Hayek and the movie reveals a more complex articulation of Latina identity. Additionally, I examine two Mexico City newspapers (*Reforma* and *La Crónica de Hoy*) to further illustrate how different audiences interpret and sometimes oppose the movie's production of ethnic authenticity. The Mexico City journalists' use of strategic essentialism stands in stark contrast to a majority of IMDb discussion participants who often propose more fluid constructions of ethnic and racial identity. Together, the analysis of U.S. Latina/o media, online audiences, and Mexican news accounts demonstrate the potential for symbolic ruptures of commercialized media constructions of Latinidad.

Celebrating 'Frida'

The movie premiered in the United States amid a void in mainstream programming about Latinas/os and an increase in social tensions over Latina/o immigration. In 2002, with the exception of the movie *Selena* (1997) and the *George Lopez* television show (2002–2007), the U.S. television and film media landscape remained a relatively barren space for Latina/o images, much less representations produced by Latinas/os themselves. According to a National Association of Hispanic Journalists annual *Network Brownout Report*, only 0.75 percent of the news stories aired on ABC, CBS, CNN, and NBC in 2002 were about Latinas/os, a majority of which were about crime, terrorism, and illegal immigration.[48] In 2005, that number rose to 0.83 percent on the three major networks.[49] Figures for 2006 and 2007 are not yet available. Entertainment representations did not fare much better. A Chicano Studies Research Center report found that in 2004, only 4 percent of regular characters on prime-time shows were Latinas/os, down from 4.2 percent in 2002.[50] As of 2007, Latina/o actors and writers remained woefully underrepresented in the television and film industries.[51] Amid this hostile representational void, *Frida* appeared.

Because of the culture of invisibility that surrounds Latinas/os in the mainstream media, it is not surprising that an overwhelming majority of the movie's public reception in the United States celebrated the cultural importance of Kahlo as well as Hayek's role in making the movie.[52] U.S. Latina/o news coverage often extolled Kahlo's and Hayek's visibility by replicating the discourses of ethnic identity and authenticity embedded in the film. Most IMDb discussion participants also reveled in the women's cultural visibility. On a personal note, I can vividly remember viewing *Frida* when it premiered at my local theater in Champaign, Illinois. Accompanied by Ecuadorian and Chilean friends, the three of us sat spellbound as we watched images of Hayek, Mexico, and Kahlo's life and art flash before our eyes with both a dignity and beauty that was rarely visible in U.S. cinema. We left the theater with the belief that we had seen something truly special, a sensitive representation of Mexican, Latin American, and Latina/o culture, and we joyfully toasted that unprecedented visibility. Despite its directorial omissions and simplifications, *Frida* still remains one of the few "positive" representations of Latinas in global Hollywood cinema. My personal reaction is illustrative of the *burden of representation* that faces most cultural representations of marginalized communities.[53] Because there are so few cultural representations of Latinas to begin with, those that do exist are often asked to speak for the entire community. The burden to represent an entire community and its complexity is rarely asked of dominant media depictions of men, heterosexuals, or white people.

The majority of Latina/o media journalists and posters in the discussion thread I analyzed lauded one of the few globally available images produced by Latinas/os, starring Latina/o actors, about a Latina and Mexicana.[54] For instance, in response to a posting that Salma Hayek's *Frida* had "sold-out" Mexican culture, one poster argued, "Salma did not sell Mexican culture . . . she exposed it to the world and in my mind, added more layers to dismantle gringo-fied, stereotypical portrayals. My friends and I are all Chicana or Mexican-American from Mexico, and we loved the film."[55] A majority (16 out of 23) of the IMDb posters for this thread self-identified as U.S. Latina/o or Latin American. All sixteen of those participants described the movie as an important cultural intervention that helped to demonstrate the cultural depth, beauty, and complexity of Mexico and its people. For these posters, the movie ruptured symbolically colonizing discourses of Latina/o and Mexican identity simply by existing and giving visibility to a strong feminist Mexicana portrayed by a strong Latina/Mexicana actor. It did not matter that Mexican culture had to be homogenized to be commercially viable. To them, the movie's cultural visibility (in particular the visibility of an iconic figure who challenged dominant notions of Latinidad) within a mainstream media environment defined by erasure was the intervention.

A similar discourse of visibility and cultural respectability dominated U.S. Latina/o news coverage of Hayek and *Frida*. Latina/o journalists identified both women as belonging to Mexico and U.S. communities of Mexican and Latina/o descent. In all of the fifty-one U.S. Latina/o news stories I collected about the movie, Hayek's Mexican nationality by birth was described as an important element of her identity and the movie's success. Simultaneously, Hayek, who was a legal U.S. resident at the time of the movie's release and who is now a U.S. citizen, was also identified as belonging to the U.S. Latina/o community, despite her own ambivalence regarding the term. Thus, the desire to identify Hayek as both Mexican and Latina by U.S. Latina/o journalists disrupts syncretic notions of Latina identity. Both women come to occupy an in-between transnational space—Hayek and Kahlo are both from here/*aquí* and from there/*allá*.[56] Hayek in particular was characterized as a Mexican woman living in the United States whose identity as a Latina immigrant made her vulnerable to racial discrimination based on national origin, and she was a Mexican citizen proudly representing her nation of origin. The transnational construction of Hayek's identity in the U.S. Latina/o media as both a U.S. Latina and a Mexican national further complicates the reception of Latina/o authenticity.

Although at the time of the movie's release Hayek had been living for more than a decade in the United States, to U.S. Latina/o journalists, Hayek's Mexican identity remained an essential aspect of the news story. For example, Miami's *El Nuevo Herald* discussed Hayek's nationality as pivotal to the role: "By large coincidence, this is the same project that almost went to Madonna. Later, Laura San Giacomo and Jennifer Lopez were mentioned as possible candidates for the role, but it was Hayek, as a Mexican, who received the privilege of representing her compatriot."[57] Interestingly, the journalistic emphasis on country of origin displaced any identity problems raised by Hayek's mixed Mexican and Lebanese heritage. What mattered most in these news stories was where Hayek was born, not the heritage of her parents or what country she currently resides in. Picking up on the language of authenticity in Hayek's publicity campaign, the news stories framed Hayek's ethnicity by virtue of her birthplace as more authentic to the role than the identity of other white or Latina actors. Not only did her ethnic identity make Hayek more authentic, but that authenticity also enhanced her artistic performance. By drawing attention to place of birth as the source of Hayek's authenticity, the U.S. Latina/o news media reaffirmed the transnational experience of millions of Latina/o immigrants who no longer live in their homeland but still identify it as home.[58] Journalistic accounts of authenticity play a significant role for U.S. Latina/o newspapers because they must carefully speak to their specific ethnic-national readerships (usually Cuban, Mexican, and Puerto Rican) without excluding any particular national backgrounds to draw the largest revenue stream.[59] Invoking Hayek's nationality allowed the Latina/o media to foreground her Mexican identity while still celebrating the movie as a panethnic success. U.S. Latina/o journalistic coverage demonstrates the production of news that builds panethnic U.S. Latina/o national identities while recognizing the specific transnational identities of their audiences.

Before its release in November 2002, national identity also was a central component of Mexico City coverage of the movie. Journalists demonstrated a desire to claim or reclaim, given Hayek's U.S. residency status, the actor as one of their own with articles such as "Salma muestra su espíritu en *Frida*" ("Salma shows her spirit in *Frida*") or "*Frida* de Salma, una película mexicana" ("Salma's *Frida*, a Mexican film") that highlighted Hayek's Mexican identity as proof of the movie's cultural value.[60] For example, the "*Frida* de Salma" article foregrounded Taymor's claim that *Frida* is intrinsically a Mexican film because, despite its U.S.-based financing, it was made possible only through the labor and efforts of Hayek, a Mexican woman. The "Salma muestra su espíritu" piece suggested that Hayek's efforts to embody Kahlo allowed her to explore her own identity as a Mexican woman, presumably an experience that neither Madonna nor Jennifer Lopez could have shared. Similar to the U.S. Latina/o news coverage, the Mexico City newspapers initially described Hayek's Mexican identity as central to producing Mexican authenticity. However, unlike the U.S. Latina/o media, the Mexico City coverage actively worked against a transnational reading of Hayek and Kahlo in favor of the women's local and ethnic-specific identities. That both the U.S. Latina/o and Mexico City media claim Kahlo and Hayek in different ways demonstrates how audiences (in this case journalists) engage in subjective readings of media representations of Latinidad.

Rupturing Hayek's 'Frida'

If the mainstream media function through a set of social and institutional practices that manufacture globally familiar ways of understanding Latina identity, then online audience responses to the movie redefine the popular contours of that identity. Consequently, the symbolic colonization of authentic ethnic identity in the film stands in tension with less stable hybrid identity discourses circulated among some Latina/o audiences. Expressions of fluidity and multiplicity among Latina/o audiences emphasize the symbolic rupturing of U.S. ethnoracial classifications. In particular, the online IMDb discussion thread I analyzed characterized Latinidad as existing at multiple and shifting intersections of identity. Unlike the movie's commodification of Latina authenticity that is predicated on the long-term stability of identity categories through cultural homogenization, identity discourses among the online audiences assumed the continual dynamism of ethnicity, race, and nation.

Specifically, the majority of IMDb posters engage the complicated ethnic and national identity of both women to think through their own identities. As ethnic hybrids, both women embody the problematic nature of national identities based on essentialistic definitions of ethnic origin. Néstor García Canclini suggests that Latin American hybridity is best characterized as liminality, as the border spaces where stabilized homogenous notions of identity and culture are decentered and negotiated.[61] Kahlo rejected her mother's Catholic faith and embraced her father's Jewish identity. A self-avowed communist from middle-class roots, she never enjoyed her visits to the United States. Hayek, the daughter of an upper-class Mexican mother and Lebanese father, is now a naturalized U.S. citizen. While she claims to fight against the discrimination she has faced as a Mexican woman in Hollywood, she continues to live an economically privileged lifestyle in the United States and Europe.

Hayek's and Kahlo's fluid and unclassifiable identities are integral to deployments of strategic essentialism in the IMDb discussion thread I analyzed. The discussion, which continued for several months, dealt with a range of arguments about the politics of ethnic, racial, and national identity. With the exception of two participants, all of the posters who responded to the initial post critical of Hayek's right to represent Kahlo challenged attacks on the movie while putting forth more complicated definitions of ethnic, racial, and national identity than those produced in the film. Their reading of the movie used knowledge about Kahlo's and Hayek's life to recuperate the movie's homogenizing constructions of Mexican identity. Defending Hayek's right to claim a Mexican identity, AlexThomas17, who identified himself as Mexican American, wrote:

> Thank you for perpetuating the stereotype that all Mexicans are the same, having brown, Mestizo skin and Spanish surnames. . . . I have commented to many people that Salma is in fact the ideal match for Frida. If you hadn't noticed, Kahlo is not Spanish either. It is German. Frida's father was from an Ashkenaicz Jewish, east-European-immigrant family in Mexico.[62]

Although the movie does not delve into Kahlo's multiethnic background, the poster engages Hayek's mixed-ethnic background to disrupt an essentialized definition of Chicana/o and Mexican nationality. For this poster, both Hayek and Kahlo inherently trouble binary or essentialist constructions of ethnic, racial, and national identity as pure, fixed, and stable. Like the majority of the posters, AlexThomas17 uses a discourse of hybridity to make sense of Kahlo, Hayek, and the movie.

Continuing discussion about the fluidity of Mexican/Latina/o identity, another poster who identified herself as Mexican American argued:

> Mexican/Chicano culture is Mexica or "indigenous," African, and Spanish. AND German (in the case of Frida Kahlo) AND Lebanese (in the case of Salma Hayek), AND whatever other ethnicities one happens to be. ALL of these ethnicities have contributed to Mexican culture as a whole, as well as to many individual Mexica (in whatever combination and to whatever degree).[63]

Another poster succinctly responded, "Her [Salma's] father is Lebanese. Her mother is Mexican. So, Salma Hayek IS Mexican. She is also Lebanese. So, she is Mexican/Lebanese,"[64] and yet another said, "I hate to break this to YOU, but regarding ethnicity, both Tiger and Salma are of mixed heritage, and can't be labeled 'black,' 'asian,' 'middle eastern' or 'mexican' so easily."[65] To online audiences, racial and ethnic identities are fluid and complex. The rich, sometimes violent, continual mixture of cultures brought about through colonization, imperialism, and global-ization thus influences audience sense-making of contemporary media depictions of Latinidad. Hybridity is not relegated to the historical or theoretical but is infor-mative of the everyday experiences of Hayek, Kahlo, and audience interpretations of *Frida*. Symbolically rupturing the commodified constructions of authenticity and Latinidad, both women are heralded by the online posters as embodied mani-festations of communities that share ethnic ties but racially, geographically, sym-bolically, and politically straddle multiple, shifting identity locations.

Challenging Hayek, Opposing 'Frida'

The celebratory U.S. Latina/o and online audience reception of Hayek, and to some extent Kahlo, stands in stark contrast to the women's more com-plicated cultural reception in Mexico. Once the movie was released, Mexico City journalists began critiquing Hayek's strategic essentialism grounded in a biological claim to authenticity (i.e., If you are born in Mexico, you are Mexican) by proposing an oppositional definition of Mexican identity based on culture and politics rather than ethnicity and national origin. Given the economic and political tensions between Mexico and the United States, it is not surprising that despite the movie's critical success, Hayek and *Frida* met with both protest and adulation in Mexico and the United States. Glo-balization and transnational policy mandates such as the North American Free Trade Agreement (NAFTA) stitch Mexico and the United States in an interdependent yet unequal economic relationship that contributes to a social and material environment where movies about culturally iconic Latin American figures find themselves in uneasy territory. The syncretic produc-tion of ethnic identity in a film designed to reach global audiences succeeded and failed, particularly among Mexico City and Chicana/o cultural critics. Such responses once again demonstrate that the process of symbolic coloni-zation is not totalizing or complete; instead, it continually speaks to ongoing power negotiations regarding identity and the nation. While Kahlo unequiv-ocally stands in for the authentic ethnic body within the transnational space of global commodity culture, Hayek's and Taymor's cinematic representation of Kahlo does not.

Although Mexico City journalists originally saluted Hayek and the movie, the coverage shifted quickly and dramatically after the movie's press screen-ing in Mexico. Hayek and her film were protested by government officials, journalists, and fellow actors decrying her performance of Kahlo and the cinematic production of Mexican culture as offensively inauthentic. Cultural critics in Mexico, including Dolores Olmedo, former director of the Frida Kahlo Museum, further muddied the movie's reception by arguing that Kahlo was an insignificant figure within the history of Mexican art.[66] A plethora of columns and articles also criticized the film's U.S.-based production, its use of English, and its negative portrayal of Rivera. Ticket sales (about $3.6 million U.S.) in Mexico—one of the world's best theater markets—paled in comparison to its take in the United States (about $26 million U.S.) and Germany ($6 million U.S.).[67] In Mexico, *Frida*'s ticket sales never topped its Mexican-produced cinematic competitors, *El Crimen del Padre Amaro* ($16.3 million U.S.) and *Amor que duele*, or U.S. blockbusters *Harry Potter and the Chamber of Secrets* ($17 million U.S) and *The Lord of the Rings: The Two Towers* ($16 million U.S).[68]

Frida, as one of the few popular representations of Mexican icons circulated through the global media, provoked a fierce debate about identity and authenticity, the burden of representation, and the cultural rights to representation. The U.S. Latina/o news coverage celebrated and affirmed the movie's syncretic notion of Mexicana/Latina ethnic identity, but both the Mexican news coverage and online discussions used a more complex construction of nationality, language, race, class, and geographical space to interpret the movie. Specifically, Mexican journalists and cultural critics accused Hayek of selling out Mexican culture and behaving like a Malinche, a reference to the controversial Aztec figure who is simultaneously described as the mother and betrayer of the Mexican nation. *Malinchismo* is often used as slang for the selling out of Mexico and the Mexican people to outsiders. A similar discourse contesting the cinematic commodification of Mexican culture initiated the IMDb discussion thread I examined for this chapter.

A month before the movie's Mexico City premiere, two Mexico City newspapers (*Reforma* and *La Crónica de Hoy*) published the same Notimex wire story about a U.S.-based protest regarding the lack of Mexican actors in the movie. Each of the newspapers' headlines focused on the group's accusation of racism ("Salma Hayek, una racista" and "Salma Hayek, racista: Mexica Movement," which translate to "Salma Hayek, a racist" and "Mexica Movement: Salma Hayek, racist") as well as claims that Hayek engaged in the same type of discriminatory actions she argues others in the movie industry have committed against her.[69] Particularly offensive to the Los Angeles–based group Defense of Indigenous Rights was the casting of European actors Alfred Molina and Antonio Banderas as two of the main characters. As one protester cited in the story argued, "Because Salma contracted two Europeans to play the roles of Rivera and Siquerios, *Frida* is an insult to the almost 30 million Mexicans who live in the United Sates and 100 million who live in Mexican territory."[70] Alongside other news stories about protests against the film in Mexico City, the news and editorial coverage opposed *Frida's* and Hayek's construction of authenticity. At the very least, the Mexico City coverage points to a multiplicity of perspectives about ethnicity and nationality. Mexico City journalists and critics argued it was not enough to be Mexican (Hayek) or to have Latina/o roots (Molina) or to be Spanish (Banderas). One must be Mexican and demonstrate an ongoing political and cultural commitment to Mexico by living and working in Mexico. Hayek's national identity was of little significance. As one Mexico City news source argued, "*Frida* is a gringo movie. It's of no consequence to me. It is not Mexican cinema. That is to say, it does not matter that Salma is in it."[71] Because the movie featured only a few Mexican actors, was directed by a U.S. director, and was financed by U.S.-based conglomerates, the Mexico City coverage framed the film as a U.S. rather than a Mexican cultural production.

Not only was it insignificant to Mexico City journalists that Hayek starred in the film, but Hayek's residency in the United States was called upon to discredit her strategic claims to authenticity and Mexican identity. News stories such as "Frida made in USA" and "Dice que daña a Frida" ("She ruined Frida, they say") further framed Hayek as a cultural interloper and the movie as a homogenized and distorted U.S. commodification of Mexican culture.[72] Significantly, the coverage did not suggest, as I would, that authenticity is an impossible and problematic identity construction but instead argues that it is impossible for the U.S. media to get Mexican authenticity correct. The use of accented English may have made the movie more attractive to international and English-speaking audiences, but it infuriated Mexican journalists, activists, and critics who interpreted the practice as a betrayal of an authentic Mexican cultural icon.

Hayek was labeled by cultural critics as the new Malinche, the historical figure accused of speaking the enemy's language (Spanish) to help Spain and sabotage the country's indigenous nations. To these critics, everything from the appearance of traditional Mexican foods to the look of the folkloric costumes is tainted by the movie's economic imperative and desire to target a global audience. Language and national identity are once again front and center in the debate over *Frida*. One film critic wrote of the movie's Mexico City premiere, "Scarcely a few minutes into the movie screening, the first sounds of laughter rose in the darkness. The reason: the use of a few Spanish words in a movie predominantly filmed in English."[73] The movie's use of

Spanglish and Spanish slang to establish Mexican authenticity is sarcastically read as a superficial and offensive attempt to woo Mexican audiences. Mexican journalists and public figures argued that given Kahlo's political beliefs, she never would have supported an English-language adaptation of her life, especially if it meant increasing movie sales to English-speaking audiences. Of course, such arguments by the Mexico City press ignore the fact that Rivera's and Kahlo's primary art patrons were wealthy U.S. industrialists and philanthropists. Nevertheless, the contemporary rebirth of Mexican cinema, Kahlo's iconic cultural status in Mexico, and the fraught political and economic relationship between the North American neighbors complicates the movie's reception in Mexico.

However, opposition to the movie did not rest solely on Mexican notions of national identity and authenticity. U.S. Chicana/o activists relied on a strategic essentialism based on fixed and stable constructions of identity to disrupt both Hayek's and *Frida*'s production of Mexican authenticity. In the IMDb discussion thread, the initial poster and most active participant, who identified himself as an indigenous Mexican living in the United States, argues for a biological definition of nationality determined by biological purity, specifically indigenous blood lineage. The poster uses *lo indigena* to place Hayek outside the borders of cultural Mexican citizenship:

1. Salma Hayek felt very strongly that a "mexican" should do the film about Frida (Madonna had been wanting to do the film for a while).
2. Salma Hayek is not Mexica—she is Lebanese.
3. She refused to hire any Mexicans to play Mexicans in the lead roles.
4. She refused to allow the Mexican Press during filming in Mexico.
Conclusion: She sold Mexica culture and a Mexican Icon to win friends and awards in hollywood.[74]

Much like Kahlo's politics of *indigenismo*, this poster privileges the "racially pure" bodies of indigenous people as the site of Mexican racial and ethnic authenticity. Embedded in the poster's discussion is a hierarchical value structure that defines authenticity through racial and ethnic fixity and stability above fluidity and hybridity.

On the surface, the poster's discourse of ethnic identity is not much different from the movie's use of the indigenous or the U.S. Latina/o news media's privileging of nationality. Calling upon his racialized experiences of U.S. economic oppression, the poster disrupts the media discourse of Latinidad by privileging a strategically essentialist identity grounded in the national-

ist and Marxist politics of the Chicano movement, which positions indigenous Mexico as a source of collective power against U.S. racial and economic
oppression.[75]

> Hayek has never lived a day in a "barrio"—she was born to a wealthy Arab
> family. . . . Hayek does not exclusively have "guts, talent, beauty, brains
> and spirit." The person struggling to raise a family with limited means has
> "guts, talent, beauty and brains." That is "spirit"—look THAT up.[76]

Throughout his postings, *lo indigena* is inserted into a broader discussion of economic conditions in Mexico and the United States—drawing a
class distinction between Hayek and the communities that he identifies as
authentically Mexican. Hayek's economic wealth and ability to become a U.S.
citizen thwart her claims to Mexican authenticity. Through strategic essentialism based on race and class, the poster creates another symbolic rupture
by defining a politics of transnational identity based on racial and economic
discrimination.

Latina Bodies in Global Commodity Culture

Because of the film's global circulation and Kahlo's cultural role as a
feminist, bisexual, Latina, and Mexican icon, she becomes one of the primary sites through which constructions of Latina identity and Latinidad are
performed, contested, and negotiated.[77] Latina bodies are a primary visual
symbol for panethnic identity formations among U.S. Latina/o communities as well as a commercialized symbol of an exotic racial difference that is
socially acceptable and consumable by domestic and global audiences. It is
the ethnic female body that is most often the site of ideological contestation
over national identity. As Ella Shohat notes, "Whereas a white female body
might merely undergo surveillance from the reproductive machine, the dark
female body is subjected to what I would call a *disreproductive* apparatus
programmed by a hidden racially coded demographic agenda."[78] The media
and audience negotiations over the symbolic colonization of iconic Latinas
inform how the bodies of ethnic women are used to discipline definitions of
race, ethnicity, nation, and national identity.

At the center of the instability surrounding ethnic identity, nation, and
culture is the notion of authenticity. In the case of *Frida*, the interdependent
economic relationship between Mexico and the United States—driven by the
U.S. need for scarce resources such as Mexican oil and inexpensive human

labor—informs the cultural politics surrounding the production and reception of the movie both in the United States and Mexico. For Mexican and some U.S. Latina/o audiences, the making of *Frida* was yet another form of exploitation that used a Mexican icon and precious Mexican locales—but not local Mexican acting talent—for the pleasurable consumption of non-Mexican audiences. For others, the movie recuperated a culture and a racialized ethnic group often erased or marked as foreign, alien, and marginal within U.S. culture. The movie's complicated audience reception points to *Frida* as a movie that speaks to multiple subjectivities. Kahlo eludes or defies borders for some but simultaneously establishes borders for others.

Thus, the demand for global audiences required *Frida's* producers and director to make creative decisions dependent on homogenized definitions of ethnic, specifically Mexican, identity to meaningfully communicate authenticity. Privileging one set of characteristics and values over another, such as Kahlo's sexuality over her leftist politics, to sell the movie contributes to the symbolic colonization of Mexicanas and U.S. Latinas. In other words, the movie reaffirms dominant values and beliefs associated with Latinas—consequently maintaining the status quo. A story about a politically and artistically radical Mexican woman who openly opposed the imperialist policies of the United States can be sold to global audiences, but only if her life is framed and reduced to familiar homogenizing tropes.

Tapping into more facile constructions of Latina identity grounded in notions of authenticity did provide increased visibility to a woman and cultures rarely depicted with sensitivity in the mainstream media. Through their institutional participation in the publicity machinery surrounding Hollywood films, U.S. Latina/o entertainment journalists are problematically implicated in the circulation of syncretic identity discourses. Nevertheless, they are simultaneously invested in defining Latina/o ethnic identity in more complicated ways, as transnational, as simultaneously ethnic-specific and panethnic. However, as the divergent readings by U.S. Latina/o and Mexican audiences demonstrate, ethnic identity is fluid. Chicana/o activists and Mexico City media opposed the cinematic commodification of Kahlo and Mexico by interjecting a different yet equally unsustainable criterion for authenticity grounded in race, citizenship, and politics—to be authentic is to be a Mexican citizen who rejects "Americanization." Such a construction of authenticity ignores both the global nature of media production and the transnational experiences of millions of Mexican citizens who live or cross the border to work in the United States. Finally, online audiences eager for representational visibility applauded and reimagined the movie's depiction of ethnic authenticity in terms that made sense to their lives, which resulted in definitions of Latina/o and Mexican identity that were more complicated and dynamic.

This chapter reflects on my conceptualization of symbolic colonization to think about the question: Under what conditions can ethnic authenticity be deployed by Latina producers? Clearly, using familiar signifiers of Latina authenticity helps sell media, capture larger audiences, and provide more visibility. Nevertheless, the politics of representation surrounding ethnic women in the media (films, television, newspapers, Web sites) challenge us to think through reductive representations that inevitably discipline the boundaries of identity categories. As competing ideas about ethnic and racial identity disseminated through the online discussion thread illustrate, more complex definitions of ethnic identity and culture are possible and desirable. Ethnic identity is not fixed; rather, it is in a constant state of formation and reformulation as it responds to the ever-shifting terrain of postcolonial global culture. *Frida*, the U.S. Latina/o news coverage, Mexican news stories, and the IMDb discussion thread show how the complex act of crossing borders—geographical, symbolic, and imagined—provide an opportunity for reflexivity, a moment in which to question the often unconscious reification of racial, ethnic, and national hierarchies. In particular, the discussion thread exemplifies the struggle for recognition and legitimacy through more complex constructions of Latina bodies and identity.[79] Transnational and diasporic cultures are continually engaged in shifting categories of authenticity, difference, and identity. The debate over Hayek, Kahlo, and Mexican ethnicity exemplifies the tensions for communities whose competing definitions of identity challenge dichotomous thinking. By questioning how we are represented, we are provided the opportunity to redefine ourselves, and in redefining ourselves critique dominant systems of social signification. Competing constructions of ethnic identity provide an opportunity to negotiate the symbolic colonization of Latinidad and open up more fluid understandings of the mediated performance of gendered Latinidad.

"Ugly" America Dreams
the American Dream

In 1997, then MTV Networks chairman Tom Freston was quoted as saying that the future of mainstream television programming was "the tale of two continents—the bringing together of North and South America."[1] Spurred by the demographic explosion of the U.S. Latina/o television market throughout the past twenty years, U.S. media conglomerates are trying to unlock U.S. Latina/o ratings by looking south to the most popular form of programming in Mexico and Latin America—the telenovela.[2] It is no surprise then that one of the biggest new network shows in 2006 featured U.S.-born Honduran actor America Ferrera in an ABC prime-time dramedy (a combination of drama and comedy) based on the international telenovela megahit *Yo Soy Betty, La Fea*.[3] Global media integration, the desire for synergistic programming, and the success of cross-promotional strategies such as dual-language programming are encouraging the development of shows and entertainment personalities that can easily move across multiple audience demographics.[4] Latinas and Latina/o programming are at the forefront of global media integration. Television scholar John Tomlinson argues that globally syndicated television shows demonstrate the characteristics of contemporary programming that crosses linguistic and national borders, thereby participating in a complex web of media production and reception.[5] *Ugly Betty* is no exception.

The original 1999 Colombian telenovela was readapted by Mexico's Televisa in 2000 and 2006, and both of those productions were later distributed by multinational conglomerate Univisión to its stations in the United States, Latin America, and elsewhere. Finally, the 1999 telenovela was developed and adapted for mainstream English-language programming by U.S. Cuban Silvio Horta, network executive Ben Silverman, and Salma Hayek. *Ugly Betty* demonstrates the transnational flows and interconnections of global media and audiences. The international popularity and portability of programs such as *Ugly Betty* depend on the production of universally appealing story lines that captivate multiple audiences regardless of age, gender, race, nationality, and language.[6] In interviews publicizing the show, the producers often highlighted its broad liberal ideology and universal themes by describing it as "an ugly-duckling story of a girl who's working in this world of beauty and fashion where getting people to see past her appearance isn't an easy thing."[7] In other words, the show is about more than a Latina or a Mexican woman from Queens trying to fit into white corporate culture. It is about the trope of the "American dream," a familiar story grounded in the ideological belief that free choice, individualism, equality, and hard work under limited government intervention will allow all to succeed according to their abilities. Consequently, part of *Ugly Betty*'s global triumph is the program's careful production and, I would argue, the ideological sublimation of Latina identity and Latinidad.

The ideology of liberalism, as one of the foundational and continually dominant ideologies of the United States, presupposes a society defined by fair competition and individual rights. Liberalism is the ideology at the center of conservative arguments against affirmative action and equal opportunity programs. By proposing that, all things being equal, everyone has the same opportunity to compete in the U.S. marketplace, success is determined by how hard someone works and not by their economic class, gender, sexuality, ethnicity, or race. Ethnic and racial identities are to be assimilated, lost, and erased through the celebrated "melting pot" of U.S. culture. Liberalism thus devalues the importance of communitarian experiences and social identities as determinants or barriers to individual success. Instead, it proposes that all individuals are fundamentally equal and that, regardless of their social identity, everyone can control his or her fate through hard work, learned skills, and acquired education—the foundational myth of a U.S. meritocracy. At its core, the American dream relies on the assumption that the United States is a nation founded on the ideals of liberalism in which individuals compete and succeed based on their unique merits. People are ultimately rewarded for the "merits" they earn and not those they are born into. Part of the backlash against Jennifer Lopez, as detailed in chapter 2, is the public perception that she has not earned her privilege—that she is benefiting economically simply because of her ethnoracial identity and body and not because of her talent and skill. The ideological framework of the American dream mandates that, to be successful as a mainstream television show, *Ugly Betty*'s character development and story lines must revolve around earning "it" the hard way.

In this chapter I explore the symbolic colonization of Latina bodies in *Ugly Betty* through the show's production of Latina ethnic ambiguity and panethnic universalism, both of which make the program more marketable. Through the lens of the American dream, Latinidad becomes coded as a "positive" depoliticized identity because it exists outside preexisting U.S. racial binaries and therefore cannot be coded as white or black. Before I continue discussing the way Latina ethnic ambiguity and panethnicity function to produce Latinidad, I must briefly return to my previous arguments regarding ethnic authenticity. The *Frida* chapter documents how media outlets that are dependent on performances of Latina ethnicity often rely on constructions of authenticity that ultimately reinforce racial and ethnic differences based on established social hierarchies and globally familiar stereotypic characteristics, such as accented English, dark hair, and dark eyes. Because of the dearth of complex images about ethnic and racial minorities in films and on television, the few mainstream media performances of ethnic identity that do exist are often held to high standards of authenticity and imbued with social significance by audiences in their respective communities. *Ugly Betty* negotiates the competing cultural demands for authenticity with the demands of globalization by situating its Latina characters and their story lines not within the production of ethnic authenticity but through depictions informed by deracialized liberalism and grounded in a campy performance of panethnic Latina identity.

In particular, the program's Betty-as-Horatio Alger premise relies on the careful sublimation of an authentic ethnic Latina or Mexican identity into a globally consumable, symbolically colonizing assimilated *pan*ethnicity (emphasis on the pan and de-emphasis on the performance of ethnicity). I purposefully use the word *sublimation* throughout this chapter to indicate that Latina ethnicity is not erased but rather turned into a more ethereal form, a form that is not easily located within U.S. racial formations and therefore easier to disseminate to audiences on a global level. The sublimation of a specific Mexican ethnic authenticity in *Ugly Betty* also moves the program away from the contemporary cultural politics surrounding immigration and Mexican identity. Ethnicity and race are not the raison d'être of the lead characters or the motivation behind the main story lines. Rather, it is the logic of the American dream, which assumes the hard-working Betty and her more wayward sister, Hilda, will eventually achieve personal, professional, and economic success regardless of their class or ethnic background. It is a story line that has become increasingly apparent in the 2008–2009 season as Betty gets a promotion and moves out of her family's house, Hilda operates her own home business, and Ignacio enters the low-wage workforce as a U.S. citizen.

I begin this chapter by mapping out the show's location within the contemporary landscape of global programming. Next, I combine textual analysis with a discussion of journalistic coverage and audience responses to the show during its premier season (2006–2007). The program's depictions of the lead character as a heterosexual second-generation Mexican woman living in New York City draw upon socially acceptable definitions of assimilated ethnic women. Not surprisingly, media critics, trade journalists, and audiences often affirm the program's liberal logic and panethnic universalism. The promotional campaign and journalistic coverage of the show further illustrate the role of liberalism in the symbolic colonization of Latinidad in a mainstream television show produced by several Latina/o professionals (Salma Hayek, Silvio Horta, Jose Tamez). Finally, I explore the influence of Horta, an openly gay U.S. Cuban producer and writer, on negotiating the characters' ethnic identity and introducing a queer sensibility that potentially symbolically ruptures the show's construction of Latinidad. In particular, I focus on audience readings of ethnic and sexual difference in a show whose story lines depend on sublimating those differences. O. Hugo Benavides argues that the program's global appeal depends on the ambiguous performance of ethnic, racial, and sexual difference, noting "*Ugly Betty* thus speaks to a large hybrid audience beyond Latinos, who see themselves enmeshed in a postmodern world where difference is being articulated in new ways."[8] Consequently, I analyze public discussions about the program's performance of identity through audience negotiations on blogs and Internet discussion boards.

Readings of ethnic difference within the show have one provocative exception. The program's use of queer camp and queer sexuality—especially in the mainstream context of Latina/o representations that are usually grounded in heterosexuality—provides an interesting example of symbolic rupture. Similar to audience reception of *Frida*, positive Latina/o media visibility, particularly of queer Latinidad, in an environment of invisibility and hostility once again appears to be a transformative moment with the potential to rupture dominant constructions of Latina/o identity, specifically representations of Latina femininity, Latina heteronormativity, and the Latina/o family. Examining the program's story lines and journalistic writings about the show creates a unique opportunity for studying how the media use Latinas and Latinidad to capture global audiences. Analyzing online responses to the program explores audience negotiations of Latina panethnicity, Latinidad, and multicultural flavors to sell products and programming.[9]

Globally Programming Latinidad

During the last ten years, the lucrative potential of the U.S. Latina/o and Latin American markets—along with the long-term success of Spanish-language conglomerate Univisión—has increasingly drawn the attention of U.S. mainstream media producers. Because Univisión was not rated in the Nielsen Television Index until 2005, it often did not have the data to compete on a par with the other four major U.S. networks (ABC, CBS, Fox, NBC). Univisión has since established itself as the fifth major network in the United States, and its Los Angeles station, KMEX, was the nation's No. 1 station among adults 18–49 in 2008. In addition, KMEX's local 6 p.m. newscast has been No. 1 nationally since 1995.[10] The current ratings landscape proves John Sinclair's observation that "to the extent that Spanish speakers in the United States can be thought of as a single audience for television in that language, the United States forms the fifth largest, and the wealthiest, domestic television market in the Spanish-speaking world."[11] Among major entertainment media conglomerates, the economic and global dominance of Univisión has upped the ante for capturing U.S. Latina/o and Latin American television markets and turned attention to Univisión's No. 1 form of global programming, the telenovela.

Telenovelas are hourlong daily melodramatic serials, much like U.S. soap operas, but with one set of lead actors and one primary story line that begins and concludes within a period of about six months. Some telenovelas are romances, others are dramadies or historical re-creations. As one of the most powerful multinational media conglomerates in the world, Mexico's Televisa Corporation is a central player in Spanish-language television. Mexico's largest television network, Televisa also is the world's largest producer of telenovelas, and it exports them to the United States, Latin America, Europe and Asia.[12] Among Latin American and U.S. Latina/o audiences, telenovelas handily top the ratings.[13] During its peak viewership in 2000, the original Colombian production of *Yo Soy Betty, La Fea* drew as much as a 72 percent market share in its home country.[14] Its popularity spread across Latin America, reaching 59 percent of audiences in Ecuador, 57 percent in Panama, and 42 percent in Venezuela in March 2001.[15] On Univisión in 2006, Televisa's most recent *Betty* reincarnation, *La Fea Más Bella*, delivered more 18–49 Latina/o adults in its time slot than all the five English-language networks combined. According to Nielsen's National Hispanic Television Index (NHTI), *Bella* was drawing 3.3 million viewers among bilingual households in 2006 compared with 855,000 for ABC's *Ugly Betty*. [16] In June 2007, *Bella*'s series finale drew an average audience of 7.4 million viewers to Univisión, while *Ugly Betty*'s season finale a month earlier drew more than 10.5 million for all viewers.[17]

Because of the consistent ratings success and built-in audience for Spanish-language telenovelas, the major networks have been shopping for crossover programming based on the popular genre. A U.S.-based version of *Yo Soy Betty, La Fea* had been pitched to the major networks for several years before ABC, in collaboration with Hayek's Ventanarosa Productions, finally picked it up in 2006.[18] The need to target larger, more diverse audiences during an era of global media integration has further encouraged three of the four major U.S. networks (ABC, CBS, and NBC) to develop telenovela-based programming.[19] Beginning in the 1980s, U.S. media companies followed in the steps of other corporations by actively pursuing media markets outside the United States.[20]

The movement of U.S. television production companies toward telenovela-like programming and the initial success of *Ugly Betty* signal the popularity of the genre not only in Latin America and the United States but throughout the globe. The original Colombian production of *Yo Soy Betty, La Fea* has been locally adapted in India (2003), Israel (2003), Germany (2005), Russia (2005), Netherlands (2006), Spain (2006), and Greece (2007).[21] ABC's current incarnation of *Ugly Betty* has aired in England, Australia, Spain, and Germany, among other locations. The online availability of the program on ABC's Web site further adds to its global reach. Such potential for broad national and global distribution is also driving the networks to develop crossover Latina/o-themed programming with multicultural casts inclusive of Latina/o characters. Historically leading the way, most industry experts argue, is ABC, which holds six of the Top Ten programs among U.S. Latinas/os 18–49 with shows such as *George Lopez*, *Desperate Housewives*, *Grey's Anatomy*, *Lost*, and *Ugly Betty*, which came in second only to CBS's *Survivor* in its 2006–2007 Thursday night time slot.[22]

However, scholarly audience research actually indicates that wooing Latina/o audiences is more complicated than was once believed.[23] First-generation Spanish-dominant Latina/o audiences are loyal viewers of Spanish-language media for news and entertainment, while second-generation Latina/o audiences often move between Spanish- and English-language media.[24] Moreover, Nielsen Media Research indicates that the mainstream viewing patterns for Latinas/os born or raised in the United States are closer to white audiences than to other ethnic or racial minority audiences. Ethnic or racial minority audiences are more likely to watch shows and networks categorized as "minority programming," such as BET (Black Entertainment Television).[25] Thus, there is more overlap in the viewing patterns of top mainstream shows for second-generation U.S. Latina/o audiences and white audiences than there is between Latina/o and black audiences, with some notable exceptions such as *George Lopez* and, more recently, *Ugly Betty*.

Given *Ugly Betty*'s focus on fashion, family, career, and romance, it is no surprise that most of its viewers are women. What is perhaps more interesting is that the women come from diverse ethnic, racial, and age backgrounds, a desirable but rare feat in television programming. For the 2006–2007 season, Nielsen Media Research reported the show among the Top Twenty programs for 18–49-year-olds and audiences who earn more than $100,000 per year, two of the most coveted television and advertising demographics. In its first season, the show averaged 11.3 million viewers a week with 72 percent of its audience composed of women, 10.5 percent African Americans, and 9.25 percent Latinas/os.[26] Like Jennifer Lopez's movie *Selena, Ugly Betty* illustrates that Latina actors and characters may be employed to capture an ethnically, racially, and linguistically diverse global audience. With the adoption of SAP (secondary audio programming that allows audiences to watch shows with audio in another language) by the mainstream networks, it is expected that Latin American and Spanish-dominant U.S. Latinas/os may be increasingly attracted to English-based programming, further raising the stakes for both Spanish- and English-language media in capturing audiences.

Producing a Panethnic Latina from Queens

In 2006, Salma Hayek and Ben Silverman, who co-owned the U.S. rights to *Yo Soy Betty, La Fea*, brought in U.S. Cuban Silvio Horta to create an English-language version of the telenovela.[27] Whereas class, ethnicity, and ethnic humor were often the source of comedy on *George Lopez*, both ethnicity and ethnic humor are carefully sublimated on *Ugly Betty*. In an interview with the *Washington Post*, for instance, Horta explained the shared vision of the program: "And creatively we [Horta, Hayek, Silverman] were all on the same page—telling the story of Betty as a young woman straddling these two worlds, trying to make her way in the American world, the gringo world, as this . . . Latina and this ugly duckling."[28] I argue that while the Betty character clearly must negotiate the demands of her white workplace with the demands of her Latina/o family, her ethnic-specific Mexican identity is rarely the focus of the story lines. Indeed, it is most often her panethnic albeit campy perfor-mance of beauty and class that is the main source of humor and conflict.

References to Betty and her family's ethnic identity are rarely mentioned or significantly incorporated into the show's publicity and story lines, with the exception of the story line dealing with her father Ignacio's citizenship status. However, even the Ignacio Suarez (Tony Plana) story depoliticizes the immigration debate by handling it in a humorous and melodramatic fash-ion. For example, in the first season's over-the-top finale, Betty and her sister, Hilda Suarez (Ana Ortiz), travel to Mexico to help their father obtain a legal visa ("A Tree Grows in Guadalajara," originally aired May 10, 2007, and "East Side Story," originally aired May 17, 2007). The episode's story line mostly focuses on Hilda's search for a wedding dress and Betty's questions about her romantic life. While the sisters' trip to Mexico is one of the only instances in which their ethnic identity is the explicit source of humor, the comedy is mostly based on their adept acculturation to U.S. society and foreignness in Mexico. In particular, Betty's lack of Spanish fluency and knowledge about her Mexican heritage—undoubtedly a situation many young U.S. born Lati-nas/os can relate to—acts as a comedic and subtle marker of her outsider status in Mexico. In the only episodes set in Mexico so far, Hilda and Betty are depicted as much cultural fishes-out-of-water in Mexico as they are in the United States.

Interestingly, the decision to cast the New York family as specifically Mex-ican is perhaps more indicative of audience aspirations than its centrality to the show's story lines. Mexican residents make up the largest U.S. Latina/o ethnic group and the largest Latin American population in the United States, even though they are not the majority Latina/o population in New York City. When responding to an audience question about how the U.S. *Betty* charac-ter compares with those in other versions of the telenovela, Horta answered, "[S]he is vastly different. This comes from cultural differences, my writing choices, America Ferrera's acting choices, and so on. The shape and prem-ise of the series is the same, but the characters, their stories, their voice, etc. are different."[29] Betty is not the Latin American heroine of the telenovelas or the Latina archetypes familiar in U.S. popular culture. As a career-oriented, second-generation college graduate, Betty is defined by her more assimilated behavior, in particular her inability to speak Spanish and her lack of inter-est in Spanish-language music and television. Although negotiating the two cultures is a part of the program's story lines, the show's central stories pay little attention to Betty's Mexican identity, focusing instead around the fam-ily's perseverance, moral rectitude, inevitable success, and inherent nobility. Consequently, the producers' ethnic-specific focus on an English-fluent Mexican character who has incorporated the cultural practices of living in the United States is a conscious and deliberate choice.

By tapping into a more assimilated construction of Mexican identity as well as more universal story lines regarding the human condition, the show produces a less ethnically and racially marked Mexican family that is more internationally marketable. Similar to the show's characters, the Latina/o actors who play them also occupy complicated identity spaces. Indeed, none of the key actors on the show identifies as Mexican—Ferrera identifies as Latin or Honduran, Plana as Cuban, and Ortiz as Puerto Rican. Ferrera, born and raised in Los Angeles, came of age identifying as white or "American." Ortiz, whose father is a major Puerto Rican politician in Philadelphia and who wed her husband in Puerto Rico, has only recently acknowledged her Irish American maternal roots. Finally, the Cuban Plana made a career playing Mexican characters in U.S. television and film. *Ugly Betty*'s Latina/o characters and the three actors who play them demonstrate the blurring of Latina/o ethnic distinctions and privileging of panethnicity necessary for globally commodifiable television depictions of Latinidad.

I Am Betty, La Global Latina

Horta widely credits the pilot's rave reviews at the 2006 Television Critics Association for initially saving *Ugly Betty* from the dead zone of Friday night television.[30] As the previous chapter discussed, journalists function as textual mediators who speak to broader cultural readings of the show. In particular, television critics, as journalists who specialize in writing about media culture, actively participate in defining popular tastes and determining what programs are culturally acceptable. What is emphasized by television critics in reviewing *Ugly Betty* is therefore informative of how critics make sense of the program and simultaneously frame the program for audiences.

U.S. television critics initially emphasized the show's more universally compelling story lines, such as the continuing "fish out of water" theme. With headlines such as "Likable 'Betty' Aided by a Lovable Lead," "The Main Character May Not Be Pretty, but Her Show Is," and "A Plucky Guppy among the Barracudas," newspaper reviews highlighted the more universal appeal of the show.[31] Foregrounding the program's American dream ideology, mainstream television critics of the pilot rarely mentioned the specific Mexican ethnicity of Betty or her family as significant to audiences enjoying the show.[32] On the rare occasion Betty's ethnicity is mentioned, it is more often than not conflated with a panethnic "Latin" or "Latin America" identity. Tom Shales of the *Washington Post*, for example, described Betty "as a very Americanized Latin American, one partial to such fashion statements as a huge red poncho with the word 'Guadalajara' embroidered across the front" (see figure 4.1).[33] Betty and her poncho are not Latin American. She is a U.S.-born citizen, and the poncho is from Mexico. Yet, in one brief sentence, the ethnic specificity of Betty and the Guadalajara poncho are sublimated. Guadalajara, located in the Mexican state of Jalisco, has an established history of immigration to the United States. Nevertheless, Betty and her attire are decontextualized as one more "Americanized Latin American" sign of her gauche taste and naïve, oddball personality. Overall, the journalistic discussion of the program encouraged viewers to focus on Betty as an "ugly duck," not Betty as the daughter of Mexican immigrants from Guadalajara. She is rarely labeled by the reviewers as Mexican, a more racialized ethnic identity; she is a safely assimilated Latin or Latin American.

Television critics such as Maureen Ryan of the *Chicago Tribune* further reaffirm the show's liberal ideology, noting, "Those who can identify with Betty's plight—anyone who has ever felt like the ugly duckling among swans, any veteran of battles fought not with fists but with cutting remarks and exclusion—should find a lot to like."[34] International journalists also emphasize the "underdog quality" of the show, such as a 2007 story in London's *Sunday Express* that quotes Ferrera as saying, "It's all about wanting her to succeed against the odds because she tries so damn hard."[35] By situating the Betty character as the oddball, reviewers define the show as "more than" a new take on Latina/o programming. While Hilda (in what is perhaps a reference to the more racially coded Latina harlot stereotype) is described as Betty's "slutty sister,"[36] Betty is always defined through ethnic and racially neutral terms. For example, a *Denver Post* critic described Betty as "Jane Doe, a woman who is a little overweight, a bit klutzy, and could use a bit of help in the style department. In other words, you and me."[37] For the television reviewers, the essence of Betty is that she can be anyone, you *and* me. Betty's ethnicity, race, and sexuality—her social identity—is less significant to the heart of the show than her actions, work ethic, and idealized morals. My analysis of journalistic reviews of the program is not meant to suggest that television journalists unproblematically circulate the intended messages of the program's producers. Rather, it draws attention to how the show's themes and story lines align with well-established media renditions of the American dream.

Journalists reinforce the ideology of the American dream by sublimating interpretations of the show based predominantly on specific ethnic or racial

Figure 4.1. The photograph of Betty Suarez (America Ferrera) wearing her red and yellow Guadalajara poncho to work was widely used by entertainment journalists in stories about the show. Not only did the Guadalajara poncho mark Betty as Mexican, or at the very least Latina, but the class signifiers of her clothes also situated her within a more universal working-class sphere.

identity. Minimizing the importance of ethnic specificity in favor of a more homogenized characterization of Latina identity contributes to the symbolic colonization of Latinidad. In her essay on Jennifer Lopez's representation of Selena, Frances Aparicio argues that the homogenization of Latina identity is typical of most mainstream media, noting a Latina actor "is discursively defined in the public sphere because of her generalizability as a Latina rather than because of her uniqueness as a Boricua or a Mexican American or Cuban American."[38] *Ugly Betty* reviews similarly engage in a blurring of Latina ethnic distinctions. Most reviewers did not discuss the ethnic identity of the characters, but some journalists did point to the program's use of stereotyped Latina/o characteristics.[39] However, even journalists who were critical of the producers' attempt to homogenize the ethnic identity of the characters still applauded the show for its universal telenovela appeal across ethnic and racial groups.[40]

America: A Real Woman Like Betty

A central component of the program's global appeal is the universal, likeable title character and the seemingly authentic celebrity persona of America Ferrera. Both journalists and producers consistently draw attention to the convergence between actor and character. For example, in interviews, Ferrera often describes herself as average, a misfit, one of those people who don't quite belong but who are inherently good and valuable. During an interview with *TV Guide*, Ferrera argued: "The truth is, we are not all people who look like we belong on television. But every single person you look at, they are the heroine of their own lives. There are people who love them and desire them and need them."[41] Ferrera is Betty and Betty *is* Ferrera; both can relate to the personal struggle of fitting in.

As the sixth and youngest child of Honduran immigrants, Ferrera says she had plenty of fish-out-of-water moments growing up in the predominantly Caucasian community of Woodland Hills, California. "As early as second grade I remember feeling really different and isolated," she says. "I had the hugest crush on a boy, and my best friend had a crush on him too. One day he said to me, 'I like your best friend more because she's paler and she has freckles.' And it was right then that I began to feel like, Oh wow, I'm different." At the same time, she says, she never felt like she fit in with the Latino community. "I mean, I grew up in the Valley," she says. "All my friends were white Jewish kids. So the Latino kids thought I was this white girl."[42]

Ferrera's willingness to share these seemingly intimate accounts about her life allows journalists and audiences to read her as a sincere and "real" person. Public performances of Ferrera as a "real woman" are key for producing positive publicity about the show. Discussing the appeal of the program, for example, Salma Hayek and Silvio Horta consciously blur the differences between Ferrera and Betty's life, between "reality" and fiction. In a May 2007 *W Magazine* article, Hayek said Ferrera is "one of the most charismatic people I've ever met. . . . She's also authentic. That's a rare characteristic nowadays, and that's why people are falling in love with her."[43] Ben Silverman, an executive producer of the show, reiterated the same sentiment, saying "there's no bulls--- with her. . . . It doesn't matter what makeup or hair or clothing she has on, she's so real that she grabs you. She's a very connected human being, and that really empowers her as an actor."[44] The merging of actor and character is not a new or novel publicity strategy, but it is nevertheless significant in framing public reception of the program.

In his book about celebrity culture, Joshua Gamson argues that promoting the emotional sincerity of actors by drawing attention to the similarity with their characters is a well-established strategy going back to the golden studio age of Hollywood.[45] Audiences want to believe that the actors who portray the sassy and naughty or good and noble characters they admire are themselves actually sassy and naughty or good and noble. In the case of *Ugly Betty*, online discussion boards, blogs, and entertainment coverage are pivotal to establishing the link between the actors and the characters. That Ferrera embodies genuine and wholesome "American" values makes it easier to promote Ferrera, Betty, and the program. The close relationship between the "good" qualities of the character and those of Ferrera as a "real" woman is thus significant to fans and audiences of the program. Many of the early postings on the ABC Web site's *Ugly Betty* discussion board consciously or subconsciously conflate the actor with the character, such as the post, "Is ugly betty ugly,ok,or beutiful?????"[46] Although the initial posting asks if "Betty" is beautiful, it is clear by the responses that what audiences want to know is if the actor is really like Betty. All the responses to the initial post center around discussions of America Ferrera, the actor who portrays the character, her real physical appearance, and her off-screen personality.[47] Some fans wanted Ferrera to be "ugly" as evidence of the show's sincerity, while others quickly wanted to affirm Ferrera's beauty as proof of the show's quality and her acting ability. Regardless, a majority of the posters desired to know that Ferrera's real-life beauty, morals, and values matched those of the television heroine they adored.

Consequently, among fans there is a careful filtering of information about Ferrera that might work against their readings of the character and actor. For instance, in a post entitled "America Ferrera should stick with acting and stay out of politics," a fan disciplines Ferrera for her involvement in Hillary Clinton's presidential campaign. Such postings point to the conventions that surround the blurring of actor and character.[48] Fans wanting to maintain the suspension of disbelief that character and actor are one sometimes police Ferrera for actions that do not fit their assumptions. Additionally, to maintain the aura that Ferrera is just like Betty, Ferrera must carefully manage information about her real life. After all, Ferrera as Betty cannot perform the role of everywoman if she too closely embodies an ethnic identity or holds specific political beliefs.

The carefully managed publicity accounts of Betty and Ferrera as "real" people once again depend on the universal appeal of both character and actor. Ferrera's persona as an average woman is key to her global appeal and *Ugly Betty*'s popularity. Perhaps a few pounds lighter and more glamorous than when she first appeared on the Hollywood scene as the provocative, slightly overweight, burgeoning high school feminist in *Real Women Have Curves* (2002), Ferrera's audience appeal continues to rest on her ordinariness. To the show's fans, for instance, Ferrera's tearful acceptance of her first acting award for best actress at the 2007 Golden Globe Awards added to their perception that she was a real woman portraying real women like them:

> Thank you so humbly for recognizing this show and this character, who is truly bringing a new face to television and such a beautiful, beautiful message about beauty that lies deeper than what we see. And it's such an honor to play a role that I hear from young girls on a daily basis how it makes them feel worthy and lovable and that they have more to offer the world than what they thought, and it's such an honor to play this role.[49]

Demonstrating the importance of Ferrera's and Betty's authenticity to her fans, this open letter to Ferrera regarding her acceptance speech illustrates the emotional link between the fans, the actor, and the character.

> I found myself openly weeping with you as you took the stage to accept your Golden Globe award for "Best Actress" on Monday night. . . . As a young Latina feminist, I wanted to shout from the rooftop of my building my congratulations to you and to say thank you—thank you for exemplifying the class, ethnic and body ideals of this woman and of real women the world over.[50]

Although the blogger draws attention to the Latina panethnicity of the actor and character, more importantly she engages emotionally with Betty's supposed "ugliness" and Ferrera's "real life" social consciousness as the real women at the heart of the program's reception.

Her acceptance speech affirmed the connection between actor and character for journalists as well, such as in the lead to this Australian profile of the show: "When an emotional America Ferrera thanked her 'mummy' during her acceptance speech as this year's Golden Globe Award winner for Best TV Actress (Comedy or Musical), her tears were the real thing."[51] Ferrera and Betty become interchangeable; one embodies the other. The emphasis on the down-to-earth nature of the actor and character allows *Ugly Betty* to resonate globally within and across national, ethnic, racial, and gender subjectivities.

However, Betty's and Ferrera's global popularity require that the ethnic-specific context of Ferrera as a second-generation Honduran and Betty as a U.S. Mexican be sublimated into the more common experience of and desire for social acceptance. The sublimation of ethnic specificity is duly emphasized by journalists, both in the United States and internationally, as well as by the show's producers and lead actor. For example, in an interview with the *Sunday Mail* in Australia, Ferrera emphasizes Betty's universality when she says, "what I love most about Betty being a Latina is that it's not a banner she carries with her. . . . It's not a show about a Latina girl; it's a show about a girl with problems who just happens to be a Latina."[52] It is precisely Betty's universality, not her specificity, that appeals most to fans across gender and national identities, as is evident in this *Los Angeles Times* story about a Trinidadian fan of the show:

> "We all like the show, and nobody should be ashamed of that," said Seon McDonald, 20, a Trinidad and Tobago native who lives in Brooklyn, N.Y. "Betty is someone who is trying to fit in. It goes to how I felt on my first day of college, you know, you feel a little bit odd. I can relate to her in the sense that she's not like everybody else."[53]

McDonald is neither a woman, nor Mexican, nor Latina/o. He does not mention his racial or ethnic identity, yet it is important for interpreting his response. An immigrant from a predominantly Afro-Caribbean island, McDonald is presumably the outsider trying to socially and economically move upward in a foreign culture, the outsider trying to achieve the American dream.

Writing about the character he most identifies with, another male fan wrote on the popular Web site uglybettynews.com:

> I am most like Betty. I was the kid who didn't go to proms, from a working class family, with no sense of style. I have gone into the world as I am (if they ever "pretty" Betty up, you'll find the worst rant you've ever seen on this site). . . . I love Betty Suarez, I see myself in her, because she just goes out there and does it, and makes people question what they think about "the way things are."[54]

Like McDonald, this fan's commonality with Betty is not so much about her gender or ethnoracial identity but about her more universal appeal and the seductive call of the American dream. Betty's working-class roots, non-normative performance of beauty, and desire to make it against the odds tap into global demands for more universally compelling stories. The responses of these male fans illustrate how the program's, actor's, and producers' performance of deracialized panethnicity inform readings of the show across national, gender, ethnic, and racial lines.

Symbolically Colonizing the Latina Dream

If Hilda functions as the more racialized ethnic character (the bilingual, telenovela-loving, strong-willed, hot-headed, curvaceous daughter who gets pregnant outside marriage in high school), then the socially awkward Betty occupies a less racialized panethnic role, the role of the good, self-sacrificing Latina señorita. In other words, Hilda is the brown Latina "bad girl," Betty is the "good" ambiguous Latina. As the "good girl" who relegates her ethnic identity to the backstage, Betty is the cornerstone of the program's liberal logic and universal appeal.

Although Betty has become slightly more sexualized since the first season, her overall role as the deracialized, panethnic, morally good, asexual, "ugly girl" making it in the big city has remained constant. Throughout the series, the plot and dialogue carefully emphasize Betty's sexually innocent, morally good, and maternal nature. For example, in the first season episode "Four Thanksgivings and a Funeral" (originally aired November 16, 2006), her caregiving responsibilities at work and home pull her in opposite directions. On the home front, Betty must cope with shopping and cooking for Thanksgiving dinner as well as finding a lawyer for her undocumented immigrant father. At the same time, she must juggle her "work" responsibilities, simultaneously nurturing her heartbroken boss, Daniel Meade (Eric Mabius). When Daniel pulls her away from Thanksgiving dinner to ask for dating wardrobe advice, Betty responds by walking out and stating, "I know that this might be a surprise to you, but I have a life, too, and a family that counts on me a lot. They already think that I put you in front of them. My dad has immigration problems. My sister may have hired a shady lawyer. And it's up to me to fix it." Similar to many working women, Betty must balance her nurturing role at home with the demand of work without letting go of her maternal status and obligations—the ultimate self-sacrificing woman. Although her ethnicity is sublimated in the dialogue and plot—with the exception of the immigration lawyer subplot—her racially unmarked panethnic Latina identity subtly informs the character's immigrant work ethic and almost suffocating commitment to family.

After Hilda loses the family's savings in an immigration lawyer scam, it is Betty who performs the symbolic role of mother and nurturer. Preparing her mother's traditional Mexican dessert for Thanksgiving, Betty takes responsibility for her sister's mistake:

BETTY: Well at least you've been trying to help. I didn't make it to Justin's pageant. Maybe this stupid job isn't worth it.

HILDA: You can't live your life for your family, Betty. You've been taking care of us since mom died, and maybe it's time for us to stop relying on you so much.

BETTY: Well, I like that you rely on me. Taking care of the family is the one thing I knew I could do. I wasn't ever going to be the pretty one.

Betty may not shine at *Mode* or in her romantic relationships, but her symbolic role as self-sacrificing nurturer is solidified. This episode, like many others during the first two seasons, significantly draws out Betty's role as mother/nurturer through the established archetypes of panethnic Latina femininity without racializing the character.

In the 2008–2009 season, the show's producers are slowly moving away from more familiar representations of Latinidad and Betty's symbolic role as the self-sacrificing Latina. Drawing on the more universal trope of the American dream, in the third season Betty leaves her family and strikes out on her own in a cross-country trip, rents an apartment in downtown Manhattan, and achieves professional success at *Mode*. Still providing the moral compass of the show, Betty is less defined by the archetype of the self-sacrificing Latina mother. Evocative of the trajectory of millions of young U.S. adults,

Betty's role as the family's maternal nurturer and main financial provider becomes less significant. She still must balance her work with the needs of her family, but the parameters of her personal life have become more universally similar than ethnically distinct from the diverse audiences who watch the program. The audience expectations for the character's ethnic assimilation and upward mobility might explain the backlash against the creative decision to have Betty return to her father's house after his hospitalization later in the third season.

Betty could be any working woman struggling to juggle family and work, and in that sense the universal themes that define her story lines associate the character with a more assimilated and less racialized performance of ethnic identity. Betty's successes are the achievements of anyone struggling to make better lives for themselves and their families. When she's at home she is ethnically contextualized by panethnic signifiers of Latina identity and culture, but at work Betty's more assimilated performance of Latina femininity, her subtle difference, is brought to the foreground through a failed performance of white middle-class social acceptability. As she spends more time away from home and her family, Betty's panethnic performance of Latinidad is less pivotal to the story lines. She is a Latina, sometimes, but an ugly-duckling working-class girl always. Betty's duality allows the program to market itself as a Latina/o show with broad global appeal to universal values and the ideology of liberalism.

For example, in the show's premier episode, Betty tries to fit in at the glamorous magazine by reporting to her first day of work with a bright red poncho purchased by her father in Guadalajara (see figure 4.1). A splash of red and yellow in an otherwise monochrome white environment, Betty is immediately surveyed and disciplined by the show's arbiter of white upper-class femininity, Amanda Tanen (Becky Newton). Amanda, who often serves as a comedic foil to emphasize Betty's ethnoracial- and class-outsider status within the elite world of high fashion, greets Betty and her Guadalajara poncho with the ethnically coded question, "Oh, my God. Are you the before and after shoot? (In slow, loud English) Are—you—de—li—ver—ing—some—thing?" Betty's initial introduction to Amanda sets the tone for the program's consistent use of class markers to sublimate her ethnic and racial difference. By placing the white Amanda in a position of power and privilege, Betty's treatment can be interpreted as racially motivated. Amanda's character assumes that only a "non-American" and presumably nonwhite Latina unable to speak English would wear such a hideous clothing item. However, the dominant reading of the poncho by most reviewers and audiences has actually been based on class and not ethnic notions of difference. Betty's class difference is further emphasized in the episode through a previous scene featuring a white model's more acceptable Prada version of a poncho. Betty is a foreigner to the corporate white world and economically elite world of high fashion. Her fashion sense, not her ethnicity, defines her as working class and not ethnically white.

Invoking class signifiers to communicate Betty's difference allows the producers to avoid associating her with the more racialized constructions of Latinidad that mark her sister, Hilda, such as speaking in Spanish, Spanglish, or English with a Spanish accent. When Betty shows up for work in an over-the-top outfit put together by Hilda, Wilhelmina responds by quipping, "It looks like Queens threw up." Such a carefully crafted line foregrounds Betty's class difference and shifts her ethnic identity to the story's background. Among New York's racially and economically segregated boroughs, Queens has historically been associated with working-class white ethnic immigrants. Indeed, it is interesting that the program locates Betty's family in Queens, a borough not usually linked with Latinas/os in the popular media. According to a 2006 U.S. Census estimate, Queens is still predominantly non-Latina/o white, making up 31.3 percent of the population, with Latina/o residents the second largest category at 26.5 percent.[55] Additionally, Mexican immigrants are most likely to live in Manhattan's East Harlem barrio, a particularly classed and racialized space once predominantly inhabited by Puerto Rican migrants.[56] By choosing to cast the characters as Mexicans living in Queens, the show acknowledges that U.S. Mexicans make up the country's largest Latina/o population but erases the current racialized geopolitics of New York City. Puerto Rican migrants followed by Dominican immigrants are the city's largest two Latina/o groups. Constructing a New York space with a Mexican family living in a historically non-Latina/o neighborhood allows the show to situate Betty's character within a less racially determined and more universally resonant setting.

Ugly Betty carefully manages the two sisters' performance of panethnic Latinidad. The hyperfeminine urban, working-class acculturated Hilda constantly wears and performs her classed and racialized Latina identity. Betty, however, must increasingly occupy an assimilated ethnic identity. Unlike Hilda, Betty's academic and cultural education allows her to move and work, albeit problematically, within a world of white wealth and privilege. Furthermore, Betty's inability to normatively perform neither Latina nor white beauty becomes part of a more universal story line grounded in the logic of liberalism by focusing on the themes of self-pride, social acceptance, and the value of individuality. Employing Betty and her family's ethnic identity as a unique but sublimated marker of difference allows the program to speak to broader audiences inside and outside the United States.

The Cosbying of Latinidad

In their pioneering audience study on *The Cosby Show*, Sut Jhally and Justin Lewis conclude that the characters' upper-class identity and the story lines' middle-class values encouraged white viewers to ignore race in such a way that it permitted white audiences to absolve themselves of social responsibility for ongoing racial prejudices and discrimination in the United States and allowed black audiences an escapist moment of media pleasure.[57] Although elements of U.S. black history and culture were consistently incorporated into the show, the plot lines and characters' development revolved around issues faced by many middle-class families regardless of race. Heteronormative story lines about high school romances, wedding anniversaries, and family dinners overshadowed the program's always-present but subtle acknowledgments of Martin Luther King, Jr. or the civil rights movement. White audiences comfortably tuned in to watch *The Cosby Show* in record numbers, allowing them to romanticize racial equality and the normalcy of their own families. On the other hand, for U.S. black audiences, the program's success depended on its uncompromisingly positive depiction of black middle-class respectability.[58] Because so few positive images of the black middle class existed in the mainstream media, the show's portrayals of respectability, dignity, and nobility resonated with black audiences long excluded from the semiotic world of television. On a global level, *Cosby*'s international appeal stemmed from the logic of U.S. liberalism grounded in media representations of idealized racial equity. The show's record-setting international syndication set the standard for other situation comedies featuring ethnic and racial minority characters—depicting an ethnic or racial minority family that is respectable and well behaved, not too racial or too ethnic, preferably middle class, and always heteronormative.[59]

Ugly Betty clearly follows some of the elements of the *Cosby* formula. Betty's ethnic identity is neither a central part of her character's development nor the program's central story lines, especially during the 2008–2009 season. The more ethnic-specific story lines, such as Ignacio's undocumented

immigration status, nod to the contemporary politics of immigration domi-
nating the U.S. public sphere but do so in an entertaining and ideologically
safe manner. Ironically, the first season story line regarding Ignacio's immigration status played out against a real-world background where the United
States came close to approving virulently anti-immigration congressional
legislation. Millions of news viewers watched record-breaking numbers of
immigration-rights activists mobilize for the right to remain in the United
States as Ignacio voluntarily returned to Mexico in first-class accommo-
dations. The producers' and writers' decision to reduce Ignacio's story to a
melodrama of extramarital romance, family feuds, corporate intrigue, and
Disneylike images of Mexico and the border diffuses any potential political backlash against the show. That is, the surreal or unreal characterization
of undocumented immigration neutralizes overtly political readings of the
show. In 2009, there is growing speculation on the discussion boards that
Ignacio will be killed off—allowing the producers to further situate Hilda's
and Betty's trajectory away from brownness.

The program's treatment of Ignacio's undocumented status is representative of televisual practices that symbolically colonize Latinidad through the
seemingly benevolent trope of the American dream rather than through the
gendering and racialization evident in the book's first three case studies. For
instance, in the episode "Trust, Lust and Must" (originally aired November 2, 2006), the Suarez family visits an immigration lawyer. Upon learning that the father could be deported, Betty responds by saying, "But he has
a family; he pays taxes; he's a Mets fan." To which Hilda adds, "He's in the
Oprah Book Club." The sisters' dialogue characterizes Ignacio as an "average American" instead of an "illegal alien" by humanizing him in ways that
resonate with audiences across ethnic, racial, and gender categories. Ignacio
may not be a citizen, but he's a moral and law-abiding man who pays his
taxes. He may be Mexican, but unlike Hilda's hypermasculine fiancé, Santos (Kevin Alejandro), his racialized masculinity is coded as less brown and
therefore less threatening. After all, Ignacio cooks the family's meals, nur-
tures his daughters, and reads Oprah's women-centered book selections. *Ugly
Betty* effectively humanizes Ignacio as a globally familiar and idealized father
figure. Ignacio's love for his daughters, grandson, and deceased wife trumps
any negative associations with his ethnic identity or legal status. Like Cliff
Huxtable of *The Cosby Show*, both men soothe dominant gender constructions of black and Latino masculinity through their deracialized, acculturated, and sensitive affect.

Sublimating Ethnicity, Resisting Race

Because ethnicity and race are not central to the show's American dream premise, it is not surprising that the most interesting fan discussions revolve around the disciplining of potential ethnic and racial readings of the show. On the ABC discussion board, for instance, a poster's claim that a line by Wilhelmina was racist toward white people drew numerous and heated responses. The original post argued: "Twice in one week an ABC Racist remark in Primetime Show. The line by the Queen BEE 'Standing here like a couple of White [crackers']. But then maybe it is ok to slur 'White People' NOT!"[60] Responses to the post contradicted the racialized reading of the dialogue by claiming that the remark was inoffensive because the show was an "equal opportunity offender."[61] Since the program is critical of everyone without respect to ethnicity, race, gender, or sexuality, posters suggested it is not possible for the show to be racist. In other words, posters claimed the show was not and its audiences should not racially code its characters or humor. Reading race into a show premised on a Mexican family living in the United States was resisting the program's message of universality.

Some audiences' resistance to ethnic or racial readings of the program is further evidenced in their discussion of Betty's relationships. Betty has never dated an identifiable Latino character. Throughout the series, Betty has taken part in a series of multiracial/multiethnic romances and crushes, in particular her long-term romance with Henry Grubstick (Christopher Gorham). Yet on a now-defunct fan Web site devoted to fan fiction and depictions of the Betty-Henry romance, nary a reference to the characters' ethnic and racial identities could be found. The screenwriters' decision to highlight the characters' awkward similarities as social misfits over their ethnoracial differences resonates more easily with audiences than any representations of potential cultural differences.

Indeed, the second season's introduction of an ethnically ambiguous romantic rival, Gio, played by Puerto Rican actor Freddy Rodríguez, threatened the show's liberal color-blind premise, creating tensions among some fans on the ABC discussion board. Gio troubled race-neutral readings of the program by introducing an uncomfortable level of ambiguity. Although *Ugly Betty*'s writers carefully kept Gio's ethnic identity neutral (his name, Giovanni Rossi, could be Latina/o or Italian), his previous Latino roles, such as Federico Diaz on HBO's *Six Feet Under*, clearly led some audiences to read him as ethnic. Unlike the WASPy Henry, the signifiers surrounding Gio (his accent, clothes, and mannerisms) produce an ethnic working-class identity.[62]

On the ABC discussion board, fans' reactions to Gio have been strong, with many eager to subtract ethnicity and race from the conversation:

> As other posters have noted, Gio is no bum. He's a hard-working, fairly honest, funny, nice guy (c'mon, he gave the extra ticket to his bratty sister!). There's no real stereotype except the ones people choose to highlight. Besides, the whole show is a caricature, so why aren't people complaining more about Marc being a stereotypical gay character, or Amanda being a stereotypical skinny monster, or Hilda being a stereotypical Latino woman? Because the show is about the idea of stereotypes.[63]

Critiques of Gio as stereotypically Latino, Italian, or ethnic are contested, not on the grounds that they are offensive but rather on the belief that racial readings are irrelevant. Because every character is a stereotype, no stereotypes matter on the show.

Fans who engage in racialized readings of the characters or story lines are in turn policed on the discussion board. For instance, in fan discussions about which character is a better fit for Betty (Daniel, Gio, or Henry), the characters' ethnic and racial identities are rarely mentioned as important.[64] Love, romance, and sexual desire are incorporated into the race-neutral liberal logic of the program. When ethnicity is brought into the fan discussion, audiences often negate its importance, such as this discussion regarding Gio:

> I don't think that a guy being a better fit into the family is a way to judge who is better for betty. Duh Gio is might be a better fit then Henry, he is latin so there is not cultrue differences to deal with. I also think Betty's family is not that keen on Henry b/c of the whole baby thing. Being latin myself and having dated white guys it can be a little wried but all that matters is that they care to try, like Henry looking a fool while dancing.[65]

The more universal theme of fitting in supersedes stories about ethnic or racial conflict. If Gio is indeed Latino, the poster raises a valid concern regarding potential differences in cultural values; nevertheless, her comments inevitably argue against the importance of ethnic or racial identity. The majority of the comments in response to the above post, however, would rather discuss the proper use of the terms *Latin* and *Latina* than the issue of mixed-race dating or the ethnic and racial differences between the characters. Most who responded agreed that, in the end, the ethnicity of Gio or Henry did not matter because love, after all, is a universal human experience.

Postings about perhaps the most ethnically and racially marked character, Hilda, equally demonstrate the complicated negotiations surrounding the show. Hilda's hyper-stereotypical performance of Latina identity is recuperated by the program's liberal logic and the trope of the American dream. Although some posters might not look, sound, or dress like Hilda, they relate to her insecurities, emotional vulnerability, struggle as a single mother, and equally ambitious desire for economic and professional success. Discussion board responses to the 2007–2008 season premiere in which her fiancé's death is confirmed exemplify the complex ideological manner through which her character is read.[66] Fans exchanged emotional stories, often reflecting on their personal vulnerability and sincere grief over Santos' death. Without mentioning the stereotypical markers of Latina femininity that overwhelmingly define the character, audiences resonated with Hilda's working-class nobility, lost chance at love, and the unpredictable nature of life. Having patiently watched Santos blossom from a "neighborhood thug" into a good father and loving fiancé, fans felt betrayed by the producers' denial of Hilda's Cinderella ending. To discussion board participants, Hilda was not a Latina spitfire but another working-class everywoman trying to succeed against the odds. Once again, racial and ethnic readings of the character are sublimated in favor of a more universal, classed and gendered reading of the show. Hilda might provide the program's Latin spice, but both women's ethnic difference is mediated by the program's overall message of universal worth and social acceptance.

Queering "America's" Dreams

My analysis thus far explores the sublimation of ethnic specificity in the production of globally commodifiable panethnic Latina/o cultural visibility. However, for the remainder of this chapter, I would like to shift gears by examining how the representations of gender and sexuality partially rupture the homogenized deracialized representation of Latinidad. I purposefully use the word *partially* because the program's representations of gender and sexuality also contribute to the ideology of meritocracy central to the trope of the American dream.

I invoke the term *queer* as more than a word used to identify gay, lesbian, bisexual, and transgender people. Instead, I build on Michael Warner's discussion of the term as problematizing identity politics by looking at the intersections of ethnicity, race, gender, and sexuality in ways that challenge dominant assumptions about identity.[67] In particular, I focus on

Ugly Betty's use of queer camp. Queer camp engages in humor based on irony, melodrama, exaggeration, and bad taste.[68] It takes what is perceived as "normal" and makes it self-referentially funny and strange and sometimes tragically sad. Throughout the final section of this chapter, I think through the lens of queerness and queer camp to suggest they can symbolically rupture the deracialized homogenization of Latinidad, Latina/o family, and Latina identity. Specifically, I argue that writer-producer Horta, an out gay U.S. Cuban, introduces a queer sensibility to the program that potentially troubles the homogenizing depiction of a deracialized and heteronormative Latinidad.

Betty's in Universal Drag

Describing the lead character's public appeal, Horta once said, "I think there's a bit of Betty in all of us. It doesn't matter what you look like or how much money you have; everyone at some point in their life feels like they're an outsider."[69] Most of Betty's story lines, therefore, can be read through the performance of the queer outsider, the person who is just a little bit strange, who is similar and Other. Summarizing the queer text of *Ugly Betty*, Michael Jensen, editor of the GLBT Web site AfterElton.com, argues that the program's queerness does not rest on the show's recurring GLBT characters, representations of gay Manhattan, or the politics of the high-fashion world but instead on the message of self-worth and social acceptance that informs the stories about its title character, Betty:

> Ironically, the character who most embodies the show's (queer) sensibility isn't Marc, Alexis, or Justin; it is the straight Betty Suarez herself. Betty is quintessential outsider: the ugly duckling whose beauty is on the inside waiting to be spotted by the right guy. She is the outcast with her nose pressed to the window waiting to be on the inside with the cool kids who reject her.[70]

Betty is the ugly duckling, the outsider, the one hiding underneath gaudiness. Her outsider status—her slight degree of strangeness—present barriers in love and at work. Indeed, the entire premise of the show is based on the fact that Daniel Meade's father hires Betty as Daniel's assistant because she would never be sexually attractive to his promiscuous son. Betty is not feminine enough—or is too weirdly feminine—to be sexually desirable to Daniel.

Betty's queer performance is evident in her unusual sense of fashion and style that echoes a drag queen aesthetic. Drag queen aesthetics, such as those employed by black drag queen RuPaul, take familiar signifiers of femininity accepted as normal and beautiful and exaggerate them to reveal their artifice. In drag, the hair is a little bigger, the makeup a tad more garish, the breasts larger, the curves rounder, and the clothes more revealing than what is generally socially accepted in white heterosexual culture. Drag performance employs exaggeration to draw attention to the constructed nature of beauty, sexuality, gender, and race. By employing a drag aesthetic, the program subverts or symbolically ruptures preexisting notions of heteronormative Latina identity.

From clothing to shoes to hairstyles, every production decision is carefully planned and executed to maximize the emotional, visual, and queer impact of the show. As Horta, who is responsible for maintaining a cohesive vision of the character and the show, notes, "We treat the clothes . . . as seriously as the characters."[71] Similar to the original telenovela heroine, Betty's exaggerated enjoyment of gaudy colors, textures, and jewelry are key elements of manufacturing the show's queerness. Not coincidentally, one British journalist makes a pejorative queer reading of the show by arguing Betty is "styled to appear not merely ugly but gay man grotesque."[72] It is queer and grossly different from dominant mainstream media signifiers stereotypically coded as Latina. Although Betty has long black hair, it is frizzy and untamed (see figure 4.2). Her dark, thick eyebrows are bushy and unmanicured. Her lips are full but she also sports metal braces. She wears bright tropical clothing but in garishly clashing colors and patterns. She is feminine, but, at least in the first two seasons, did not wear makeup or high heels. Betty embodies exaggerated Latin flavors without the stereotypical media resonances of Latina heterosexual femininity. Her sense of fashion is familiar and funny and slightly wrong—a little bit queer—by the standards of Latinidad familiar to television audiences.

Consequently, like the telenovela upon which it is based, Betty's changing fashion sense in the 2008–2009 season is also symbolic of her journey toward upward mobility and ethnoracial assimilation. As Betty has become more of the independent "American girl" throughout the third season of the show, her queer sense of style has been toned down. Commenting to *Variety* on Betty's evolving wardrobe in the third season, Horta said, "Betty's new wardrobe illustrates the changes Betty is making in her life—not the changes *Mode* is making in Betty's life. That is to say, Betty is evolving—she's growing up according to her own ideals, but she's changing nevertheless."[73] Although Betty remains the outsider, later seasons of the show have made her more familiar through the character's performance of a socially acceptable con-

Figure 4.2. Betty Suarez (America Ferrera) undergoes a makeover at the hands of her sister, Hilda (Ana Ortiz), and Hilda's black stylist to fit into the high-fashion world of *Mode*. The socially awkward Betty is transformed from a no-fashion geek into an ethnic urban fashion template. This scene is one of a few that locate Betty within a more classed and racialized ethnic space.

struction of middle-class whiteness. Her colors are not as garish, and her hair and makeup are tasteful. She wears fashionable shoes and more expensive clothes. Indeed, as the show's future became precarious in early 2009, one critic suggested that Betty's quick class transformation into middle-class femininity has made the show less funny.[74]

Before the third season, what queered Betty's presentation of panethnic Latinidad was her in-between status—not quite Latina but never quite white, never particular yet always universal. For example, in the episode "Queens for a Day" (originally aired October 12, 2006), Betty, with the help of Hilda's black stylist, submits to her sister's beauty rituals. Her transformation into Latinidad during this episode is queerly exaggerated (see figure 4.2). She gets artificial nails in brightly colored red, teases her hair into a high bouffant with big curls, and puts on an outfit that looks like something of a cross between a drag queen and a ghetto-fabulous home girl. Throughout the scene, salsa, Latin pop, and reggaetón play in the background, reaffirming Betty's entry into an over-the-top rendition of working-class urban Latinidad.

Foregrounding Betty's drag-like performance of Latinidad is the episode's juxtaposed scene featuring Wilhelmina Slater's tony salon visit, where Wilhelmina (Vanessa Williams) subjects herself to an upper-class regimen grounded in white beauty practices and upper-class notions of taste. At the end of the episode, Betty disavows her sister's outlandish working-class performance of Latinidad as well as expectations by her boss to perform upper-class whiteness. She safely returns to her campy but undefinable style. Black Wilhelmina can improve her symbolic capital by transcending her blackness, but Betty neither fits into her sister's ethnic working-class world nor the elite white world of the high-fashion magazine she works for. Reminiscent of drag queen performances, Betty's style, beauty, and identity remain always in between—outside the beauty and class practices of urban Latinas and the beauty and taste standards of a fashion world grounded in white heteronormative privilege. Her rejection of both brown and white beauty practices ruptures the commodification of Latinidad and emphasizes her queer location. One of the consequences of Betty's third-season modification of her outrageous drag aesthetic is her move away from what some audiences considered the compelling queer outsider theme.

Queering Latina Motherhood

With its global distribution in more than 130 countries through Disney-ABC International, *Ugly Betty* depicts a loving, functional panethnic

Latina/o family that worldwide audiences can relate to regardless of their ethnic, racial, or national identity. Additionally, the show's representation of motherhood and family also contributes to the queer symbolic rupturing of mediated Latinidad. Representations of the Suarez family are unlike that of other Latina/o families seen on television and film. The young career-minded Betty performs a campy working-class panethnic Latina, and the sexualized Latina Hilda fiercely protects her Broadway-loving, fashion-diva son, Justin (Mark Indelicato). The sexually ambiguous Justin does not act or behave like the stereotypical hyper-masculine Latino, and neither does the heterosexual Ignacio, the enlightened Latino patriarch who loves to cook for and nurture his family. In his book *Next of Kin*, Richard Rodríguez calls for a reimagining of popular conceptions of the Latina/o family away from the patriarchal, heteronormative kinship system that defines its representation in the media.[75] Rodríguez suggests that queer aesthetics contribute to a rearticulation of media depictions of the Latina/o family while still maintaining its social, cultural, and political importance. Thus, as a show created, produced, and written by openly gay Horta and queer-friendly Hayek, perhaps the most radical element of *Ugly Betty* is its queering of Latina/o familial heteronormativity through its production of Latina motherhood and young Latino masculinity.

One queer reading of Hilda is that she's a self-referential campy reinvention of dominant mainstream media stereotypes, in particular that of the Latina spitfire and self-sacrificing Latina mother. Hilda's comedic, sometimes tragic performance of Latina motherhood, femininity, and sexuality and unequivocal acceptance of her non-normative son symbolically rupture the dominant tropes of the hot-headed Latina spitfire and the self-sacrificing Latina mother in a patriarchal Latina/o family. The show's producers generally avoid dressing Betty in tight-fitting, physically revealing, tropically colored clothing, but Hilda consistently wears those very clothes. She is Jennifer Lopez on a budget. Hilda celebrates her body and sexuality and is rarely depicted without exposed cleavage, tight-fitting pants, red lipstick, long, painted nails, and high-heeled shoes. Hilda almost marries her son's father and carries on an affair with a married man. She unconditionally celebrates her body and sexuality and strives to meet her emotional need for love. Yet Hilda is also the unconditionally loving mother who places the needs of her sexually ambiguous son at the center of her life. She regularly encourages her son's love of fashion, acting, theater, and potentially homosocial friendships with other boys. When his biological father, Santos, disciplines Justin for not being masculine enough, Hilda staunchly comes to Justin's defense.

After the boys at his school make fun of him for asking another boy to a Broadway musical—with tickets his mother purchased as a gift—it is Hilda who once again picks up the pieces without judging the possible homosocial aspects of the relationship. As one blogger commented, Hilda is the ideal queer-friendly mother:

> When she finally coaxes the truth out of Justin, we are treated to one of the most touching and heartfelt scenes between mother and gay son since—well since Mark and his mom (as played by Patti Lupone) reunited. Hilda tells Justin that he's perfect just the way he is and anyone who doesn't think so is an idiot. I know, I know, every mom worth her mettle has tried this line on us—but somehow Hilda really makes Justin and us believe it. [76]

This blog, similar to other journalistic and audience writings, assumes Justin is gay, even though the show's producers have purposefully left it queerly ambiguous.[77] Hilda performs a construction of Latina motherhood not readily visible in U.S. mainstream media. She symbolically ruptures dominant constructions of Latinidad through her complex representation of Latina motherhood and acceptance of her non-heteronormative family. She is the *nueva* Latina mother.

The show's engagement with queer camp, sexually queer characters, and queer-themed story lines together symbolically rupture the media's homogenous commodification of Latinidad. *Ugly Betty* features an openly gay male character (Marc/Michael Urie), one male-to-female transgender character (Alexis/Rebecca Romijn), and throughout its first three seasons has aired several explicitly gay-themed story lines ("I'm Coming Out," originally aired February 1, 2007, and "Don't Ask, Don't Tell," originally aired March 22, 2007, among others). Furthermore, in another public blurring of actors and characters, many of the show's cast members, such as Vanessa Williams, Ana Ortiz, and Becki Newton, are actively involved in supporting equal rights for the GLBT community.[78] Discussing the program as it relates to the GLBT community in *Out* magazine, Ferrera argues that people who are intolerant "miss out on the truly beautiful because they can't see through the stereotypes they live their lives by. Betty really proves that; if you don't love Betty, *you're* the asshole."[79] GLBT audiences are among the show's most ardent fans.[80] On fan Web sites, gay participants celebrate the show and its queer-friendly ideology of social acceptance and the American dream. For instance, on the ABC discussion board, one participant who identified as a gay man responded to an anti-gay posting about the show by arguing:

Ugly Betty is the best written television show since Designing Women and is meant to be fun . . . nothing more. It is well acted, unbelievably well written and adored by millions worldwide. After Will and Grace, I never dreamed that such a wonderful portrayal of gay characters would make its way back to primetime television.[81]

The program's socially conscious, intelligent sense of humor and sensitive portrayal of GLBT characters present a moment of symbolic rupture by troubling the generic conventions of ethnic and racial minority programming and dominant signifiers of Latinidad and Latina families as heteronormative.

Recuperating the American Dream

Textual readings, media responses, and audience writings about the show affirm the ideological success of its Latina Cinderella theme even as the show's queer aspects threaten to disturb popular understandings of Latinidad, Latina femininity, and Latina domesticity. However, in the end, sexuality, gender, ethnicity, race, class, and beauty do not matter in the search for the "American dream." Despite her more racialized performances of ethnoracial identity, Hilda remains as committed as Betty to achieving the American dream on her terms. In his 2007 Golden Globe acceptance speech for best comedy, Horta spoke of the relationship between his immigrant background and the program's message: "This show is a testament to the American dream. And that the American dream is alive and well and within the reach of anyone in the world who wants it."[82] The universal themes of unconditional acceptance and hard-won success provide a shared space for audiences across different backgrounds.

Despite the characters' development throughout the first three seasons, the liberal ideology of the show has remained constant and dominant. In the third season, when Betty learns that she was selected for a premier editing program because she is Latina, she withdraws from the program ("When Betty Met YETI," originally aired November 20, 2008). Encapsulating the show's ideological message, Betty decides she will only participate if she earns entry based on her merit, not her ethnic identity. Ethnic and racial identities are ideologically policed in the service of attaining the American dream through skill, merit and perseverance. Likewise, Betty's third-season decision to move back with her family—thereby once again occupying the more ethnically marked role of the family's Latina matriarch—has met with a strong backlash from audiences ("Sisters on the Verge of a Nervous Breakdown," originally aired January 22, 2009). An entire thread on the ABC discussion board was devoted to complaints about Betty's seemingly backward mobility in the episode:

> Her family just does not GET Betty—her sister Hilda is whiny and selfish—and should have understood why Betty had to miss her opening party!!! Betty helped enough with her input and gift bags—she even sent her friend Christina to help! The fact that her father had a heart attack was NOT her fault—her being there wouldn't have helped—or prevented it!!!
> AND—did she quit the Mentor program? What is going on? surprised
> AND—she's working at MODE for goodness sake—when is she going to get a makeover? Can't she tell her clothes don't match? Although lately they are at least a better quality of clashing colors and patterns!!![83]

Such responses illustrate the careful negotiations the show's producers must make between producing a safe, familiar, and consumable representation of Latinidad and maintaining the ethnoracial neutrality of the show's liberal logic. Audiences are contesting Betty's return to more panethnic story lines after a shift toward ethnoracial universality, which ultimately may be contributing to the show's plummeting ratings.

The contradictions surrounding the production and reception of Latina lives in *Ugly Betty* demonstrate the complicated process of symbolic colonization in the media. On the one hand, the show symbolically ruptures preexisting media representations of Latina/o lives through its queerness and sensitive portrayal of Latina loss, grief, and motherhood. On the other hand, much like *The Cosby Show*, it depends on the assimilation of ethnicity and race and the commodifiable nature of ethnic ambiguity for its global success. Foregrounding the liberal ideology of the American dream ultimately demands the safe containment of the potentially threatening growth of ethnic and racial difference, in this case Latinidad. U.S. Latina/o identity might not be understandable to audiences in Australia or England, but a story about a working-class family trying to make it in the big city translates across the world.

5

Maid in Hollywood

Producing Latina Labor in an
Anti-immigration Imaginary

Audiences in the United States are continually exposed to contradictory media narratives about Latinidad.[1] While evening news broadcasts
remain fixated on the economic, demographic, and cultural invasion of
Latina/o immigrants, such as news coverage about the Elián González case,
contemporary film and television often provide more romantic stories about
Latinas, such as the film *Frida* or the television program *Ugly Betty*. Generally absent from news reports, Latina/o faces dot the backgrounds of television show story lines. According to a 2001 report by the National Hispanic
Foundation for the Arts, Latina/o characters are generally invisible on television, making up only 2 percent of all prime-time characters in the 2000–
2001 season. When Latinas do appear, they are usually secondary characters
playing nurses, maids, and nannies.[2] For instance, in programs such as *Law
and Order*, Latina domestic workers in New York City often function as use-
ful witnesses or sympathetic crime victims.[3] Other secondary Latina characters on television are commonly the source of ironic humor in shows such as
Will and Grace, which featured the award-winning Shelley Morrison as the
caustic maid Rosario. As the previous two chapters indicate, the entertainment landscape is slowly changing with programs such as *Ugly Betty* and the
more racially diverse casts of programs such as *Grey's Anatomy*, too often
Latina bodies remain confined to laboring roles as domestic caretakers. And
as the Jennifer Lopez tabloid news case study illustrates, productive "laboring" Latina bodies are not always coded as safe or good.

In this final chapter, I bring together the arguments of this book through
a discussion of the cultural conditions under which Latina migration and
Latina domestic labor are constructed as socially acceptable in Hollywood
cinema and the ongoing audience negotiations over commodified depictions
of Latinidad within the context of a global anti-immigration backlash. By

analyzing the cinematic and IMDb audience discourse about Latina migration and labor in two romantic Hollywood comedies, I document how the symbolic colonization of Latinidad in the mainstream media carries both cultural and political consequences. *Maid in Manhattan* features Jennifer Lopez and Ralph Fiennes in a contemporary rendition of the Cinderella story. Lopez plays a New York chambermaid who falls in love with and captures the heart of one of the hotel's elite guests. *Spanglish* takes place in California, where Paz Vega plays Flor, a maid and nanny to a wealthy white family. While coping with the growing pains of her only daughter, Flor also falls in love with and captivates the heart of the family's patriarch. In the end, she places her daughter ahead of her job and walks away from the man she loves. Specifically, I argue that *Maid in Manhattan* (2002) and *Spanglish* (2004) represent Hollywood cinema's continual incorporation of laboring Latina characters through the romanticized and politically nonthreatening roles of maids and domestic workers. Finally, throughout the chapter I weave in IMDb discussions about the movies: the first dealing with the politics of language in *Spanglish* and the second dealing with representations of domestic labor in *Maid in Manhattan*. Both discussion threads affirm the significant relationship between the real world and cinematic fiction through audience interpretations grounded in their readings of the political environment and their everyday experiences.

Despite the anti-immigration news environment of the past two decades that contributed to such events as the repatriation of Elián González,[4] Latina characters in Hollywood stories are often depicted as filial committed workers and inherently morally good. The first section of this chapter maps the symbolic currency and cultural conflicts regarding constructions of Latina labor during a historical and political period when immigration is increasingly constructed as a potential site of terrorism. I document how the romantic cinematic discourse surrounding Latina migration and labor in *Spanglish* and *Maid in Manhattan* erases the diverse, sometimes violent trajectories of transnational Latina immigrants and workers within contemporary U.S. culture and politics. The second and third sections of the chapter examine the cinematic production of Latina bodies as workers safe for cultural and economic consumption. My analysis of the movies and selected IMDb discussions provide a final opportunity for reflection on the questions that guide this book: Under what conditions are Latina bodies desirable, consumable, or dangerous? What are the consequences of Latinas' contemporary global marketability?

Reimagining the Nation through Hollywood Cinema

I focus on Hollywood films because, as Ella Shohat and Robert Stam have long held, cinema is a central component of narratives about the nation. I thus build on their work by defining contemporary Hollywood movies as illustrative of ongoing social and cultural tensions.[5] As my discussion of *Frida* illustrates, English-language Hollywood films provide a dynamic site for studying contemporary social formations about ethnicity, race, nation, gender, and sexuality. Movies are informative of ideologically dominant and conflicted constructions of Latina femininity, domesticity, and citizenship. This chapter returns to film as a critical component of the public sphere that provides a site of popular contestation and popular knowledge about ethnic, racial, national, and gender identity.[6] Heeding Vivian Sobchack's call for a more nuanced understanding of the complexity through which ethnicity functions in contemporary Hollywood cinema, I focus on the storytelling contradictions within the movies and the points of ethnic and racial discomfort for their online audiences.[7] Additionally, I analyze each film and its reception by situating both within the media's economic and cultural demand for Latina bodies and the anti-immigration political environment. In doing so, I do not make general claims about representations of Latinas or Latinidad within the movies but rather demonstrate how the particular characters and narratives of each film function in concert with or in opposition to broader public discourses about Latina migration and labor.

As I have articulated throughout this book, symbolic colonization depends on media storytelling practices that reaffirm dominant norms, values, and beliefs about Latinidad. Film, television, and news stories grounded in the practices of symbolic colonization produce a homogenizing construction of Latinidad, therefore reinforcing the border between the nation as white, Anglo-Saxon, and Protestant and its marginalized subjects as ethnic and racial others. Contestations about the movie *Frida*, for instance, point to the important storytelling role cinema plays in cultural imaginings about the nation and national identity. Indeed, as Shohat and Stam argue, cinema remains an important part of the nation-building project "in the sense that beliefs about the origins and evolution of nations crystallize in the form of stories. The cinema, as the world's storyteller par excellence, was from the outset ideally suited to relaying the projected narrative of nation and empires."[8] To maintain ideological dominance and control, the colonized in mainstream movies must be continually and inventively reimagined as Homi

Bhabba's "the Other"—the object that is simultaneously desired and disciplined, the subject who is almost the same as those who seek to control her but not identical to those bodies in power.[9] Subsequently, in this chapter I once more take up Myra Mendible's call for Latina feminist scholarship that maps "the contours of the Latina body in the interstices where lived reality and public fantasies converge, in those myriad encounters and pleasures that embody the 'politics and erotics of culture.'"[10] I return to my arguments regarding Latinas as stand-ins for the imaged nation by examining romantic comedy depictions of Latina workers and immigrants in the context of Latinas' lived realities.

To do so, I propose that throughout the 1990s and the 9/11 context, Hollywood romantic comedies about Latina migration and labor have been informed by the continuing imperialistic relationship between the United States and Mexico, Latin America, and the Caribbean. It is an economic relationship that—particularly since the General Agreement on Tariffs and Trade (GATT), North American Free Trade Agreement (NAFTA), and Central American Free Trade Agreement (CAFTA)—is increasingly dependent on the unequal flow of U.S. commodities southward and the uninterrupted flow of cheap and increasingly feminized Latina labor northward.[11] It is a contemporary flow described by feminist immigration scholars as the "racialized feminization of labor":

> In the search for ever cheaper, more "flexible," labor pools, this reorganization also produces a greater "pull" for new Asian and Latino immigrants, especially for Asian and Latina women, to fill the insecure assembly and service sector jobs in the United States that have emerged largely as a result of restructuring and "re-engineering."[12]

In 2009, the global economic recession disrupted the transnational flow of money and goods, and researchers have found that the number of unauthorized immigrants in the United States has declined since 2007.[13] However, decades of unequal movement of money, objects, and people across U.S. borders has resulted in a polarized environment where the demand and desire for "real" and cultural Latina labor perform a vital economic role—even as "real" Latina bodies are politically disciplined through unfair labor practices and anti-immigration policies.[14] In this political and economic terrain, the generic practices of Hollywood romantic comedies contribute to the symbolic colonization of Latinidad by homogenizing and sanitizing gendered ethnic and racial difference.

Theorizing the Southern U.S. Border in
Contemporary Popular Discourses

As border theorists Gloria Anzaldúa, José Saldívar, Alejandro Lugo, and others recognize, the border is a highly contested geopolitical and cultural space.[15] Borders also are the physical space through which people, culture, goods, and services flow. They are also a contact zone, a zone of linguistic, cultural, and social crossings and mixtures that allow for a multidirectional and complex rearticulation of social relations. In the United States, the transnational flow of immigration has the potential to challenge the binary discourse of racial identity through which nation and citizenship are defined. For example, Néstor García Canclini argues that the unique and routine experience of working in one country and living in another, of crossing through geographical boundaries and living in zones of cross-cultural contact, produces hybridized cultures disruptive of dominant definitions of citizenship and ethnic and national identities.[16] While the news media focus on furtive crossings along the U.S.-Mexico border, more than 800,000 Mexicans legally cross and recross the border daily to attend schools and work in low-wage jobs in the United States.[17] This legal Latina/o immigration to and from the United States challenges the very definitions of what it means to be "American" or what it means to perform "American" culture. Consequently, along with increases in the U.S. population of those who identify as more than one race, the transnational flow of immigration through the United States is creating symbolic ruptures in how we think of and perform Latinidad.

Influencing the flow of documented and undocumented Latina/o workers into the United States is what Zaragosa Vargas calls "global economic integration" or globalization.[18] Globalization accompanied by U.S. deindustrialization has restructured the labor pool, weakened the permanent job market, and decreased unionization—lowering wages and shifting low-skill jobs once held by poor and working-class white, African American, and U.S. Latinas/os to undocumented Latina/o immigrants.[19] Mexico, like other parts of Latin America and the Spanish Caribbean, is undergoing a similar economic transformation that drives its labor pool north in search of better economic opportunities—mainly low-wage, low-skill manufacturing, construction, service, and domestic labor jobs scarce within Mexico's economy.[20] Because of its proximity to Mexico and its traditional demand for agricultural, construction, and domestic labor, California continues to be the main destination for many Mexican and Latin American immigrants and a major site of hybrid cultural production.[21] Since the 1990s, the ethnic and racial destabilization of dominant U.S. culture and society along with the ongoing threat of terrorism since the 9/11 attacks have contributed to a backlash against immigration.

None of the 9/11 terrorists were of Latina/o descent, yet in the United States the backlash against immigration has focused predominantly on Latinas/os and securing the southern U.S. border, a 1,951-mile-long stretch adjoining Texas, New Mexico, Arizona, and California. It is a highly regulated and deadly militarized zone patrolled by U.S. and Mexican border police, unmanned drones, and Blackhawk helicopters. While some areas of the border are made up of cement walls, watchtowers, and electronic wires, other areas are only separated by barbed-wire fences across deserts and mountains. Along the Arizona border, more than 154 deaths due to natural and criminal causes were reported in 2005.[22] While it is difficult to say exactly how many undocumented immigrants enter the country through the southern U.S. border, in 2005 the Pew Hispanic Center estimated that 400,000 successfully cross and 1 million to 3 million immigrants try to cross the border from Mexico each year.[23] New undocumented and documented immigrants to the United States total about 1.2 million per year. Pew estimates that Mexicans make up 5.9 million, or 57 percent, of the estimated 10.3 million undocumented residents living in the United States.[24] So while undocumented Mexican immigrants are a majority, they are by no means the only undocumented population living in the United States. The anti-immigration discourse linked to anti-terror policies and the increased militarization of the southern U.S. border is pivotal to making sense of contemporary romantic Hollywood depictions of Latina labor and border-crossers.

The southern U.S. border is not explicitly mentioned in the Patriot Act of 2001 or the Department of Homeland Security Act of 2002, but it is nevertheless the southern U.S. border and undocumented Mexican immigration that is often reimagined in the news as a significant threat, particularly in conservative news coverage. The conservative framing of the southern border as a potential site of terrorist activity is increasingly seeping into the mainstream news and informing U.S. immigration policy. Perhaps the best illustration of this phenomenon is the news coverage dealing with the Border Protection, Anti-Terrorism, and Illegal Immigration Control Act of 2005 (H.R. 4437), otherwise known as the Sensenbrenner bill. The bill did call for an examination of potential problems along the U.S.-Canada border, but most of the news coverage focused on policing and defending the United States against undocumented immigrants entering from Mexico. The 2006 *Brownout Report* from the National Association of Hispanic Journalists found news coverage of Latina/o immigration remains one of the most popular news stories in television news, so much so that a 2006 Fairness and Accuracy in Reporting article about the Sensenbrenner bill observed:

> Unfortunately, despite the global significance of immigration legislation and immeasurable effects on individual lives, there have been deep flaws in media coverage of the legislative debate. In particular, large segments of the media have biased their coverage towards a pro-business standpoint on the debate, which is misleadingly portrayed as a pro-immigrant position; the opposition to this view is a racialized, nativist perspective that is misrepresented as advocacy for U.S.-born workers. Actual pro-immigrant, pro-worker and international points of view have been almost entirely absent.[25]

No domestic terrorist to date has been identified as Mexican (José Padilla is a U.S.-born Puerto Rican) or as having entered through the southern U.S. border. Yet the virulent association between terrorism, Mexican immigration, and the U.S. border continues to circulate in the conservative and mainstream news media. By framing immigration from the south as a large cultural and criminal "invasion," conservative political discourses reposition Latina/o immigrants and communities as a threat.

As a result of the Immigration Reform and Control Act of 1986, the Illegal Immigration and Reform Act of 1996, and the Patriot Act, emigrants from Mexico are pushed to make the journey through more hostile and isolated territory, resulting in increased violence against them.[26] Since 1986, deaths from hypothermia, drowning, suffocation, and border patrol shootings at crossing points have increased from 8 percent to 16 percent among undocumented immigrants.[27] For women traveling alone, the journey is even more dangerous, as they face the threat of physical and sexual violence in Mexico, at the border, and in the United States. Border activist Claudia Smith identifies U.S. policy toward women migrants as one of the most important human rights issues, noting the U.S. program of lateral repatriations has made unaccompanied women "all the more vulnerable to physical and sexual violence by deporting them to Mexican cities where they had no contacts. The height of folly was to deport them to Ciudad Juárez, where hundreds of women have been murdered or have disappeared during the past decade."[28] Under the lateral repatriations program, undocumented immigrants were transported to another U.S. border location and involuntarily deported to Mexican cities often far from their original point of crossing.[29] So a woman crossing the border at Tijuana/San Diego, for instance, would be handcuffed and involuntarily repatriated to the Ciudad Juárez/El Paso crossing. The pilot program ran for one month at an approximate cost of $1.3 million. It continues today on a voluntary basis, with the exception of violent criminals, who are automatically deported to Mexico.[30]

Taming the Southern Border: Hollywood's Romantic Depictions of Latina Immigration

Partly as a response to U.S. demands for cheap domestic and service labor, more undocumented women from Mexico and Central America are making the dangerous journey alone.[31] A contradictory discourse about Latina immigration and labor as both threatening and consumable thus arises in the media. On the one hand, the southern border is constructed in the mainstream and conservative news media as a dangerous zone of criminality, terrorism, disease, and environmental pollution.[32] For instance, in an online video produced by the conservative Arizona-based organization American Border Patrol,[33] the use of infrared technology shows a "bomb" being smuggled through the U.S.-Mexico border in a commercial van filled with human cargo. Additionally, accounts of invasion and terrorism associated with Mexico and Mexican immigration can be easily found through basic Internet searches. On the other hand, contemporary romantic comedies featuring Latinas and Latina workers often elide the anti-immigration politics and violence surrounding Latina immigration and Latina labor by reimagining the border and its crossers as safe, consumable, and docile.

For example, in *Spanglish*, the main character, Flor (performed by Spanish actor Paz Vega), makes the journey from Mexico to the United States accompanied only by her young daughter, Cristina (Shelbie Bruce). Flor's motivation for crossing into the United States appears personal and is only subtly informed by economics. She consciously makes the decision to remain in Mexico long enough to allow Cristina's cultural roots to develop and leaves only when it is clear that it is the best or last opportunity for them to cross. In departing her beloved Mexico, Flor says goodbye to what would be considered by most a comfortable middle-class existence presumably for a better existence in the United States. Both Flor and Cristina live alone in a well-constructed, colorful house full of pretty furniture, flowers, and paintings, among other signifiers of Western middle-class status. Their home in the United States is equally comfortable if not nearly as beautiful.

The economic exigency of poverty and unemployment that drives most undocumented Mexican immigrants to make the hazardous journey is not visible in the film. Audiences are shown only a brief montage of their border crossing—Flor and Cristina are dropped off in the desert by an unidentified male driver in an old truck; they walk through the desert in clean, ironed dresses with rolling suitcases in tow; and they finally cross the border into the United States via comfortable seats in an air conditioned bus. At the end of the montage, Flor and Cristina arrive unquestioned, untroubled, and refreshed in Los Angeles, where they immediately wander into a Latina/o neighborhood filled with music, colorful flowers, and the Spanish language. Although Cristina, the movie's narrator, hints in her college essay that their journey was illegal, their border crossing is portrayed as uncontested, easy, and safe—there are no border patrol police, border security stops, or male threats of violence against their bodies. To maintain the generic conventions of romantic comedies, the movie represents the border as safe and easily penetrable. The typically hazardous crossing is tamed by cinematically drawing attention away from the reality experienced by undocumented women crossing the southern U.S. border, and U.S. audiences are allowed to safely consume Flor's journey without social or political discomfort.

Spanglish temporarily soothes the U.S. national imaginary—the stories and images we create about the nation and those who live within it. The fear of undocumented immigration and the U.S.-Mexico border so prevalent in the news and Web sites, among other locations, is allayed by cinematically harkening back to familiar, less threatening images about the border and the archetype of the Latina señorita dating back to the "Good Neighbor Era" of the 1930s and 1940s. In the face of World War II and the United States' growing isolation from Europe, the economic, political, and military importance of Mexico, the Caribbean, and Latin America increased. At the peak of their financial success and in response to potential government regulation, Hollywood studios agreed to become cultural ambassadors through the tenets of the Hayes Code, which forbade provocative sexual scenes, profanity, and "the defamation both of foreign nationals and of the histories of their countries."[34] Among the more popular of the Good Neighbor-era Latina actors were Mexican-born Lupe Vélez and Dolores del Rio.

I briefly focus on one of the earlier Good Neighbor movies to draw linkages to more modern depictions of Latina border-crossers. In *Girl of the Rio* (1932), a romantic drama starring Dolores del Rio, she plays "Dolores," a virginal Mexican chanteuse working as a cabaret dancer in a U.S. bordertown bordello. *Girl of the Rio*, like other Good Neighbor movies, was a conscious attempt by the major Hollywood studios in the 1930s and 1940s to facilitate U.S. foreign policy by "positively" depicting Latin Americans. The characters and story lines of most Good Neighbor movies were fairly similar—either featuring a tragically doomed but morally noble señorita or a comedic, singing, dancing, and lovelorn spitfire. Sometimes, as in *Girl of the Rio*, it was a blend of both characters. Dolores portrays a socially acceptable Mexican character who sings and dances and is desired by both her Mexican and U.S. white male bordello customers. She moves easily through the U.S.-Mexican border during a historical period of highly regulated labor traffic between the two countries. Typical of Good Neighbor cinematic diplomacy, Dolores eventually rejects her "violent" but wealthy Mexican suitor and marries the poorer but "civilized" white U.S. male citizen she has fallen in love with. Both men agree to set aside their differences and be friends for the benefit of the woman they love—becoming idealized symbols of cultural diplomacy. Although the old Hollywood studio system has long been dead and the demands of World War II have long been over, the contemporary need for a "friendly" economic, if not political, relationship with Mexico remains. Contemporary Hollywood romantic comedies, in particular, continue to fill their goodwill ambassador role by allaying domestic fears and making the unknown familiar.

More than fifty years after the first Good Neighbor movies, Salma Hayek's U.S. Mexican character Isabel in the romantic comedy *Fools Rush In* (1997) continued the project of cultural ambassadorship. She also travels carefree across geopolitical and cultural borders during a time of increased militarization. Throughout the movie, Isabel journeys to Mexico several times, but audiences never see her stop at border inspection sites. The ease with which Flor and Isabel travel across the border, one an undocumented Mexican immigrant and the other a U.S. citizen, produces a consumable and desirable cinematic construction of the border and border-crossers. In romantic comedies, the dangerous and surveilled nature of the border is depoliticized. Latina bodies become consumable zones of cross-cultural contact and sites of heteronormative romance and white sexual desire. Like Dolores, Flor and Isabel are the noble and morally "good" Latina señoritas who serve as cultural bridges for the Latino or non-Latino male characters who desire them. Although Dolores works in a bordello, she remains chaste until marriage. In spite of her emotional and sexual desire for her white boss, Flor walks away from a potential extramarital affair, leaving his marriage intact. The accidental pregnancy from a one-night stand is portrayed as a moral anomaly that ultimately brings the traditionally Catholic Latina Isabel together with the Anglo-Saxon Protestant man she was fated to marry. To commodify Latina bodies as the comedic and acceptable object of cinematic romantic desire in contemporary Hollywood, the border must be sanitized from violence and military regulation. Nonthreatening Latina border-crossers must exude sexual allure while maintaining their moral purity. In other words, the "ugly" dangers of the border must be disciplined and symbolically colonized to make Latina immigration familiar, desirable, and socially acceptable for white desire and heteronormative romance.

Reinforcing a socially acceptable construction of Mexican immigrant femininity requires the mediated regulation of Latina sexuality. The Latina señorita must therefore be rendered different from more threatening Latinas marked as socially undesirable by the contemporary anti-immigration discourse. Therefore, Flor and Isabel distinguish themselves from other Latinas, specifically Mexican and Puerto Rican women, who are depicted in news and entertainment as hypersexual and hyperfertile.[35] Instead, the Latinas of Hollywood's romantic comedies are defined by their hyperfemininity (Flor rarely wears pants); conservative domesticity (Isabel is a devout Catholic); and regulated sexuality (Dolores presumably maintains her virginity until she marries the man she loves). Although Flor and Isabel each have a daughter, the sexuality of all these women is ultimately constrained by religiously informed morality. To render these border-crossing cinematic Mexican women consumable, especially in the contemporary anti-immigration context, their sexuality must be contained while their bodies remain eroticized visual spectacles. Undocumented Mexican immigrant Flor, for example, can function as the object of romantic and sexual desire because she is simultaneously different from the film's white characters and from the racialized bodies of undocumented Latina immigrants depicted in the evening news.

In *Spanglish*, the character's Mexican difference is rendered familiar, accessible, and sexually safe through the politics of language and U.S. racial formations. Her initial reticence to learn English is depicted as a protective cultural mechanism—allowing her to work in a world dominated by the white family she cares for while still maintaining those aspects of her identity she defines as essential. Flor's conscious decision to learn English allows her to communicate directly with her employers, marking a turning point in her relationship with the family and the United States. The importance of her decision to learn some English is emphasized through her daughter's voice-over narration: "A simple request from my mother startled me. Her rules were bending. She was losing her battle to remain uninvolved with the

Claskys. *¿Como se dice pruebatelo en ingles?*" Through learning the English phrase "just try it on," Flor makes the deliberate decision to communicate with her employer's daughter in the language of the white English-dominant family she serves. As Cristina notes, it marks the moment of her mother's cultural border crossing.

Flor's linguistic crossing is meant to signal her acculturation—her incorporation of U.S. culture while still maintaining her Mexican cultural values. However, some English-dominant speakers only see racialized Latina difference and perpetual foreignness in Flor's resistance to learn English. As one IMDb poster wrote:

> But damn if I'm not annoyed by immigrants who make the USA their home and find every excuse to not become Americans or learn English. I imagine some of them think that it's good enough to have "made the move" to create a better life for their kids, knowing that the kids will speak both languages. But no, I don't think it's sufficient. If they want to live here, they should learn our language.[36]

The poster's reading of *Spanglish* is informed by his own understanding and perception of Latinidad. Although Flor's resistance to learning English is not constructed as a political act of resistance to the United States, his reading of the movie speaks to an everyday, more general discomfort with immigration, Latina/o immigrants, and demographic and cultural change. The poster was not alone in his discomfort with the movie's depiction of Latina labor and language as Flor's unwillingness to learn English became the focus of at least one lengthy and at times contentious IMDb discussion thread titled "why cant every latino learn english?"[37] Such audience readings point to the complex readings of romantic representations of Latinidad in the broader anti-immigration context.

Spanglish functions as more than commercial entertainment by unwittingly tapping into the contemporary unease with demographic and cultural changes brought about through Latina/o immigration and Latina/o incorporation in the U.S. nation. Anti-immigration readings of the movie also highlight the pitfalls of cinematic attempts to negotiate Latina difference in more acceptable and consumable ways. Paz Vega's whiteness might not resemble the racialized Latina immigrants on the evening news, and Flor's border crossing might not be like those described on conservative anti-immigration Web sites, but the political anti-immigration discourses that surround the movie's reception can never be fully erased, only tamed.

Cleaning Up the Hollywood Latina Domestic

Borders and border crossings are not the only cinematic constructions of Latinidad that must be disciplined through generic conventions of Hollywood romantic comedies. Romantic cinematic depictions of Latina labor must also be negotiated in the service of maintaining dominant hierarchies of ethnicity, gender, citizenship, and power. In her study of television representations of Latina domestic workers,[38] L. S. Kim notes that news and comedic depictions of Latina maids in the 1990s helped displace economic, sexual, and racial anxieties during another period of political backlash against undocumented immigrants.[39] Romantic comedies about Latina immigrants or Latina domestics succeed only when they contain cultural anxieties about undocumented immigration through humor. But for the humor to work, the domestic labor of cleaning and caring for others must be cleansed of its high stigma and low status.

Therefore, racially stigmatized domestic labor is reimagined in film and television as a morally noble profession. Either as helpmates of working white women or desexualized domestic partners of widowed white fathers, popular representations of Latina domestic workers, especially Latina immigrants, are once again informed by the historical archetype of the señorita. Latina domestic workers in romantic comedies, such as Flor in *Spanglish* and Marisa in *Maid in Manhattan*, are simultaneously more glamorous and more maternal. They are thin, sexy, and modestly but stylishly dressed. The contemporary Latina maid character reinforces popular beliefs about ethnic domestic workers as more hygienic, more maternal, more "naturally" domestic, and therefore more occupationally suited for domestic work than the biological mothers of white children.[40] Popular U.S. television and romantic cinematic representations of Latina maids often depict them as exceptional surrogate mothers who are naturally nurturing, devoted, and honest. It is the campy reference to this stereotypical assumption that informs the humor in the character of Rosario as the caustic Latina maid on *Will and Grace*.

Overall, the romantic cinematic discourses surrounding Latina domestic work elide the powerful inequities that subordinate the lives of Latina domestic workers to those of their predominantly, but not exclusively, white middle- to upper-class employers. Similar to depictions of the border and border crossings, Hollywood representations of Latina maids and nannies in romantic comedies sharply contrast with the reality of domestic labor as racialized dirty work. Discussing the racialized dimensions of domestic work, Pierrette Hondagneu-Sotello writes:

Relationships between domestic employees and employers have always been imbued with racial meanings: white "masters and mistresses" have been cast as pure and superior, and "maids and servants," drawn from specific racial-ethnic groups (varying by region), have been cast as dirty and socially inferior. The occupational racialization we see now in Los Angeles or New York City continues this American legacy, but it also draws to a much greater extent on globalization and immigration.[41]

On the West Coast, domestic work is mostly carried out by recent arrivals from El Salvador and Guatemala. On the East Coast, the "dirty job" of cleaning spaces and caring for children is mostly the domain of immigrants from the Dominican Republic and other Caribbean nations. Throughout the 1990s, immigrant women in the United States, predominantly from Central America and the Caribbean, have filled the growing demands of hoteliers and single-parent and dual-income households. Across the United States, the racial demography of domestic workers has changed dramatically, with U.S.-born white and black women now making up less than 1 percent of the domestic workforce.[42] For the "real" women who care for the families and homes of predominantly middle- and upper-class U.S. citizens, the hours are long and unregulated, and the work itself is fraught with complex class and racial dynamics. The anti-immigration backlash combined with linguistic discrimination has further exacerbated the contemporary racial meaning surrounding domestic work.

To some extent, the depiction of Latina domestic labor in *Spanglish* and *Maid in Manhattan* does acknowledge the uneasy social position of Latina domestic workers within U.S. society. Much of *Spanglish*'s story line, for instance, centers on the gender, racial, ethnic, and class conflicts between Flor and Deborah. The white matriarch Deborah ignores her socially awkward daughter, instead showering her cultural and economic privilege on the thin, pretty, and respectful Cristina. She provides Cristina with cosmetic makeovers and a scholarship admission to a prestigious, predominantly white private school, enabling her acculturation. Meanwhile, Flor's idealized nurturing labor enables Deborah's emotional distance from her husband and children. Flor becomes a more suitable and desirable wife and mother than Deborah. The movie's conclusion is inevitable. It is Flor who must walk away to protect her daughter from complete assimilation and to leave the heteronormative white family intact. The opposition between Flor and Deborah subtly draws out the difficult power relationships surrounding the domestic co-existence of families from different ethnic and economic backgrounds, a relationship exacerbated in the movie by Cristina's youthful desire for economic and cultural assimilation.

The romanticized performance of racialized domestic work in *Maid in Manhattan* raises a different set of ironies and contradictions. While Flor is clearly marked as Mexican, *Manhattan's* main character, Marisa Ventura (Jennifer Lopez), is only ambiguously coded as Latina and is specifically articulated as "American" rather than immigrant. Her name could be of Spanish or Italian descent. And although she lives in a traditionally Puerto Rican neighborhood that has more recently become occupied by Dominican immigrants, Marisa is never explicitly identified as either. The only cues to her ethnic difference rest with the character's occasional and isolated use of Spanish. For instance, Marisa calls her son "papi," and she is sometimes referred to by her mother as "mija." There are no complete sentences or extended dialogue in Spanish. At best, Marisa's ethnicity as a second- or possibly third-generation Nuyorican can only be coded through subtextual signifiers. Because of the ambiguous ethnic coding surrounding her, Marisa's journey, like that of Betty Suarez in *Ugly Betty*, is primarily one of deracialized class mobility.

Marisa's ethnically ambiguous identity is not accidental. The movie, produced by her then-manager Benny Medina, was supposed to be a star vehicle for Lopez to reaffirm her status as a marketable actor. Maintaining the character's ethnic ambiguity situates Lopez within a commodified racial flexibility that speaks to multiple audiences—a cinematic identity that Lopez has consciously cultivated since her role in *Selena* (1997). Marisa is an assimilated Latina, not quite white but not black. She experiences moments of discrimination presumably because of her class and ambiguous ethnic difference yet still remains exotic and desirable to the white object of her affection, in this case politician Chris Marshall (Ralph Fiennes). Speaking about her role in the movie, which she was heavily involved in developing, Lopez said:

> I can definitely identify with that, in a lot of ways. You know, being from the Bronx and being Puerto Rican. I even told them on the set exactly how that man would look at her. It's just a weird kind of thing. It's a class thing. It's a social thing. It exists. To say that it doesn't exist would be a lie. It would be like trying to sugar coat the truth. So I can understand what it's like. And not even in a romantic way, but to have people respect you in a certain way. You know, because you're a minority.[43]

Lopez acknowledges the ethnic identity of the character she portrays to the interviewer, which is apparently a subtle homage to her own history. However, in the interview, Lopez also clearly affirms the primary message of the movie is about class and achieving the American dream. Consequently, the movie's conscious containment of ethnoracial Latina identity shifts the cinematic discourse of difference to class, a more universally compelling story line. The liberal ideology of the film is reinforced in mainstream reviews about the movie. In the *New York Times* review, for instance, the main theme is described as follows: "Marisa does not lose her tough, determined attitude. The film's message, like the song's ["Jenny From the Block"], is that upward mobility is not a betrayal of working-class values but rather their ultimate fulfillment."[44] Once again, the global demands of marketability require a focus on a cleansed depiction of Latina domestic labor that moves beyond ethnicity and race to class.

The movie's melodramatic performance of domestic labor contributes to the universal message of the movie. For instance, the hotel maids are not just underappreciated—they are depicted as nameless, interchangeable bodies, exhorted to do exceptional work without attracting physical attention. When a wealthy white female hotel guest calls Marisa "Maria," the character demurs without correcting the mistake. Indeed, working-class Marisa only becomes visible and desirable to the male protagonist when she takes on the cultural signifiers of white wealth and privilege, among them haute couture clothes and designer jewelry. The official Web site for the movie summarizes it best: "After an enchanting evening together, the two fall madly in love. But when Marisa's true identity is revealed, issues of class and social status threaten to separate them."[45] According to the movie's official Web site, Marisa's "true identity" is not that she is Latina, it's that she is a working-class maid. Marisa must be transformed from an invisible laboring body to a commodifiable ambiguous Latina and noble panethnic mother. Indeed, Marisa's motherhood and relationship with her son are central to a globally consumable cinematic production of a working-class panethnic domestic worker. By the movie's conclusion, Marisa's class trajectory and maternal goodness—after all, she raises a clever, intelligent, ethical son who admires Republican politicians—is represented as Chris's moral equal (see figure 5.2). Using cinematic framing almost identical to that of *Spanglish* (see figure 5.1), Marisa faces off against her white object of desire. Their mutual love for her child, Ty Ventura (Tyler Garcia Posey), bridges the economic and social distance between the two. Marisa's noble goodness and love recuperates Chris's political hypocrisy. She in turn is cleansed of her ethnic and working-class roots through her son's actions and hard-won success based on the ideals of meritocracy.

Figure 5.1. Mexican maid Flor Morena (Paz Vega) mediates the growing marital tension between Deborah Clasky (Téa Leoni) and her husband, John Clasky (Adam Sandler). Flor and John never consummate their physical attraction. Despite the ethnic differences, the inherent conservative morality of Flor and John is used as a narrative point of commonality.

Similarly, by the end of *Spanglish*, Flor and John Clasky (Adam Sandler) are likewise recuperated through her noble goodness and love for her child. Flor learns English and falls in love with the family patriarch, John, whose feminized white masculinity is comedically depicted in the movie as the antithesis of white and Latino heteronormative masculinity. Although Flor privileges and maintains an ethnic difference marked as more traditionally maternal and feminine than her white counterpart, Deborah Clasky (Téa Leoni), her decision to learn English makes her already romanticized and homogenized difference less threatening and accessible to the man she loves. Flor, John, and Deborah form their own relationship triangle (see figure 5.1). It is Flor who saves the Claskys from themselves. Flor's unwavering conservative morality reaffirms John's goodness, and her traditional femininity and maternal nature provide a mirror for Deborah to recognize her own faults. And John's unconsummated emotional and sexual desire for Flor presents her with a morally pure moment of pleasure. Unlike the emotionally unstable and selfish Deborah, who ignores the emotional needs of her family to carry on an extramarital affair, Flor sacrifices the opportunity to have a physical and emotional relationship with John to protect the stability of both families. Together Flor and John discover that despite linguistic and ethnic differences, they share common cultural values, such as privileging the heteronormative family over their sexual and emotional needs. Flor's nobility transforms the family even as she and her daughter are transformed by them. Picking up on the depiction of Flor as moral guide, Roger Ebert writes:

> When it comes to the experiences of a Latino maid in an Anglo household, nothing is likely to improve on the adventures of Zaide Silvia Gutierrez in "El Norte" (1983), where the space-age automatic washer-dryer proved so baffling that the young maid just spread the washing out on the lawn to dry in the sun. But "Spanglish" isn't really about being a maid, it's more about being a lifeforce, as Flor heals this family with a sunny disposition and an anchor of normality.[46]

Flor's role in the movie, as Ebert points out, is not to function as the Latina domestic but to stand in as a symbol of an idealized motherhood outside ethnic and racial borders. Flor is as morally good as John. Both value family above physical or emotional desire. Like the noble lead character in *Ugly Betty*, Flor's morality defines her ethnic difference and panethnic universality. Both Flor and Marisa are rendered socially and culturally safe through the cleansed depictions of their physical and moral labor.

Figure 5.2. Using a cinematic frame almost identical to the *Spanglish* scene, Ty Ventura (Tyler Posey) stands between his mother, Marissa Ventura (Jennifer Lopez), and her love interest, Chris Marshall (Ralph Fiennes). Lopez plays an ethnically ambiguous, racially flexible hotel maid who transgresses her ethnic and class background to fall in love with a wealthy politician.

Not surprisingly, in an IMDb discussion thread dealing with the discourse of race and class in *Maid in Manhattan*, posters debated the movie's seemingly contradictory ideological messages.[47] Some audiences responded positively to the movie's deracialized storyline of upward class mobility based on meritocracy while others had more negative reactions to the depiction of class and ethnoracial identities as sites of romanticized difference. As an example of a negative reading of the film, one poster on IMDb questioned the movie's depiction of domestic labor by arguing against its liberal race-neutral ideology: "Am I nuts, or is this Cinderella tale the cinematic equivalent of the McDonald's commercial that suggests that if African-Americans work really, really hard one day they too can become fast-food managers?"[48] Problematizing the very ideal of a meritocracy, the poster suggested that the ongoing inequalities that define the ethnic and racial minority experience in the United States should not be reduced to a commercialized Hollywood plot. Pointing to the economic context of poverty and unfair labor practices that define the lives of most Latina domestic workers, the poster troubled the very premise of the American dream central to the movie.

To others, the idealized liberal ideology significant to the story lines of romantic comedies overrode concerns about realism and the contemporary context. In response to critiques of *Maid in Manhattan* as racist and unrealistic, one poster argued, "Where's the difference? The moral about 'work ethics' is still the same; so no, it's not 'racist' . . . 'Clichéd' and 'opportunistic,' maybe; but not racist."[49] For these posters, in the end the movie was about love, hard work, and meritocracy, and not the ethnic and racial identities of the women who performed the labor or the clients who benefitted from it.

The range of responses both for and against the movie's depictions of ethnoracial minority identity and domestic labor points to the ways lived experience informs audience expectations of entertainment content. Joining the discussion over the racialized message of domestic labor, one poster argued, "Racism is big in this movie. Notice all the maids in the hotel? They are all hispanic, asian , & black. Only the high ranking hotel staffs are white."[50] Central to this poster's desire for a melting-pot vision of a sustainable and achievable meritocracy was more "positive" representations of ethnoracial minority women. While the poster wanted to see the American Dream represented in a more visible way, for others the romantic comedy's depiction of racialized domestic labor seemed acceptable and natural. Cognizant of the ethnic and racial demographics of domestic service, another poster responded, "I dont necessarily think that this was racist . . . its just that in general most maids are of those ethnicity."[51] The movie was simply depicting the world the way it functions or the way it is perceived to function by the poster.

For some audiences, the global context of a service and domestic labor industry that depends on the bodies of ethnic women seemed natural. To others, the cost of Latina invisibility in the mainstream media demanded "positive" depictions that move beyond the stereotype of the noble Latina domestic worker. Yet to others the hypervisibility of Lopez, who at the time had recently announced her engagement to Ben Affleck, and her conscious use of the movie as a global mainstream star vehicle disrupted the universal themes of upward mobility and the "American dream."[52] Overall, the online discussion of the movie signaled the complicated terrain Hollywood cinema must negotiate in producing globally consumable narratives of Latinidad. Romantic comedy depictions of Latina domestic labor might stabilize U.S. racial formations and appease racial anxieties regarding the U.S. low-wage labor force, but the symbolic colonization of Latinidad is read by audiences in uneven and sometimes contradictory ways.

The Cinematic Nurturing of the Nation

Like millions of hotel workers around the world, the laboring bodies of women are often invisible to those who benefit from their work. Both *Spanglish* and *Maid in Manhattan* reinforce Latina difference by inviting audiences to celebrate the inherent nobility and moral goodness of the Latina maid despite the asymmetrical power relationships based on race, nationality, citizenship, language, and class that define domestic workers' lived conditions.[53] Cleansed depictions of Latina domestic labor as noble and morally good contribute to the cultural erasure of unfair wage, labor, and citizenship practices faced by workers who are often hired precisely because their immigration status and linguistic limitations make them more vulnerable.[54] For example, the racial makeup of the domestic staff in *Maid in Manhattan* (most of the workers in the movie are U.S. citizens of white or black descent) is out of synch with the actual demographics of domestic and hotel workers (mostly Latina and African immigrants).[55] Likewise, Flor's weekly wage of $600 for a non–English fluent domestic worker who lives outside the home exceeds the average income of English-fluent Latina non–live-in domestics who earn an average $240 per week, or $6 per hour.[56] The often denigrating labor experiences faced by immigrant and migrant domestic workers is stripped from the more subtle class and racial conflicts faced by the maid in *Spanglish* or the hotel staff of *Maid in Manhattan*.[57] It is an ideological effort best described by one reviewer as "so committed to inoffensiveness and to hammering home its uplifting, bootstrap message that it lacks the necessary element of malice."[58] To sell Latina bodies, Latina immigration, and Latina domestic labor, the lived experiences of Latina domestic workers and conservative anti-immigration discourses must be carefully translated into a more consumable story.

Hollywood's romantic comedies sanitize the physically dirty and emotionally difficult work of caring for other people's children by actually erasing the work. The long days and low wages of domestic workers, particularly for live-in nannies and maids, leave them little time to spend with their children, and as a result of the long hours and low pay, for many immigrant women in the domestic workforce, mothering their own children is often not an option. As Hondagneu-Sotelo notes, "The substantial proportion of Latina domestic workers in Los Angeles whose children stay in their home countries of origin are in the same position as many Caribbean women working in domestic jobs on the East Coast, and as the Filipinas who predominate in domestic jobs in many cities around the globe."[59] When the children of immigrant women are mothered by others in their home countries, transnational motherhood becomes the reality for many domestic workers. Nevertheless, these romantic comedies present Latina domestic labor as providing dignified and living wages, as viable occupations for nurturing their families—eliding the emotional and financial costs of domestic labor in the United States.

Drawing attention to the disparities between the fiction and the reality of domestic work is not meant to discredit the commercial and emotional constraints of films that are produced as a form of lighthearted capitalist and globally consumable entertainment. Rather, by discussing the discursive disjuncture between fictional portrayals and lived experiences, I am foregrounding the ideological work of romantic comedies featuring Latina domestics at a time when the economic success of globalization increasingly depends on their labor. During an era defined by heightened racial anxieties, moral panic about immigration, and economic discrimination targeted at Latina immigrants, identifying the way Latinidad functions in globally distributed and consumed romantic comedies becomes a politically important act.[60] Global Hollywood's constructions of Latina migration and labor cleanse the dirty work of a global economy that falls on the marginalized to wash, clean, and care for others' children.

The depictions of Latina bodies, Latina border crossing and Latina labor analyzed in this chapter and throughout the book serve as an ideological salvo for a nation undergoing economic and demographic transformations. It is thus no surprise that in both *Spanglish* and *Maid in Manhattan* the romantic stories of a Mexican maid/nanny and a presumably Nuyorican maid recuperate patriarchal whiteness. Flor teaches her white employers to nurture each other and stops the father, John, from committing adultery and walking out on his dysfunctional wife. Likewise, Marisa's love, honesty, and desire to improve her economic status rescue Chris from a future filled with materialism and hypocrisy. The women's real labor is not the work they presumably perform in the kitchen or the bathroom—indeed, we hardly see Flor perform any work at all—but the emotional growth their work as surrogate nurturers enables in those around them. In these two films, the "real" work of the Latina domestic revolves around the emotional salvation and moral transformation of the white characters.

Writing about depictions of mothering in popular culture, Sau-ling C. Wong writes that in a society "undergoing radical demographic and economic changes, the figure of the person of color patiently mothering white folks serves to allay racial anxieties."[61] Flor's inherent goodness works in opposition to the neurotic behavior of her boss, Deborah, who eventually takes stock of her life and acknowledges that she does indeed love her caring husband. By the movie's end, Flor has not only saved her mother-daughter relationship with Cristina, but she also has enabled the heteronormative Clasky family to love themselves and keep their family together. Likewise, Marisa's honesty and self-dignity force Chris to face the lies and hypocrisies within his life. Through recapturing her love, Chris presumably becomes a better politician and more honest human being. The erasure of actual domestic labor within the films allows both characters to occupy a more noble yet less threatening position. Flor's and Marisa's emotional and domestic labor serve the interests of the white characters even as it romantically erases unequal racial and economic relationships.

Interestingly, two more serious movies produced during this period—*A Day Without a Mexican* (2004) and *Fast Food Nation* (2006)—attempt to disrupt the erasure of Latina/o labor and laboring bodies typically found in Hollywood romantic cinema. *A Day Without a Mexican* was a mocumentary commissioned by Chicago's Mexican Fine Arts Center Museum and written and directed by Yareli Arizmendi and her spouse, Sergio Arau, both Mexican-born U.S. residents. The movie, where Latinas/os mysteriously disappear from California as it is surrounded by an isolating pink fog, debuted as a No. 1 box office hit in Mexico but only grossed a little more than $10 million in combined U.S. and Mexico ticket sales.[62] Depicting California's decline without its Latina/o labor force drew comedic attention to the hypocrisies of the contemporary anti-immigration discourse. At the heart of the movie is not only the importance of Latina/o labor to California's agricultural and construction industries but also the centrality of Latina domestic labor to the stability of white families and the economic productivity of working mothers. The low-grossing *Fast Food Nation*, based on the book by the same title, gives audiences a fictionalized glimpse at the real, often hazardous, bloody, and dirty working conditions faced by Latina/o immigrant workers who make up the majority of employees in the slaughterhouses and meatpacking industries. *Fast Food Nation* and *A Day Without a Mexican* both present alternative, less ideologically sanitized depictions of Latina labor. Tellingly, the combined ticket sales for the two independently produced and distributed movies ($12 million) did not come close to the global reach of Hollywood's *Maid in Manhattan* ($155 million worldwide) and *Spanglish* ($55 million worldwide).[63]

The two romantic comedies featuring a Mexican immigrant and Nuyorican domestic worker provide an intellectual space for exploring the contemporary status of Latina bodies in U.S. society and politics during a moment of increasing anxiety about the U.S. Latina/o population. In particular, romantic comedy depictions of Latina domestic labor reimagine the lives of millions of Latina laborers by constructing Latinas not as a threat to the cohesion of the U.S. imagined nation but as domestic nurturers of whiteness and white domesticity. Decades after the first Good Neighbor movies premiered in the United States, Latina ethnic difference is still employed by Hollywood and other global media to facilitate the emotional development of Anglo-Saxon characters and reaffirm the nation's inherent goodness.

Conclusion

An Epilogue for Dangerous Curves

What is most important about these mediascapes is that they provide (especially in their television, film and cassette forms) large and complex repertoires of images, narratives, and ethnoscapes to viewers throughout the world, in which the world of commodities and the world of news and politics are profoundly mixed.

—Arjun Appadurai

In the decade since I began the research for this book, the visibility of Latinas in the global mediascape has proliferated. Latina/o immigration continues to occupy the evening news and political sphere. New Latina cover girls have arisen to capture our attention. America Ferrera and Eva Longoria are as likely to appear on the glossy pages of fashion magazines as more established Latina stalwarts Jennifer Lopez and Salma Hayek. Actors who previously resisted identifying as Latina are now embracing the label, perhaps for political reasons, perhaps as a sign of the increased economic viability of Latina bodies in the global media.

For instance, Jessica Alba, who many bloggers refer to as Jessica "Don't Call Me Latina" Alba, until recently downplayed her Mexican heritage.[1] Nevertheless, in a March 2008 appearance in *Latina* magazine, Alba tentatively embraced her Latin or Latina identity, saying, "I can't change how I grew up (with parents and grandparents who did not speak Spanish or identify as Mexican), and I shouldn't have to apologize for it. I know I feel close to the Latin community, because that's what I grew up with." In the same interview, Alba privileged her multiethnic and multiracial background, arguing for the inherent unclassifiable nature of her identity as American: "When are they [media producers] going to get a clue that I am American, that this is what America looks like—people like me who are mixed, have different blood, mixed with different ethnicities?"[2] Whether she is conscious of it or not,

Alba, like other contemporary Latina actors, is transforming the mediascape of U.S. racial formations.

And, finally, new Latina stories are being told. On the news front, U.S.-born Puerto Rican Sonia Sotomayor dominated headlines. In 2009 she became the first Latina nominated to the U.S. Supreme Court. While some conservative news commentators and legislators questioned her judicial objectivity by framing her as aggressive and a "hotbench," the mainstream news media widely covered her nomination as a sign of ethnic and racial progress. Her nomination and related news coverage illustrated once again the public interest and fixation with the contemporary social and political status of Latinas.

On the entertainment front, Latina representations and story lines continue to become more prevalent and complex. Throughout the 2007–2009 television seasons, shows such as *CSI*, *Without a Trace*, *Law and Order*, and *Grey's Anatomy* incorporated secondary Latina characters into their story lines as doctors, scientists, lawyers, and other professionals. The science fiction series *Heroes*, for example, added two Mexican characters who introduced viewers to a grittier reality of Latina/o immigration. More telling still, comedy programs such as *Scrubs* pushed against established commercialized depictions of Latina identity through the complex development of the strong, intelligent, nuanced Afro-Dominican nurse Carla Espinosa, performed by Latina activist and U.S. Dominican Judy Reyes. Latinidad as performed through the ethnically ambiguous and racially flexible bodies of Latinas thus continues to capture and redefine the popular imagination.

Yet in many ways the narratives surrounding Latinidad in the global media remain the same. Throughout 2008 and 2009, the birth of her twins and rumors of another failed relationship once again landed Jennifer Lopez on the front pages of celebrity tabloids and gossip blogs. Her status as the Latina diva who "Americans" love to hate—or at the very least gawk at—remains unchallenged. A cursory review of television, films, and tabloid celebrity coverage of Latinas over the past two years indicate that the commercialized contours of the Latina body have retained their shape—curvaceous, dark hair, dark eyes, and phenotypic features that skew toward whiteness and away from blackness. Rarely do discussions of the continuing Latina boom in the media include the work of Reyes or Afro-Cuban Rosario Dawson. Indeed, Reyes' Carla Espinosa remains the only primary television Latina character in the new century to date, love, and marry a black man (Donald Faison as Christopher Turk) from the United States. The contemporary mediascape thus continues to tell a cautionary tale about the political and social consequences of the mediated manufacturing of Latinidad as a homogenized construction that can be sold to global audiences.

Despite the representational progress of some Latina figures over the past decade, the political and economic realities faced by Latinas/os and Latina/o immigrants remain unchanged. The United States, like many European countries, is coping with dramatic demographic shifts that threaten the stability of established notions of nationhood and citizenship. As a result of immigration, changes in birth rates, and the backlash toward globalization, communities of color from the United States to France face increased social and political hostilities. Citizenship and national identities are under political and cultural contestation throughout the globe, and, as a result, majority (often racially white) communities are working out anxieties about their changing status by disciplining those who embody racialized ethnic difference. In 2005, predominantly Muslim youth, many of whose parents emigrated from former French colonies (Senegal, Morocco, Tunisia), erupted in several weeks of violent protests in France, shattering dominant constructions of that country as an ethnically, racially, and culturally homogenous nation. The social acceptance of Latin American and African immigrants in Spain is falling prey to more nativist sentiments as jobs disappear throughout the country. Racial conflicts in Ireland over segregated schools and other domestic issues are on the rise as small, previously homogenous communities deal with the surge of African immigrants and their children.

Closer to home, after the 9-11 terrorist attacks, hate-crime violence against sexual minorities and ethnic and racial minorities has sharply increased, drawing into question the nation's nostalgic melting pot ideology central to several of the media texts discussed in this book, such as *Maid in Manhattan* and *Ugly Betty*. In January 2009, the *New York Times* reported on a grisly story of Suffolk County teenagers (most of them white) engaging in a pastime they called "beaner hopping."[3] The teenagers specifically hunted Latina/o immigrants, or at least people assumed to be Latina/o immigrants, to violently attack, which in one instance resulted in murder. Many of the victims were too afraid to report the crimes to the police because of their immigration status. Ongoing public debates and news coverage about the 2008 recession, public healthcare reform, national security, and immigration further reinforce the unease with changes to established notions of the United States and U.S. citizenship as predominantly English-speaking, Protestant, and Anglo-Saxon. Together, transnational economic transformations and shifting immigration patterns are rekindling long-held global anxieties about the dangers of changing definitions of citizenship and the status of women, sexual minorities, and racial and ethnic minorities in the public sphere. Thus, central to understanding the representational stakes for Latina/o communities historically erased from the national imaginary is drawing attention to the political environment underlining the global media production and consumption of Latinidad and Latina bodies. The world of news, politics, and entertainment must be analyzed together to understand how they work to create, reinforce, and disrupt commonsense knowledge about citizenship, ethnicity, race, gender, and national identity.

I would like to finish by returning briefly to the introductory questions of this book: What is desirable and consumable about Latina bodies? Under what representational conditions are Latinas socially acceptable, culturally dangerous, or politically transformative? What are the limits, possibilities, and consequences of Latinas' contemporary global marketability? From television to news to film, Latina visibility in the mainstream media informs us about the tensions surrounding immigration, globalization, and the changing role of the nation-state. Arjun Appadurai suggests that contemporary mediascapes are characterized by the convergence of fact and fiction and news, entertainment, and politics.[4] If so, then mapping the global mediascape about Latinidad through news, tabloids, film, television, online discussion boards, and blogs is significant to documenting the political and symbolic status of Latina bodies.

Throughout the case studies, I employed the concept of symbolic colonization to outline the conditions under which ethnic or racial minority women, specifically Latinas, become safe, consumable, desirable, or threatening in news and entertainment. As a set of media practices that function to reproduce dominant norms, values, beliefs, and public conceptions about Latinidad, the process of symbolic colonization demands a careful interrogation of the images, languages, and stories used by the media to construct that Latinidad. Under the symbolic colonization of Latinidad, the gendering and racialization of Marisleysis González transforms her into an unruly brown Cuban body; Frida Kahlo's story of political and sexual rebellion is packaged as a story about heterosexual romance and gendered Mexican identity; and, finally, the success of *Spanglish, Maid in Manhattan,* or *Ugly Betty* depends on representations of Latinas devoid of political challenges to dominant definitions of the United States. The racialized dimension surrounding the national origin of the women also requires that media depictions of Cuban, Boricua and Mexican women be carefully integrated into the U.S. national imaginary and U.S. racial formations through more panethnic and racially ambiguous representations. In the end, Cuban identity must be reimagined as marginal forty years after the Cuban Revolution; Mexican identity must still be contained more than 150 years after the U.S. conquest of Mexico; Puerto Rican identity must still be disciplined 100 years after the U.S. colonization of Puerto Rico; and U.S. Latina identity must be homogenized to serve the United States' continuing imperialistic relationship with Mexico, the Spanish Caribbean, and Latin America.

More often than not, the consumable Latina body whether in news or entertainment must be carefully controlled and patrolled.[5] For example, the case study of Lopez's tabloid coverage illustrates how the initial mainstream visibility of Lopez's beauty/booty is contested by entertainment journalists and audiences as she increasingly transgresses into the domain of heteronormative whiteness by losing weight, straightening and lightening her hair, and flaunting her wealth and privilege through her relationship with Ben Affleck. The common tabloid emphasis on people who beat the odds is replaced by more negative discourses of material and sexual aberrance and excess. Tabloid news stories and Internet audience discussions contain Lopez's ethnic and racial ambiguity by reincorporating it through dominant U.S. ethnic and racial signifiers. She is neither white nor black, but somewhere in between, and her in-betweenness presents a dangerous threat to established notions of citizenship and national identity grounded in whiteness.

The Elián case study further illustrates how the gendering of Latinidad disciplines competing notions of citizenship, thereby producing docile Latina bodies that can be more readily consumed. My analysis of the mainstream, Latina/o, and ethnic and racial minority news coverage of the Elián saga documents the gendering of Cuban identity and the racialized shift of U.S. Cubans from white ethnic political exiles to brown ethnics and unlawful Latina/o immigrants. Previously privileged as ethnic political exiles, news coverage about Cuban immigration now is read against the racialized anti-immigration discourses sweeping across the United States. The racialization of Cubans continues, as seen in reactions to a 2007 MSN.com news blog about the increase of Cuban refugees entering the United States through the Mexico border, where the U.S. dry foot policy grants Cubans immediate temporary citizenship status. MSN audiences responded to the news story with a virulent anti-immigration passion.[6] Of the more than fifty respondents who commented on the story, many saw little difference between Cubans and other Latinas/os, such as Yvette, who said, "They should all be deported back to their native countries, no considerations given at all. As far as Cubans are concerned, its time the US closed it's borders to them as well."[7] To MSN audiences, there remained little to differentiate Cubans from Mexicans, or any other Latina/o immigrant for that matter, since all Latinas/os are suspicious foreigners and invaders of the imagined nation.

However, as several of the case studies document, the symbolic colonization of Latinidad also produces moments of ideological instability that I call symbolic ruptures. Symbolic ruptures signal an interpretive position that allows audiences as cultural readers to disrupt the process of symbolic colonization—sometimes through language that opens up radical definitions of Latina/o identity and sometimes through more conservative ideas that disrupt the global celebration of ethnically ambiguous and racially flexible Latinidad. For instance, ethnic and racial minority journalists and columnists in the Elián case contributed to the racial reformulation of Latinidad by questioning the white exceptionalism and privilege of U.S. Cuban exiles. Jennifer Lopez challenged classifying Puerto Ricans along the United States' dominant black/white racial binary. And some U.S. Mexican audiences of *Frida* emphasized that Mexicans and Latinas are multiethnic and multiracial hybrids rather than racially homogenous panethnics. Whether these symbolic ruptures produce transformative or conservative conceptions of Latinidad, they are examples of the complex ways publics make sense of the images they consume.

I therefore conclude the book on a less skeptical note. At various moments in each case study, some audience readings decentered the very signifiers of Latinidad, of what it means to perform Latina identity in the global media. By questioning dominant definitions of ethnicity, race, and Latina identity, audiences ultimately contribute to the dynamic reformulation of contemporary U.S. culture and national identity.[8] My discussion of ethnic ambiguity and racial flexibility throughout the book suggests that some Latinas are capable of controlling how their ethnic and racial identities are read (in much the same way Raquel Welch and Rita Hayworth controlled perceptions of their identities as white in previous decades), resulting in a socially uncomfortable disruption of dominant identity categories. Racial flexibility does not assume that all Latinas are racially undetermined or racially unmarked, and it recognizes that some Latinas, such as Jessica Alba, have more flexibility than others, such as Rosario Dawson or Salma Hayek. For some online audiences, the ethnic ambiguity and racial flexibility of Latina news figures and celebrities, such as Marisleysis González and Jennifer Lopez, confirmed a looming threat to their commonsense understandings of ethnicity, race, and U.S. national identity as implicitly white, Anglo-Saxon, and Protestant. Elián news coverage in particular served as a cautionary template for ongoing negotiations over national identity and immigration throughout the world. For other audiences, the social discomfort presented a moment of pleasure as it reaffirmed their own more fluid ethnoracial identity. Media depictions of Latinas contribute to the symbolic colonization of Latinidad by maintaining safe depictions of Latina femininity, domesticity, immigration, and labor. Simultaneously, the global media create story lines that are equally transformative for some audiences. The ethnic ambiguity and racially flexible physicality of some Latinas—the very quality that makes them the ideal body to sell the exotic Latina Other to audiences across language, racial, ethnic, and national subjectivities—also produces provocative moments of symbolic rupture.

What I and other audiences expect from the media is not to get rid of commercially profitable or negative news depictions of Latinidad but instead to create more opportunities for nuanced, compelling, and diverse articulations of Latina/o identity. The respectful treatment of the mother-daughter conflict in *Spanglish* honestly speaks to the gendered and classed realities faced by the children of women who carry out domestic work.[9] Likewise, the class struggles embedded in *Maid in Manhattan* and audience discussions of *Ugly Betty* move away from constructions of Latinas as socially dangerous, heteronormative, hyperfertile immigrant threats. Additionally, more recent news coverage of the Sotomayor confirmation hearings signal shifts in news narratives about Latinas and Puerto Ricans as welcomed citizens of the imagined U.S. nation. As the hundreds of students who have moved through my classroom throughout the past seven years demonstrate, the very visibility of moral, beautiful, dignified, and productive Latina bodies—even those depictions that serve the political and economic interest of others—creates a unique opening for meaningful conversations about the media, social justice, and ethnic and racial equality.

Notes

INTRODUCTION

1. With the U.S. Census predicting demographic changes in the Latina/o population, Latina/o marketing specialists began hailing the 1980s as the decade of the Hispanic, the preferred term used by the advertising and marketing industry. Use of the term *Latina/o* gained currency in the mainstream media during the 1990s. For a more thorough discussion of terminology and marketing history, see M. Isabel Valdés, *Marketing to American Latinos: A Guide to the in-Culture Approach*, Part II (Ithaca, NY: Paramount Market Publishing, 2002).

2. Mari Castañeda, "The Importance of Spanish-Language and Latino Media," in *Latina/o Communication Studies Today*, ed. Angharad Valdivia, 51–68 (New York: Peter Lang, 2008).

3. For more information on the growth of the Latina/o market, see Hispanic Fact Sheet, University of Georgia Business Outreach Services (January 2003); Isabel Molina-Guzmán, "Latinas/os in Advertising," in *Oxford Encyclopedia of Latinas and Latinos in the United States*, ed. Suzanne Oboler and Deena J. González (New York: Oxford University Press, 2005); Valdés, *Marketing to American Latinos*.

4. For a more detailed discussion on how various industries are targeting Latina/o consumers, see Valdés, *Marketing to American Latinos*.

5. As the Latina/o media industry has expanded and demographic shifts have taken place, academic scholars have kept pace with a vibrant area of scholarship on media and mediated representations of Latinas. See Frances R. Aparicio, "Jennifer as Selena: Rethinking Latinidad in Media and Popular Culture," *Latino Studies* 1, no. 1 (March 2003); Frances R. Aparicio, *Listening to Salsa: Gender, Latin Popular Music, and Puerto Rican Cultures* (Hanover, NH: University Press of New England, 1998); Frances R. Aparicio and Susana Chávez-Silverman, eds., *Tropicalizations: Transcultural Representations of Latinidad* (Hanover, NH: Dartmouth College, University Press of New England, 1997); Jillian M. Báez, "'En Mi Imperio': Competing Discourses of Agency in Ivy Queen's Reggaetón," CENTRO 18, no. 2 (Fall 2006); Jillian M. Báez, "Speaking of Jennifer Lopez: Discourses of Iconicity and Identity Formation among Latina Audiences," *Media Report to Women* 35, no. 1 (Winter 2007); Mary Beltrán, "The Hollywood Latina Body as Site of Social Struggle: Media Constructions of Stardom and Jennifer Lopez's 'Cross-over Butt'," *Quarterly Review of Film and Video* 19, no. 1 (January–March 2002); María Elena Cepeda, "Shakira as the Idealized, Transnational Citizen: A Case Study of Colombianidad in Transition," *Latino Studies* 1, no. 2 (July 2003); Rosa Linda Fregoso, *The Bronze Screen: Chicana and Chicano Film Culture* (Minneapolis: University of Minnesota Press, 1993); Rosa Linda Fregoso,

MeXicana Encounters: The Making of Social Identities on the Borderlands (Berkeley: University of California Press, 2003); Michelle Habell-Pallán, *Loca Motion: The Travels of Chicana and Latina Popular Culture* (New York: New York University Press, 2005); Michelle Habell-Pallán and Mary Romero, eds., *Latino/a Popular Culture* (New York: New York University Press, 2002); Isabel Molina-Guzmán, "Gendering Latinidad through the Elián News Discourse About Cuban Women," *Latino Studies* 3, no. 2 (July 2005); Isabel Molina-Guzmán, "Mediating Frida: Negotiating Discourses of Latina/o Authenticity in Global Media Representations of Ethnic Identity," *Critical Studies in Media Communication* 23, no. 3 (August 2006); Isabel Molina-Guzmán and Angharad Valdivia, "Brain, Brow or Bootie: Iconic Latinas in Contemporary Popular Culture," *Communication Review* 7, no. 2 (April–June 2004); Frances Negrón-Muntaner, *Boricua Pop: Puerto Ricans and the Latinization of American Culture* (New York: New York University Press, 2004); Frances Negrón-Muntaner, "Jennifer's Butt," *Aztlán* 22, no. 2 (2000); Deborah Paredez, "Remembering Selena, Re-membering Latinidad," *Theatre Journal* 54, no. 1 (March 2002); Viviana Rojas, "The Gender of Latinidad: Latinas Speak About Hispanic Television," *Communication Review* 7, no. 2 (April–June 2004); Angharad Valdivia, *A Latina in the Land of Hollywood and Other Essays on Media Culture* (Tucson: University of Arizona Press, 2000); Angharad Valdivia, *Latina/o Communication Studies Today* (New York: Peter Lang, 2008).

6. I will use the terms *Latina, Latino,* and *Latina/o* to refer to the general population of Mexican, Latin American, and Spanish Caribbean people living in the United States. My use of the label acknowledges that each ethnic/national group has a unique and specific set of historical experiences and contemporary trajectories and at the same time recognizes the shared experiences of racialized prejudice, class oppression, and linguistic discrimination. I will refer to characters and actors by using ethnic-specific labels such as Puerto Rican, Mexican, Chicana/o, and Euro-Spanish when it is particular to the analysis. While I recognize the great diversity within each category, non-Latina/o populations in the United States will be referenced through racial labels such as black and white or ethnic labels such as Italian.

7. Roberta J. Astroff, "Capital's Cultural Study: Marketing Popular Ethnography of U.S. Latino Culture," in *Buy This Book: Studies in Advertising and Consumption*, ed. Mica Nava, 120–138 (London, New York: Routledge, 1997), 120.

8. Jonathan Xavier Inda, "Biopower, Reproduction, and the Migrant Woman's Body," in *Decolonial Voices: Chicana and Chicano Cultural Studies in the 21st Century*, ed. Arturo J. Aldama and Naomi Helena Quiñonez, 98–112 (Bloomington: Indiana University Press, 2002); Maria Ruiz, "Border Narratives: HIV/AIDS, and Latina/o Health in the United States: A Cultural Analysis," *Feminist Media Studies* 2, no. 1 (March 2002).

9. See Aparicio and Chávez-Silverman, *Tropicalizations*; Molina-Guzmán and Valdivia, "Brain, Brow or Bootie."

10. I'm using the term *queer* as queer studies scholars do to reclaim the once-derogatory descriptor as a way to politicize GLBT identity.

11. Richard T. Rodríguez, *Next of Kin: The Family in Chicano/a Cultural Politics* (Durham, NC: Duke University Press, 2009).

12. Arlene M. Dávila, *Latinos, Inc.: The Marketing and Making of a People* (Berkeley: University of California Press, 2001); Charles Ramírez Berg, *Latino Images in Film: Stereotypes, Subversion, Resistance* (Austin: University of Texas Press, 2002).

13. Aparicio, "Jennifer as Selena," 93.

14. See Richard T. Rodríguez, "Imagine a Brown Queer: Inscribing Sexuality in Chicano/a-Latino/a Literary and Cultural Studies," *American Quarterly* 59, no. 2 (June 2007).

15. Silvio Torres-Saillant, "Inventing the Race: Latinos and the Ethnoracial Pentagon," *Latino Studies* 1, no. 1 (March 2003): 124.

16. Ibid., 125.

17. In discussing racialization, Tomás Almaguer concludes that the situation of Latinas/os living in the United States "reflects a clash between two cultures of race, as a Latino/a population, racialized according to one racial regime, is reracialized in the United States according to a different racial logic." Tomás Almaguer, "At the Crossroads of Race: Latino/a Studies and Race Making in the United States," in *Critical Latin American and Latino Studies*, ed. Juan Poblete, 206–222 (Minneapolis: University of Minnesota Press, 2003), 213.

18. Today, most Latin American and Spanish Caribbean countries continue to celebrate the historical legacy of racial mixture through the ideologies of *mestizaje* (Mexico and Latin America) and *trigueñidad* (the Spanish Caribbean). See the two-volume work, Norman E. Whitten and Arlene Torres, *Blackness in Latin America and the Caribbean: Social Dynamics and Cultural Transformations* (Bloomington: Indiana University Press, 1998).

19. Yeidy M. Rivero, *Tuning out Blackness: Race and Nation in the History of Puerto Rican Television* (Durham, NC: Duke University Press, 2005).

20. Dávila, *Latinos, Inc.*

21. Néstor García Canclini, *Hybrid Cultures: Strategies for Entering and Leaving Modernity* (Minneapolis: University of Minnesota Press, 1995); María Lugones, *Pilgrimages = Peregrinajes: Theorizing Coalition against Multiple Oppressions* (Lanham, MD: Rowman & Littlefield, 2003); Angharad Valdivia, "Latinas as Radical Hybrid: Transnationally Gendered Traces in Mainstream Media," *Global Media Journal* 3, no. 4 (2004).

22. Frances R. Aparicio, "Reading the 'Latino' in Latino Studies: Toward Re-Imagining Our Academic Location," *Discourse* 21, no. 3 (Fall 1999); Suzanne Oboler, *Ethnic Labels, Latino Lives: Identity and the Politics of (Re)presentation in the United States* (Minneapolis: University of Minnesota Press, 1995).

23. *Overview of Race and Hispanic Origin*, U.S. Census Bureau, March 2001 [accessed February 17, 2008]; available from http://www.census.gov/prod/2001pubs/cenbr01-1.pdf.

24. Clara E. Rodríguez, *Changing Race: Latinos, the Census, and the History of Ethnicity in the United States* (New York: New York University Press, 2000).

25. Almaguer, "At the Crossroads of Race," 214.

26. Dávila, *Latinos, Inc.*; Marilyn Halter, *Shopping for Identity: The Marketing of Ethnicity* (New York: Schocken Books, 2000).

27. Celine Parreñas Shimizu, *The Hypersexuality of Race: Performing Asian/American Women on Screen and Scene* (Durham, NC: Duke University Press, 2007).

28. Inderpal Grewal and Caren Kaplan, *Scattered Hegemonies: Postmodernity and Transnational Feminist Practices* (Minneapolis: University of Minnesota Press, 1994).

29. Suzanne Oboler suggests that Latina/o identity in the United States has always been homogenized as foreign, in part because U.S. foreign policy toward Latin America dictates a position of superiority that defines Latinas/os as inherently different. See Oboler, *Ethnic Labels, Latino Lives*.

30. For more on the importance of examining mainstream popular culture not to the exclusion of alternative media but because of its centrality within U.S. and international life, see Molina-Guzmán and Valdivia, "Brain, Brow or Bootie"; Valdivia, A Latina in the Land of Hollywood.

31. That said, I am not suggesting that alternative, independent, or counterculture performances do not play an equally important and oppositional role. A growing body of work illustrates that studying Chicana/o and Latina/o cultural and media production outside the mainstream media is a significant site for theorizing about the production of politically significant Latina/o community formations. See, among others, Rosa Linda Fregoso and Lourdes Portillo, Lourdes Portillo: The Devil Never Sleeps and Other Films, 1st ed. (Austin: University of Texas Press, 2001); Habell-Pallán, Loca Motion; Chon A. Noriega, ed., Chicanos and Film: Essays on Chicano Representation and Resistance (New York: Garland Publishing, 1992).

32. Habell-Pallán and Romero, Latino/a Popular Culture, 5.

33. A. W. McHoul and Wendy Grace, A Foucault Primer: Discourse, Power, and the Subject (New York: New York University Press, 1997), 31.

34. George Gerbner et al., "Growing up with Television: The Cultivation Perspective," in Media Effects: Advances in Theory and Research, ed. Jennings Bryant and Dolf Zillmann, 17–41 (Hillsdale, NJ: Erlbaum, 1994); Larry Gross, "Out of the Mainstream: Sexual Minorities and the Mass Media," in Gay People, Sex, and the Media, ed. Michelle Andrea Wolf and Alfred P. Kielwasser, 19–46 (New York: Haworth Press, 1991).

35. Sut Jhally and Justin Lewis, Enlightened Racism: The Cosby Show, Audiences, and the Myth of the American Dream (Boulder, CO: Westview Press, 1992).

36. Michel Foucault and Paul Rabinow, The Foucault Reader, 1st ed. (New York: Pantheon Books, 1984), 61.

37. Dávila, Latinos, Inc., 10.

38. For a discussion of "genderization" as a linguistic and symbolic concept, see Cheris Kramarae and Paula A. Treichler, A Feminist Dictionary (London, Boston: Pandora Press, 1985). For a discussion of how genderization informs media practices and texts, see Lana Rakow and Kimberly Kranich, "Women as Sign in Television News," Journal of Communication 41, no. 1 (1991).

39. Lucila Vargas, "Genderizing Latino News: An Analysis of a Local Newspaper's Coverage of Latino Current Affairs," Critical Studies in Media Communication 17, no. 3 (September 2000): 285.

40. Jack Z. Bratich, Jeremy Packer, and Cameron McCarthy, Foucault, Cultural Studies, and Governmentality (Albany: State University of New York Press, 2003).

41. Ibid., 8.

42. Foucault and Rabinow, The Foucault Reader, 181.

43. Susan Bordo, Unbearable Weight: Feminism, Western Culture, and the Body (Berkeley: University of California Press, 1993), 26.

44. Valdivia discusses Perez's struggle to lose weight and her urban accent because her managers thought it would make her more marketable to the Hollywood industry. Angharad Valdivia, "Rosie Goes to Hollywood: The Politics of Representation," Review of Education, Pedagogy, and Cultural Studies 18, no. 2 (1996).

45. Myra Mendible, "Introduction: Embodying Latinidad: An Overview," in From Bananas to Buttocks: The Latina Body in Popular Film and Culture, ed. Myra Mendible, 1–28 (Austin: University of Texas Press, 2007), 8.

46. Usha Zacharias, "Trial by Fire: Gender, Power, and Citizenship in Narratives of the Nation," *Social Text* 19, no. 4 (Winter 2001).

47. Benedict Anderson, *Imagined Communities: Reflections on the Origin and Spread of Nationalism* (London: Verso, 1991), 36.

48. Zacharias, "Trial by Fire," 30.

49. Aparicio, "Jennifer as Selena," 99.

50. Jonathan Xavier Inda documents the disciplining of the immigrant body in particular. Inda, "Biopower, Reproduction, and the Migrant Woman's Body."

51. In making this reference, I am building on Elizabeth Spelman's discussion of Plato's discussion of the mind/soul and body binary. Elizabeth V. Spelman, "Woman as Body: Ancient and Contemporary Views," in *Feminist Theory and the Body: A Reader*, ed. Janet Price and Margrit Shildrick, 32–41 (Edinburgh: Edinburgh University Press, 1999).

52. Angharad Valdivia, "Is Penélope to J.Lo as Culture Is to Nature? Eurocentric Approaches to "Latin" Beauties," in *From Bananas to Buttocks: The Latina Body in Popular Film and Culture*, ed. Myra Mendible, 129–148 (Austin: University of Texas Press, 2007).

53. For a discussion of symbolic violence in the literary canon and how the privileging of certain works erases the value inherent in other genres of literature, see Spelman, "Woman as Body," 20. For discussions of how white, male heterosexual media producers impact media content, see Gross, "Out of the Mainstream"; Michael Schudson, *The Sociology of News* (New York: Norton, 2003).

54. Aihwa Ong, "Cultural Citizenship as Subject Making: Immigrants Negotiate Racial and Cultural Boundaries in the United States," in *Race, Identity, and Citizenship: A Reader*, ed. Rodolfo D. Torres, Luis F. Mirón, and Jonathan Xavier Inda, 262–294 (Malden, MA: Blackwell, 1999), 267.

55. Ellen McCracken, *New Latina Narrative: The Feminine Space of Postmodern Ethnicity* (Tucson: University of Arizona Press, 1999), 12–13.

56. Rodolfo D. Torres, Luis F. Mirón, and Jonathan Xavier Inda, *Race, Identity, and Citizenship: A Reader* (Malden, MA: Blackwell, 1999).

57. Lisa Lowe and David Lloyd argue that neocolonial or global capitalism does not result in homogenous cultural forms but rather "that 'culture' obtains a 'political' force when a cultural formation comes into contradiction with economic or political logics that try to refunction it for exploitation or domination." Lisa Lowe and David Lloyd, *The Politics of Culture in the Shadow of Capital* (Durham, NC: Duke University Press, 1997), 1.

58. Jacqueline Bobo, *Black Women as Cultural Readers* (New York: Columbia University Press, 1995).

59. Lugones, *Pilgrimages = Peregrinajes*.

60. *2002 National Survey of Latinos*. Pew Hispanic Center (December 2002).

61. As a grassroots political and academic term, the gender-neutral and panethnic label *Latino* first gained widespread use and acceptance in the Midwest, where sizable generations of Puerto Ricans and Mexicans historically have shared urban and rural work and educational and residential spaces. The term, which many scholars and activists see as resisting the Europeanized legacy of the term *Hispanic*, became an officially recognized label in the 2000 U.S. Census. The use of *Latina/o* is a grassroots attempt to address the multiplicity of identities and comparative historical and contemporary experiences of both U.S. immigrants and U.S.-born citizens with ties to more than twenty Caribbean and Latin American countries in ways that more regional- and ethnic-specific labels, such

as the U.S. Mexican-derivative label *Chicana/o,* do not. Angharad Valdivia's writing on Penélope Cruz further complicates this discussion. See Valdivia, "Is Penélope to J.Lo as Culture Is to Nature? Eurocentric Approaches to 'Latin' Beauties." Cruz, a white European, is often encoded in the English- and Spanish-language media as Latina, thus raising further questions about who gets defined as Latina by the media and the implications for U.S. racial formations.

CHAPTER 1

1. Throughout the book I define "mainstream" media as those outlets in English and Spanish that are accessible to a large cross-section of the population, such as ABC News or Univisión. For this chapter, I examine four major television news networks (ABC, CBS, CNN, and NBC), the *New York Times,* and the *Miami Herald.* I am defining ethnic news media as media that target specific ethnic and racial communities, sometimes in English but often in the language most likely to be spoken by first-generation immigrants of those communities. For this chapter, I examined ethnic news outlets such as *La Opinión* and African American and Asian newspapers collected through the Ethnic NewsWatch Database. Finally, my discussion of *El Nuevo Herald,* which is run in partnership with the *Miami Herald,* assumes that it is an ethnic newspaper, specifically a U.S. Cuban newspaper. As such, it puts forth a specific perspective that is at times oppositional to the mainstream media and other ethnic news media.

2. Journalism scholars such as Barbie Zelizer maintain that the news media are a cultural form open to critical examination along cultural dimensions. See Barbie Zelizer, *Taking Journalism Seriously: News and the Academy* (Thousand Oaks, CA: Sage, 2004).

3. I place "truth" and "fact" in quotations here in recognition of established journalism scholarship critiquing objectivity as an achievable or sustainable practice. For more in this area, see Michael Schudson, *The Sociology of News* (New York: Norton, 2003); Zelizer, *Taking Journalism Seriously.*

4. Serafín Méndez-Méndez and Diane Alverio, *Network Brownout 2001: The Portrayal of Latinos in Network Television News, 2000* (Washington, DC: National Association of Hispanic Journalists, 2001).

5. *2000 Year in Review: TV's Leading News Topics, Reporters and Political Jokes.* Washington, DC: Center for Media and Public Affairs (January/February 2001).

6. David W. Moore, "Public: Reunion of Elián with Father Should Have Occurred Earlier," *Gallup Poll Monthly* 415 (April 2000).

7. For a fuller discussion of the U.S. backlash against Latina/o immigration, see Wayne A. Cornelius, "Ambivalent Reception: Mass Public Responses to the 'New' Latino Immigration to the United States," in *Latinos: Remaking America,* ed. Marcelo M. Suárez-Orozco and Mariela Páez, 165–189 (Berkeley: University of California Press, 2002); Jonathan Xavier Inda, "Biopower, Reproduction, and the Migrant Woman's Body," in *Decolonial Voices: Chicana and Chicano Cultural Studies in the 21st Century,* ed. Arturo J. Aldama and Naomi Helena Quiñonez, 98–112 (Bloomington: Indiana University Press, 2002); Maria Ruiz, "Border Narratives: HIV/AIDS, and Latina/o Health in the United States: A Cultural Analysis," *Feminist Media Studies* 2, no. 1 (March 2002).

8. See Mark Gillespie, "Americans Support Resumption of Diplomatic Relations with Cuba," *Gallup Poll Monthly* 416 (May 2000). For more on the Cuban ethnic enclave in

Miami, see Alex Stepick and Carol Dutton Stepick, "Power and Identity: Miami Cubans," in *Latinos: Remaking America*, ed. Marcelo M. Suárez-Orozco and Mariela Páez, 75–92 (Berkeley: University of California Press, 2002).

9. Carol Rosenberg, "Where Should Rafter Boy Live? S. Florida Split," *Miami Herald*, December 12, 1999.

10. See Moore, "Public: Reunion of Elián with Father Should Have Occurred Earlier"; Frank Newport, "Americans Say It Is in Elián González' Best Interests to Return to Cuba with His Father," *Gallup Poll Monthly* 415 (April 2000).

11. Alex Stepick et al., *This Land Is Our Land: Immigrants and Power in Miami* (Berkeley: University of California Press, 2003), 2.

12. For a more detailed discussion of the way childhood, family, and domesticity functioned in the reproduction of U.S. national identity, see Sarah Banet-Weiser, "Elián González and 'the Purpose of America': Nation, Family, and the Child-Citizen," *American Quarterly* 55, no. 2 (June 2003).

13. For a discussion of "genderization" as a linguistic and symbolic concept, see Cheris Kramarae and Paula A. Treichler, *A Feminist Dictionary* (London, Boston: Pandora Press, 1985). For a discussion of how genderization informs media practices and texts, see Lana Rakow and Kimberly Kranich, "Women as Sign in Television News," *Journal of Communication* 41, no. 1 (1991).

14. Because several of the figures in the Elián story share the last name of González, I use first names to avoid confusion. The article uses the spelling of Elisabet Brotons most often used by the English- and Spanish-language media.

15. Louis DeSipio and James Richard Henson attribute differences in media representations of Cuban and Latina/o groups to Cubans' political status within the United States. See Louis DeSipio and James Richard Henson, "Cuban Americans, Latinos, and the Print Media: Shaping Ethnic Identities," *Harvard International Journal of Press/Politics* 2, no. 3 (June 1, 1997).

16. María de los Angeles Torres, *The Lost Apple: Operation Pedro Pan, Cuban Children in the U.S., and the Promise of a Better Future* (Boston: Beacon Press, 2003).

17. María de los Angeles Torres, *In the Land of Mirrors: Cuban Exile Politics in the United States* (Ann Arbor: University of Michigan Press, 1999).

18. Nicolás Kanellos, *Thirty Million Strong: Reclaiming the Hispanic Image in American Culture* (Golden, CO: Fulcrum Publishing, 1998).

19. It was not until the Immigration and Nationality Act amendments of 1965 (the Hart-Cellar Act), which finally privileged family reunification, that Mexican immigrants were legally allowed to bring their families to the United States.

20. María Cristina García, "Exiles, Immigrants and Transnationals: The Cuban Communities in the United States," in *The Columbia History of Latinos in the United States since 1960*, ed. David Gutiérrez, 146–186 (New York: Columbia University Press, 2004).

21. For a discussion of the ebb and flow of Mexican immigration and deportation, see Pierrette Hondagneu-Sotelo, "The History of Mexican Undocumented Settlement in the United States," in *Challenging Fronteras: Structuring Latina and Latino Lives in the U.S.: An Anthology of Readings*, ed. Mary Romero, Pierrette Hondagneu-Sotelo, and Vilma Ortiz, 115–134 (New York: Routledge, 1997).

22. For a discussion of Cuban immigration, see García, "Exiles, Immigrants and Transnationals."

23. For an in-depth discussion of race and the Mariel and Balsero exiles, see Nancy Raquel Mirabal, "'Ser De Aquí': Beyond the Cuban Exile Model," *Latino Studies* 1, no. 3 (2003); Rubén G. Rumbaut, "Origins and Destinies: Immigration to the United States since World War II," *Sociological Forum* 9, no. 4 (December 1994). For an in-depth discussion of the political and economic impact of the Mariel exiles, see Silvia Pedraza-Bailey, "Cuba's Exile: Portrait of a Refugee Migration," *International Migration Review* 19, no. 1 (Spring 1985); Alejandro Portes and Leif Jensen, "The Enclave and the Entrants: Patterns of Ethnic Enterprise in Miami before and after Mariel," *American Sociological Review* 54 (December 1989); Alejandro Portes and Alex Stepick, "Unwelcome Immigrants: The Labor Market Experience of 1980 (Mariel) Cuban and Haitian Refugees in South Florida," *American Sociological Review* 50, no. 4 (August 1985); Stepick et al., *This Land Is Our Land*.

24. DeSipio and Henson, "Cuban Americans, Latinos, and the Print Media," 60–67.

25. Otto Santa Ana, *Brown Tide Rising: Metaphors of Latinos in Contemporary American Public Discourse*, 1st ed. (Austin: University of Texas Press, 2002). Also see *Selected Social Characteristics in the United States: 2005*. U.S. Census Bureau, 2005 [accessed December 18, 2008]; available from http://factfinder.census.gov/servlet/ADPTable?_bm=y&-context=adp&-qr_name=ACS_2005_EST_G00_DP2&-ds_name=ACS_2005_EST_G00_&-tree_id=305&-redoLog=true&-_caller=geoselect&-geo_id=04000US06&-format=&-_lang=en.

26. Rosa Linda Fregoso, *The Bronze Screen: Chicana and Chicano Film Culture* (Minneapolis: University of Minnesota Press, 1993); Charles Ramírez Berg, *Latino Images in Film: Stereotypes, Subversion, Resistance* (Austin: University of Texas Press, 2002).

27. See "Three Sisters," a three-day series by the *New York Times*, published December 19–21, 2006, available at http://www.nytimes.com/ref/us/three_sisters.html (accessed January 20, 2009). Stories include Lizette Alvarez, "Fear and Hope in Immigrant's Furtive Existence," *New York Times*, December 20, 2006; Lizette Alvarez, "A Growing Stream of Illegal Immigrants Choose to Remain Despite the Risks," *New York Times*, December 20, 2006 ; Mireya Navarro, "For Divided Family, Border Is Sorrowful Barrier," *New York Times*, December 21, 2006; Mireya Navarro, "Traditional Round Trip for Workers Is Becoming a One-Way Migration North," *New York Times*, December 21, 2006; Julia Preston, "Low-Wage Workers from Mexico Dominate Latest Great Wave of Immigrants," *New York Times*, December 19, 2006; Julia Preston, "Making a Life in the U.S., but Feeling Mexico's Tug," *New York Times*, December 19, 2006.

28. Lisa Arthur, Bruce Taylor Seeman, and Elaine De Valle, "5-Year-Old Survivor Clung to Inner Tube Two More Rafters Rescued, but 11 Other Cubans May Have Died at Sea," *Miami Herald*, November 26, 1999.

29. Lisa Marie Cacho, "'The People of California Are Suffering': The Ideology of White Injury in Discourses of Immigration," *Cultural Values* 4, no. 4 (October 2000); Ruby C. Tapia, "Un(di)ing Legacies: White Matters of Memory in Portraits of 'Our Princess,'" *Cultural Values* 5, no. 2 (April 2001).

30. On ABC's *World News Tonight* a couple of weeks after Elián's rescue, the only reference to Elisabet was made during Peter Jennings' introduction of Elián as the six-year-old "whose mother died at sea as she was bringing him to Florida." Morton Dean, "Tensions Rise between U.S. And Cuba over Six-Year-Old Boy." *World News Tonight*, anchor Peter Jennings, ABC, December 8, 1999. Yet again, months later, *U.S. News and World Report's* John Leo described Elián as the boy "whose mother has perished at sea." John Leo, "Elián: The Opera," *U.S. News and World Report*, May 8, 2000.

31. "Cuban Moms: 'Return Our Son!' Havana Mobilizes Thousands as Battle for Elián Drags On," *Miami Herald*, January 15, 2000.

32. Lazaro Muñero also died on the fateful voyage. For more on different accounts about why and how the voyage was organized, see Alfonso Chardy, "Family Ties Spurred Rafters on Elián Trip," *Miami Herald*, June 23, 2000.

33. Oscar Avila, "Hunger Strikers in Pilsen Seek Halt to Deportations," *Chicago Tribune*, May 25, 2006.

34. Oscar Avila, "Act of Faith, Defiance: Activist for Illinois' Illegal Immigrants Battles Deportation by Taking Shelter in a City Church," *Chicago Tribune*, August 16, 2006.

35. For more information on the undocumented children population, see Jeffrey S. Passel, *Unauthorized Migrants: Numbers and Characteristics*. Washington, DC: Pew Hispanic Center (June 14, 2005).

36. For examples of the racially tinged debate in the *Chicago Tribune*, see Oscar Avila, "Activist Steps into Debate Pulpit," *Chicago Tribune*, August 18, 2006; Oscar Avila, "Boy Wages Fight for Mother: Critics Charge Immigrant's Son Being Exploited," *Chicago Tribune*, November 15, 2006; Oscar Avila, "Illegal Immigrant's Supporters, Foes in Made-for-TV Roles," *Chicago Tribune*, August 26, 2006; "Elvira Arellano and the Law," *Chicago Tribune*, August 17, 2006; "Should Elvira Arellano Be Deported or Allowed to Stay in the U.S.?" *Chicago Tribune*, August 18, 2006.

37. Oscar Avila, "She Refuses to Go Silently," *Chicago Tribune*, November 19, 2005.

38. The Border Protection, Antiterrorism, and Illegal Immigration Control Act (H.R. 4437) was introduced and passed by the House in December 2005. According to the National Immigration Forum, the bill "attacks the rights of immigrants, both legal and undocumented, on a broad front. Among other things, it would make 'unlawful presence' an 'aggravated felony,' making criminals out of millions of undocumented immigrant workers and family members." Although the bill passed the House, it never made it out of the Senate. See *Legislation: Enforcement Only Will Not Fix Our Broken Immigration System*. National Immigration Forum, [accessed June 20, 2007]; available from http://www.immigrationforum.org/DesktopDefault.aspx?tabid=777.

39. For more discussion on how Elisabet was discursively used by the Cuban and U.S. Cuban communities, see Isabel Molina-Guzmán, "Gendering Latinidad through the Elián News Discourse About Cuban Women," *Latino Studies* 3, no. 2 (July 2005).

40. Rosenberg, "Where Should Rafter Boy Live? S. Florida Split."

41. Marika Lynch, "Elián's Miami Relatives Say INS Is Tight-Lipped," *Miami Herald*, December 21, 1999.

42. Jasmine Kripalani and Eunice Ponce, "Protests March to Different Beats," *Miami Herald*, January 30, 2000.

43. Dean, "Tensions Rise between U.S. And Cuba over Six-Year-Old Boy"; Leo, "Elián: The Opera."

44. Sharyl Attkisson, "Five-Year-Old Cuban Boy Who Was Rescued Off the Coast of Florida Is Allowed to Remain in the United States." *CBS Evening News*, anchor John Roberts, November 26, 1999.

45. Mireya Navarro, "Grandmothers Cite Family Values in Effort to Take Cuban Boy Home," *New York Times*, January 23, 2000.

46. Connie Hicks, "Thousands of Protesters Marching in the Streets of Little Havana." *World News Now*, anchor Anderson Cooper, ABC, March 30, 2000; Steve Osunsami,

"Elián González Endures Spotlight and Adulation in Cuba and Miami." *World News Tonight*, anchor Carole Simpson, ABC, January 23, 2000.

47. Another widely circulated image was an AP photograph of an oval mirror inside Marisleysis' bedroom, where she claimed an image of the Virgin Mary appeared to her and Elián. The photograph and news footage of the mirror aired March 27, 2000, on CNN and *NBC Nightly News*. See Leon Harris, Susan Candiotti, and Carol Lin, "Government Gives Elián González's Family until Noon to Accept Speedy Appeals Process," *CNN Early Edition*, March 27, 2000; Pete Williams, "Battle over Elián González Heats Up," *NBC Nightly News*, anchor Tom Brokaw, March 27, 2000.

48. Rumbaut, "Origins and Destinies," 586.

49. For an overview of the U.S. Cuban community, see *Cubans in the United States*, Washington, DC: Pew Hispanic Center (August 25, 2006). Cuban studies scholars have documented the negative media representations and political backlash surrounding the April–October 1980 Mariel boatlift, which brought 125,000 Cubans to Miami, and the Balseros of the early 1990s. While most of the refugees were working-class laborers, the media focused on black Cubans, homosexual Cubans, and the small percentage of refugees with criminal records. For an in-depth discussion of race and the Mariel and Balsero exiles, see Mirabal, "'Ser De Aquí': Beyond the Cuban Exile Model"; Rumbaut, "Origins and Destinies." For an in-depth discussion of the political and economic impact of the Mariel exiles, see Pedraza-Bailey, "Cuba's Exile"; Portes and Jensen, "The Enclave and the Entrants"; Portes and Stepick, "Unwelcome Immigrants"; Stepick et al., *This Land Is Our Land*.

50. Scott Baldauf, "U.S. Tries Spy Tactics to Stop Human Smugglers," *Christian Science Monitor*, August 30, 2000.

51. Rick Bragg, "Haitian Immigrants in U.S. Face a Wrenching Choice," *New York Times*, March 29, 2000.

52. "Haitians Continue to Protest for Equal Treatment under Immigration Policy," *Miami Times*, January 20, 2000.

53. Charles B. Rangel, "Why Citizenship for Elián Is Wrong," *New York Amsterdam News*, February 3, 2000.

54. Ruiz, "Border Narratives"; Santa Ana, *Brown Tide Rising*.

55. Wolf Blitzer et al., "Elián González Takes Center Stage in the Political Arena," *CNN Late Edition with Wolf Blitzer*, anchor Wolf Blitzer, April 9, 2000.

56. Ironically, one of the unintended consequences of the Elián story was the formation of white and black community coalitions against the "real" and "perceived" preferential treatment of Miami Cubans. See Stepick et al., *This Land Is Our Land*.

57. Paul Brinkley-Rogers et al., "Case Provokes Harsh Feelings, Hope," *Miami Herald*, April 6, 2000.

58. For more discussion on public responses within the *Miami Herald*, see Isabel Molina-Guzmán, "Competing Discourses of Community: Ideological Tensions between Local General-Market and Latino News Media," *Journalism: Theory, Practice and Criticism* 7, no. 3 (August 2006).

59. Stepick et al., *This Land Is Our Land*.

60. Jeffrey Bartholet et al., "Grandma Diplomacy," *Newsweek*, January 31, 2000.

61. Carol Rosenberg, "Grandmas Find a Few D.C. Supporters," *Miami Herald*, January 26, 2000.

62. Ruth Behar, "Queer Times in Cuba," in *Bridges to Cuba = Puentes a Cuba*, ed. Ruth Behar, 394–415 (Ann Arbor: University of Michigan Press, 1995); Torres, *In the Land of Mirrors*.

63. Bob Jamieson, "Elián González's Grandmothers Arrive in New York," *World News Tonight*, anchor Peter Jennings, ABC, January 21, 2000; Carol Rosenberg and Elaine De Valle, "Boy May Be Sent Back: INS to Discuss Case with Elián's Father in Cuba," *Miami Herald*, December 8, 1999.

64. "Cuban Moms: 'Return Our Son!'"

65. Ron Claiborne, "Elián González Meets Grandmothers on Neutral Ground," *World News Tonight*, anchor Peter Jennings, ABC, January 26, 2000; Jamieson, "Elián González's Grandmothers Arrive in New York"; Lucia Newman, "Elian Gonzalez's Father Pleads for Son's Return," *CNN Worldview*, anchor Wolf Blitzer, CNN, January 27, 2000; Dan Rather, "Juan Miguel González Talks About Why He Wants His Son, Elián, Back," *60 Minutes II*, CBS, April 18, 2000.

66. For a critique of race neutrality in U.S. immigration law, see Ruben J. Garcia, "The Racial Politics of Proposition 187," in *The Latino/a Condition: A Critical Reader*, ed. Richard Delgado and Jean Stefancic, 118–124 (New York: New York University Press, 1998).

67. Carol Rosenberg, "Tears Flow as Grandmas Meet Reno; They Ask for Elián's Return to Father," *Miami Herald*, January 23, 2000.

68. Frank Davies, "Groups Call for Returning Elián to Father," *Miami Herald*, January 19, 2000.

69. Gilbert Dunkley, "On Stealing a Child, and Other Outrages," *Caribbean Today*, January 31, 2000; Terry Jackson, "It's Time to Take Boy Out of Spotlight," *Miami Herald*, December 9, 1999; Rangel, "Why Citizenship for Elián Is Wrong"; Rosenberg and De Valle, "Boy May Be Sent Back"; Jay Weaver, "Rafter's Case Pits Family Emotion vs. Custody Law," *Miami Herald*, November 8, 1999.

70. Byron Pitts, "Tension Building in Miami as U.S. Immigration Decides the Fate of Elián González," *CBS Evening News*, March 29, 2000.

71. Aaron Brown, "Janet Reno Leaves Decision to Elián González's Father," *World News Tonight*, anchor Peter Jennings, ABC, January 12, 2000.

72. Ron Claiborne, "Father of Elián González Says He'll Never Go to Miami," *World News Tonight*, anchor Peter Jennings, ABC, January 13, 2000.

73. Claiborne, "Elián González Meets Grandmothers on Neutral Ground."

74. Ron Claiborne, "Miami Relatives of Elián González Won't Give Permission for Elián to Live with His Father While in Miami," *World News Tonight*, anchor Peter Jennings, ABC, March 31, 2000.

75. For a more in-depth discussion of the political role Marisleysis played in the Elián case, see Molina-Guzmán, "Gendering Latinidad through the Elián News Discourse About Cuban Women."

76. *ABC World News Now*, 2000 [accessed March 5, 2004]. Available from http://more.abcnews.go.com/sections/us/DailyNews/elian_subindex.htm.

77. Myra MacPherson, "All in Elián's Family," *Salon*, April 8, 2000 [accessed December 18, 2008]; available from http://archive.salon.com/news/feature/2000/04/08/family/. Although he was 5 years old when he was rescued, Elián turned 6 on December 6, 1999.

78. Luisa Yanez, "'She Loves Elian Very Much': A Woman Is Thrown into Spotlight for Her Devotion to a Cuban Cousin Who Floated in on an Inner Tube," *Sun Sentinel, Fort Lauderdale*, March 13, 2000.

79. Meg Laughlin, "Elián's Cousin in, out of Hospitals," *Miami Herald*, April 11, 2000.

80. Byron Pitts, "Tensions Grow High in Custody Battle over Elián González," CBS *Evening News*, anchor Dan Rather, CBS, April 4, 2000.

81. DeWayne Wickham, "Elian's 'Surrogate Mother' Should Get a Grip," *USA Today*, May 10, 2000 [accessed December 18, 2008]; available from http://www.usatoday.com/news/opinion/columnists/wickham/wick091.htm.

82. John Montgomery, *Creep of the Week: Marisleysis Gonzalez*. johnmonty.com, April 29, 2000 [accessed March 1, 2008]; available from http://www.johnmonty.com/cotw/cw000429.htm.

83. *From News Highlights to Highlighting Hair*. Associated Press, August 3, 2002 [accessed March 1, 2008]; available from http://www.sptimes.com/2002/08/03/State/From_news_highlights_.shtml.

84. Michael Omi and Howard Winant, *Racial Formation in the United States: From the 1960s to the 1990s*, 2nd ed. (New York: Routledge, 1994).

85. For a snapshot of public opinion regarding Cuba post-Elián, see Gillespie, "Americans Support Resumption of Diplomatic Relations with Cuba."

86. Roberto Santiago, "Miami Cubans Lost, Big Time," *New York Daily News*, June 30, 2000.

87. Sylvia Moreno and Lonnae O'Neal Parker, "The Voice of Dispassion for U.S. Cubans," *Washington Post*, April 28, 2000.

88. Frances R. Aparicio and Susana Chávez-Silverman, eds., *Tropicalizations: Transcultural Representations of Latinidad* (Hanover, NH: Dartmouth College, University Press of New England, 1997); Kramarae and Treichler, *A Feminist Dictionary*; Ana M. López, "Are All Latins from Manhattan?: Hollywood, Ethnography, and Cultural Colonialism," in *Unspeakable Images: Ethnicity and the American Cinema*, ed. Lester D. Friedman, 404–424 (Urbana: University of Illinois, 1991); Molina-Guzmán, "Gendering Latinidad through the Elián News Discourse About Cuban Women"; Gustavo Pérez Firmat, *Life on the Hyphen: The Cuban-American Way*, 1st ed. (Austin: University of Texas Press, 1994); Rakow and Kranich, "Women as Sign in Television News"; Ramírez Berg, *Latino Images in Film*; Ella Shohat and Robert Stam, *Unthinking Eurocentrism: Multiculturalism and the Media* (London, New York: Routledge, 1994); Angharad Valdivia, *A Latina in the Land of Hollywood and Other Essays on Media Culture* (Tucson: University of Arizona Press, 2000).

89. Magdalena Barrera, "Hottentot 2000: Jennifer Lopez and Her Butt," in *Sexualities in History: A Reader*, ed. Kim M. Phillips and Barry Reay, 407–420 (New York: Routledge, 2002); López, "Are All Latins from Manhattan?"; Frances Negrón-Muntaner, "Jennifer's Butt," *Aztlán* 22, no. 2 (2000); Ella Shohat, ed., *Talking Visions: Multicultural Feminism in Transnational Age* (Cambridge, MA: MIT Press, 1998).

90. Stuart Hall, ed., *Representation: Cultural Representations and Signifying Practices* (London, Thousand Oaks, CA: Sage in association with the Open University, 1997).

CHAPTER 2

1. Frances R. Aparicio, "Jennifer as Selena: Rethinking Latinidad in Media and Popular Culture," *Latino Studies* 1, no. 1 (March 2003); Magdalena Barrera, "Hottentot 2000: Jennifer Lopez and Her Butt," in *Sexualities in History: A Reader*, ed. Kim M. Phillips and Barry Reay, 407–420 (New York: Routledge, 2002); Mary Beltrán, "The Hollywood Latina Body as Site of Social Struggle: Media Constructions of Stardom and Jennifer Lopez's 'Cross-over Butt,'" *Quarterly Review of Film and Video* 19, no. 1 (January–March 2002); Isabel Molina-Guzmán and Angharad Valdivia, "Brain, Brow or Bootie: Iconic Latinas in Contemporary Popular Culture," *The Communication Review* 7, no. 2 (April–June 2004); Frances Negrón-Muntaner, "Jennifer's Butt," *Aztlán* 22, no. 2 (2000).

2. Paul D. Colford, "J.Lo: Cover Queen Singer's Life Saga Sells Mags," *New York Daily News*, December 30, 2004.

3. *Jennifer Lopez*, Forbes.com, 2005 [accessed December 19, 2008]; available from http://www.forbes.com/lists/2005/53/X5GN.html; *Jennifer Lopez*. Forbes.com, 2007 [accessed December 19, 2008]; available from http://www.forbes.com/2007/01/17/richest-women-entertainment-tech-media-cz_lg_richwomen07_0118womenstars_slide_10.html.

4. Teresa Wiltz, "Booty Boon: Jennifer Lopez's Backside Makes an Impression on the Nation's Cultural Landscape," *Chicago Tribune*, October 15, 1998.

5. Richard Dyer, *Heavenly Bodies: Film Stars and Society* (New York: St. Martin's Press, 1986).

6. Beltrán, "The Hollywood Latina Body as Site of Social Struggle"; Christine Gledhill, *Stardom: Industry of Desire* (London Routledge, 1991).

7. Beltrán, "The Hollywood Latina Body as Site of Social Struggle," 72.

8. Larry Gross, *Contested Closets: The Politics and Ethics of Outing* (Minneapolis: University of Minnesota Press, 1993).

9. S. Elizabeth Bird, *For Enquiring Minds: A Cultural Study of Supermarket Tabloids*, 1st ed. (Knoxville: University of Tennessee Press, 1992).

10. Beltrán, "The Hollywood Latina Body as Site of Social Struggle"; Dyer, *Heavenly Bodies*; Gledhill, *Stardom*.

11. Aparicio, "Jennifer as Selena"; Beltrán, "The Hollywood Latina Body as Site of Social Struggle"; Coco Fusco, *English Is Broken Here: Notes on Cultural Fusion in the Americas* (New York: New Press, 1995); Negrón-Muntaner, "Jennifer's Butt."

12. In this chapter I use the terms *elite* and *mainstream* press to characterize the mainstream news media that define their journalistic activities as more newsworthy and therefore more legitimate and culturally significant than other forms, such as tabloid journalism. Mainstream news thus refers to mainstream English- and Spanish-language news organizations such as the *New York Times*, the *Miami Herald*, ABC News, *La Opinión*, and Univisión.

13. For instance, Bird interviewed Cliff Linedecker, a *National Enquirer* editor who worked as a reporter for the *Philadelphia Inquirer* (82), and Ruth Annan, a 16-year veteran of *Time* magazine who headed up the research department at the *National Enquirer* (93). For a detailed discussion of tabloid journalistic practices, see Bird, *For Enquiring Minds*, 79–106.

14. Ibid., 91.

15. Television perhaps best illustrates the convergence between news and entertainment. An excellent example of this content convergence is the much-covered relationship between Jennifer Lopez and Ben Affleck. For example, a BBC News story cited an ABC television news story announcing the engagement. *J-Lo Confirms Affleck Engagement.* BBC News, November 11, 2002 [accessed February 11, 2008]; available from http://news.bbc.co.uk/1/hi/entertainment/showbiz/2439307.stm. For the original ABC story, see Diane Sawyer, "Primetime Live J.Lo," *Primetime Live,* anchor Charles Gibson, ABC, November 13, 2002. A December 17, 2003, "Barbara Walter's Special" on "The 10 Most Fascinating People of 2003" also documented the couple's domestic life. Further evidence of the blurring between "mainstream" and tabloid news was an extended 2003 interview between the couple and Pat O'Brien, then anchor of *Access Hollywood,* a syndicated celebrity news show owned by NBC Universal. Not only was the interview used exhaustively on *Access Hollywood,* the much-touted "get" was aired on NBC's prime-time news show, *Dateline NBC.* See Pat O'Brien, "Ben and Jen; Ben Affleck and Jennifer Lopez Discuss Their Lives, Careers and Upcoming Marriage," *Dateline NBC,* anchor Stone Phillips, July 17, 2003. In 2004, CNN mentioned their breakup. See Anderson Cooper, "Jennifer Lopez and Ben Affleck Break Up," *Anderson Cooper 360 Degrees,* CNN, January 22, 2004. CNN also posted a long Associated Press story about the breakup on its Web site the next day. See *Lopez Announces Split from Affleck,* CNN, January 23, 2004 [accessed February 11, 2008]; available from http://www.cnn.com/2004/SHOWBIZ/01/22/affleck.lopez.ap/index.html. Even the *New York Times* got in on the story. See Adam Sternbergh, "The Year in Ideas; Flirtation by Full-Page Ad," *New York Times,* December 15, 2002.

16. Stuart Hall et al., *Policing the Crisis: Mugging, the State, and Law and Order* (New York: Holmes & Meier, 1978), 53.

17. Bird, *For Enquiring Minds*; Richard Campbell, *60 Minutes and the News: A Mythology for Middle America* (Urbana: University of Illinois Press, 1991); Martin Conboy, *The Press and Popular Culture* (Thousand Oaks, CA: Sage, 2002); Peter Dahlgren and Colin Sparks, eds., *Journalism and Popular Culture* (Thousand Oaks, CA: Sage, 1992); John Fiske, *Television Culture* (New York: Methuen, 1987); Gaye Tuchman, *Making News: A Study in the Construction of Reality* (New York: Free Press, 1978).

18. Bird, *For Enquiring Minds,* 67.

19. Joshua Gamson, *Claims to Fame: Celebrity in Contemporary America* (Berkeley: University of California Press, 1994), 98.

20. For an example of how Angelina Jolie negotiates access and publicity with entertainment journalists, see Brooks Barnes, "Story Behind the Cover Story: Angelina Jolie and Her Image," *New York Times,* November 21, 2008.

21. Allan Bell and Peter Garrett, eds., *Approaches to Media Discourse* (Oxford: Blackwell, 1998); S. Elizabeth Bird and Robert W. Dardenne, "Myth, Chronicle, and Story: Exploring the Narrative Qualities of News," in *Media, Myths, and Narratives: Television and the Press,* ed. James W. Carey, 67–86 (Newbury Park, CA.: Sage, 1988); Norman Fairclough, *Media Discourse* (New York: E. Arnold, 1995); Stuart Hall, ed., *Representation: Cultural Representations and Signifying Practices* (Thousand Oaks, CA: Sage in association with the Open University, 1997); David Thorburn, "Television as an Aesthetic Media," in *Media, Myths and Narratives: Television and the Press,* ed. James Carey, 48–66 (Newbury Park, CA: Sage, 1988); Tuchman, *Making News*; Barbie Zelizer, "Achieving Journalistic Authority through Narrative," *Critical Studies in Mass Communication* 7, no. 1 (1990).

22. Fiske, *Television Culture*, 58.

23. *Average Total Paid and Verified Circulation for Top 100 ABC Magazines*, Magazine Publishers of America, 2007 [accessed January 25, 2009]; available from http://www. magazine.org/CONSUMER_MARKETING/CIRC_TRENDS/26643.aspx.

24. *In Touch Media Kit*. in Touch Weekly 2008 [accessed January 26, 2009]; available from http://www.bauerpublishing.com/ITW/ITW_mk/ITW-MK-EMAIL.pdf; *People 2008 Rate Card*. People 2008 [accessed January 26, 2009]; available from ftp://ftp.timeinc.net/pub/people/mediakit/pdfs/ratecard.pdf.

25. Fiske, *Television Culture*.

26. Ian Connell, "Personalities in the Popular Media," in *Journalism and Popular Culture*, ed. Peter Dahlgren and Colin Sparks, 64–83 (London: Sage Publications, 1992).

27. Gamson, *Claims to Fame*, 190.

28. Ibid., 146.

29. Bird, *For Enquiring Minds*, 129.

30. *Us Weekly Demographics*, SRDS Media Solutions, 2008 [accessed December 19, 2008]; available from http://www.srds.com/mediakits/us_weekly/demographics.html.

31. For circulation, demographic, and advertising information about the five tabloids, see *In Touch Media Kit*; *National Enquirer Media Kit*, National Enquirer, 2007 [accessed January 26, 2009]; available from http://www.americanmediainc.com/mediakits/ne/pdf/ne_mediakit_all.pdf; *People 2008 Rate Card*; *Star: Why Star*, Star, 2008 [accessed January 26, 2009]; available from http://www.americanmediainc.com/mediakits/star/pdfs/star_mediakit.pdf; *Us Weekly Demographics*.

32. Jillian M. Báez, "Speaking of Jennifer Lopez: Discourses of Iconicity and Identity Formation among Latina Audiences," *Media Report to Women* 35, no. 1 (Winter 2007).

33. Gamson, *Claims to Fame*, 58.

34. Jim Farber, "The High 'J.Lo' Country: Two No. 1s Jennifer Tops Music, Movie Charts," *New York Daily News*, February 1, 2001.

35. The 2004 salary figure was for the movie *Shall We Dance?* See *Jennifer Lopez Star Bio*. Tribute Entertainment Media Group, [accessed December 19, 2008]; available from http://www.tribute.ca/people/JenniferLopez/1526.

36. On March 25, 2008, MSN.com ranked Lopez as the fourth most searched female celebrity on MSN UK and Live.com over the previous six months. See *MSN Hotlist Presents: Top 100 Most Searched for Women*. uk.msn.com [accessed March 25, 2008]; available from http://hotlist.uk.msn.com/2007/top-100-women-2008.aspx.

37. Barrera, "Hottentot 2000"; Beltrán, "The Hollywood Latina Body as Site of Social Struggle."

38. Javier Castaño, "Los Boricuas Desafiaron La Lluvia Durante Su Desfile," *El Diario La Prensa*, June 15, 1998.

39. Beatriz Barvelo, "Con Sabor Latino: Jennifer Lopez, Enrique Iglesias, Ricky Martin Y Carlos Santana Figuran En La Lista De Nominados De Los American Music Awards Que Se Celebrara El 17 De Enero," *La Opinión*, December 7, 1999.

40. Negrón-Muntaner, "Jennifer's Butt."

41. Andrew Hindes, "WB Targets Untapped Demo with Its 'Selena,'" *Variety*, March 17, 1997.

42. Anna Marie De La Fuente, "Battle of the 'Betty' Beauties," *Variety*, October 9, 2006.

43. *Selena*. Box Office Mojo [accessed April 4, 2008]; available from http://www.boxofficemojo.com/movies/?id=selena.htm.

44. Arlene M. Dávila, *Latinos, Inc.: The Marketing and Making of a People* (Berkeley: University of California Press, 2001); Marilyn Halter, *Shopping for Identity: The Marketing of Ethnicity* (New York: Schocken Books, 2000).

45. Molina-Guzmán and Valdivia, "Brain, Brow or Bootie."

46. *Shall We Dance?* Box Office Mojo [accessed February 13, 2008]; available from http://www.boxofficemojo.com/movies/?id=shallwedance.htm.

47. The worldwide box office gross for *El Cantante* was just under $8 million. *El Cantante*, Box Office Mojo [accessed January 1, 2009]; available from http://www.boxofficemojo.com/movies/?id=elcantante.htm.

48. Negrón-Muntaner, "Jennifer's Butt," 189.

49. *The Hispanic Population in the United States: 2004*. U.S. Census, 2004 [accessed July 22, 2007]; available from http://www.census.gov/population/socdemo/hispanic/ASEC2004/2004CPS_tab1.2a.pdf.

50. María Lugones, *Pilgrimages = Peregrinajes: Theorizing Coalition against Multiple Oppressions* (Lanham, MD: Rowman & Littlefield, 2003).

51. Michel Foucault, *Discipline and Punish: The Birth of the Prison*, 2nd Vintage Books ed. (New York: Vintage Books, 1995).

52. Troy Patterson, "Rock Frock: Double Sided Tape Was This Fly Girl's Best Friend," *Entertainment Weekly*, December 19, 2000 [accessed December 19, 2008]; available from http://www.ew.com/ew/article/0,,92259,00.html

53. Marie Redding, "Too Haute to Handle: Six Designers Give Jennifer Lopez Tips on How to Dress for Oscar-Night Success," *New York Daily News*, March 16, 2000.

54. Kathleen Tracy, *Jennifer Lopez* (Toronto: ECW Press, 2000). The quoted material is text from the publisher posted on the Amazon.com Web site. See http://www.amazon.com/Jennifer-Lopez-Kathleen-Tracy/dp/1550224190 (accessed January 26, 2009).

55. Garth Pearce, "Livin' La Vida Lopez," *The Sunday Times (London)*, April 1, 2001. The subhead for the story read: "Hollywood diva, pampered pop star, Catholic good girl? Will the real Jennifer Lopez please stand up?"

56. Celine Parreñas Shimizu, *The Hypersexuality of Race: Performing Asian/American Women on Screen and Scene* (Durham, NC: Duke University Press, 2007).

57. Beltrán, "The Hollywood Latina Body as Site of Social Struggle," 79. In using the concept of the "white gaze," Beltrán borrows from the work of Manthia Diawara and bell hooks. See Manthia Diawara, "Black Spectatorship: Problems of Identification and Resistance," in *Black American Cinema*, ed. Manthia Diawara, 211–220 (New York: Routledge, 1993); bell hooks, *Black Looks: Race and Representation* (Boston, MA: South End Press, 1992).

58. Pearce, "Livin' La Vida Lopez."

59. Julie K. L. Dam et al., "September Song: Jennifer Lopez and Cris Judd Tie the Knot, Then Do What They Do Best: Dance All Night," *People*, October 15, 2001, 113.

60. Ibid., 112.

61. Michelle Tauber et al., "J. Lo Goes It Alone," *People*, June 24, 2002, 141.

62. Jim Farber, "Low Marks for Lopez: Diva's Disk Lacks 'Vida,'" *New York Daily News*, January 21, 2001.

63. Lia Haberman, *J.Lo Fires and Hires.* E! Online, June 17, 2003 [accessed December 19, 2008]; available from http://www.moviefinder.com/uberblog/b45344_jlo_fires_hires.html.

64. Martin Gould, "J.Lo Lesbian Sex Shocker: Romp Caught on Tape," *Star*, February 5, 2002. The main cover headline read: "J.Lo gay sex tape scandal: Star weeps over home video shocker." A similar story also appeared in the *National Enquirer* on June 5, 2002.

65. Ellen Goodstein, Rick Egusquiza, and Patricia Towie, "Puffy's Sex Tape Wrecks J.Lo Marriage . . . Pals Say," *National Enquirer*, June 25, 2002, 4. A small cover headline read: "J.Lo Divorce: Secret sex tape drove husband over edge."

66. With an estimated budget of $54 million, the much-panned *Gigli* only brought in about $7.3 million worldwide. See *Gigli*, Box Office Mojo [accessed January 2, 2009]; available from http://www.boxofficemojo.com/movies/?id=gigli.htm. The budget figure was from the IMDb Web site. See http://www.imdb.com/title/tt0299930/business (accessed January 2, 2009).

67. This analysis is not meant to discount potential queer audience readings of the story but rather to highlight the story's moral journalistic tone.

68. Elisa Lipsky-Karasz, "J.Lo & Ben vs. Gwyneth & Chris: With Exes Ben and Gwyn in the Arms of Others, Could Their Love Lives Be Less Alike?" *Us Weekly*, March 17, 2003.

69. Ken Baker and Jeremy Helligar, "Cris Judd: Life with & without J.Lo," *Us Weekly*, March 31, 2003. The main cover headline read: "J.Lo & Me: The truth about our marriage: The proposal, the gifts, the wild times. J.Lo's ex-husband reveals the intimate details of their roller-coaster life together." Russell Scott Smith, "J. Lo—CEO," *Us Weekly*, June 10, 2002. The main cover headline read: "J. Lo Answers—What's Rumor? What's Real? Is the marriage working? Was she emotionally abused? Is she *really* a diva? PLUS: Her 6 have-it-all secrets."

70. Ojani Noa, "The Nasty Real J.Lo: Sex Crazed . . . Selfish . . . Cruel," *Star*, December 10, 2002. The small cover headline read: "PLUS! Her first hubby tells all to *Star*."

71. Ibid., 17.

72. Joal Ryan, *Lopez, Affleck: For Real!* E! Online, November 11, 2002 [accessed December 19, 2008]; available from http://www.eonline.com/uberblog/b44157_Lopez__Affleck__For_Real_.html.

73. Leon Wagener, Bob Smith, and J.D. Robinson, "J.Lo Reads Ben His Rights: Pre-Nup Lays Down the Law on Sex, Cash—Even Cheating," *Star*, December 10, 2002. The main cover headline read: "J.Lo drops pre-nup bombshell on Ben! Insiders reveal . . . her rules: CHEATING: $5 million fine SEX: At least 4 times a week KIDS: As many as she wants."

74. For an example of positive tabloid coverage surrounding Julia Roberts, see Bob Michals et al., "Julia Roberts Bombshell! She's Visiting Fertility Clinic," *Star*, December 31, 2002. The secondary cover headline read: "Julia Roberts baby! Secret visit to fertility clinic." For an example of positive tabloid coverage surrounding Angelina Jolie, see Aimee Agresti, "Brad & Angelina Are Adopting!" *Us Weekly*, July 18, 2005. The main cover headline read: "They're adopting: They just applied to adopt a baby in Ethiopia. How Brad and Angelina are more serious than you think."

75. Jennifer Pearson, Maggie Harbour, and Roger Hitts, "J.Lo & Ben Blowup! Valentine's Day Wedding Is Off," *Star*, December 31, 2002, 20. The main cover headline read: "J.Lo and Ben put wedding on hold!—after bitter blowup."

76. Michals et al., "Julia Roberts Bombshell!" 31.

77. O'Brien, "Ben and Jen." The *Dateline NBC* segment was a shortened version of the extensive interview originally shown on NBC Universal's syndicated entertainment news show, *Access Hollywood*.

78. Aisha S. Durham and Jillian M. Báez, "A Tail of Two Women: Exploring the Contours of Difference in Popular Culture," in *Curriculum and the Cultural Body*, ed. Stephanie Springgay and Debra Freedman, 131–147 (New York: Peter Lang Publishing, 2007).

79. Michelle Tauber et al., "Destiny's Darling," *People*, August 12, 2002.

80. See Rick Egusquiza et al., "Demi & Ashton's Hot New Romance," *Star*, June 17, 2003. The cover's dominant headline read: "Demi's red hot affair—she falls in love with Ashton Kutcher." The cover also featured a smaller headline that read: "J.Lo's jealous frenzy—over Ben and Uma Thurman." Also see "Jennifer Aniston's a True Friend Indeed," *Star*, June 17, 2003.

81. "How Jennifer Won over Ben's Mom," *Star* magazine, May 25, 2005 [accessed April 9, 2008]; available from http://www.starmagazine.com/news/670?print=1.

82. Jeff Samuels and Marcia Scott Harrison, "Ben & Jen Trying for a Baby!" *Star* Magazine, May 3, 2005 [accessed December 19, 2008]; available from http://www.starmagazine.com/news/1262.

83. Sean Gannon, "Bed Rules for Ben & Jen," *Star* magazine, October 11, 2005 [accessed December 19, 2008]; available from http://www.starmagazine.com/news/5544.

84. Brenda You et al., "Ben Forces J.Lo Makeover: She's Fixin' Vixen Image," *Star*, July 1, 2003.

85. Haberman, *J.Lo Fires and Hires.*

86. Kate Stroup, "When Will He Marry Her?" *Us Weekly*, February 2, 2004; You et al., "Ben Forces J.Lo Makeover."

87. "Stepping out Alone: Are J.Lo and Ben Putting the Brakes on Their Wedding?" *in Touch*, June 2, 2003. The cover with a dominant photo of Ben and J.Lo featured a headline that read: "Wedding on hold! The real story behind the sudden change." Tom Gliatto et al., "Under Pressure," *People*, August 18, 2003. The main cover headline read: "Is the wedding still on? J.Lo and Ben deal with a box office bomb and his strip club antics. Will their love survive?"

88. Michael Cohen, "J.Lo and Ben Fall out—Again!" *in Touch*, January 19, 2004. A small headline on the cover read: "J.Lo's desperate fight for Ben." Also see Stroup, "When Will He Marry Her?" The main cover headline read: "Where's the ring? Why Ben won't marry her: They're still in love, so what's the problem—and why was she with P. Diddy? Inside the couple's new decision not to say 'I do.'"

89. "Stepping out Alone," 15.

90. Mark Coleman et al., "J.Lo & Ben: Is It Finally Over?" *in Touch*, February 2, 2004.

91. *Ben Affleck: I Should Never Have Got Engaged to Jennifer Lopez.* fametastic, November 14, 2006 [accessed January 4, 2009]; available from http://fametastic.co.uk/archive/20061114/3325/ben-affleck-i-should-never-have-got-engaged-to-jennifer-lopez/. The Web posting cited the British celebrity magazine *Now* as its source for the interview.

92. Quotes such as "The subject of Brad and Angelina is still so raw that Jennifer admits seeing pictures of his new family hurts" affirm the construction of Aniston as victim. "Jen Shuts Brad Out," *in Touch*, March 13, 2006.

93. Bird, *For Enquiring Minds*, 151. In this passage, Bird quotes from Fiske, *Television Culture*, 187. For Bird's discussion of women readers, see *For Enquiring Minds*, 139–152.

94. Eric Olsen, *About Blogcritics*. Blogcritics Magazine, October 24, 2005 [accessed December 19, 2008]; available from http://blogcritics.org/archives/2005/10/24/094437. php.

95. Cameron McCarthy, *The Uses of Culture: Education and the Limits of Ethnic Affiliation* (New York: Routledge, 1998).

96. "Bad Blood over Club Fracas," *New York Post*, December 5, 2002.

97. Eric Olsen, *Ben "Addict"—J Lo "Freak."* Blogcritics Magazine, December 5, 2002 [accessed January 28, 2009]; available from http://blogcritics.org/archives/2002/12/05/123457.php For the original *New York Post* story, see "Bad Blood over Club Fracas."

98. bookofjoe, *J-Lo Fired by Louis Vuitton for Stealing*. Blogcritics magazine, December 14, 2003 [accessed June 15, 2007]; available from http://blogcritics.org/archives/2003/12/14/091910.php.

99. Shantell Fletcher, comment posted March 9, 2005, http://blogcritics.org/archives/2003/12/14/091910.php (accessed January 28, 2009).

100. Don't Trip, comment posted December 31, 2005, http://blogcritics.org/archives/2003/12/14/091910.php (accessed February 15, 2008).

101. Juan Perez, comment posted March 11, 2006, http://blogcritics.org/archives/2003/12/14/091910.php (accessed January 5, 2009).

102. Dave Nalle, comment posted March 9, 2005, http://blogcritics.org/archives/2003/12/14/091910.php (accessed February 15, 2008).

103. Eric Olsen, *"Bennifer" History*. Blogcritics Magazine, January 23, 2004 [accessed February 15, 2008]; available from http://blogcritics.org/archives/2004/01/23/130126.php.

104. WK, comment posted September 26, 2004, http://blogcritics.org/archives/2004/01/23/130126.php (accessed January 4, 2009).

105. perineal, comment posted February 2, 2004, http://blogcritics.org/archives/2004/01/23/130126.php (accessed February 15, 2008).

106. Doc, comment posted January 23, 2004, http://blogcritics.org/archives/2004/01/23/130126.php (accessed February 15, 2008).

107. Dawn, comment posted January 23, 2004, http://blogcritics.org/archives/2004/01/23/130126.php (accessed February 15, 2008); Natalie, comment posted August 18, 2005, http://blogcritics.org/archives/2003/12/14/091910.php (accessed February 15, 2008); danyell, comment posted November 11, 2005, http://blogcritics.org/archives/2003/12/14/091910.php (accessed February 15, 2008).

108. Bob, comment posted January 1, 2006, http://blogcritics.org/archives/2003/12/14/091910.php (accessed February 15, 2008).

109. Adrian, comment posted November 6, 2005, http://blogcritics.org/archives/2003/12/14/091910.php (accessed February 15, 2008). See also Jr., comment posted August 6, 2005, http://blogcritics.org/archives/2003/12/14/091910.php (accessed February 15, 2008); Tha Truth, comment posted October 28, 2005, http://blogcritics.org/archives/2003/12/14/091910.php (accessed February 15, 2008).

110. Báez, "Speaking of Jennifer Lopez."

111. John Bambeneck, comment posted August 6, 2005, http://blogcritics.org/archives/2003/12/14/091910.php (accessed October 22, 2008).

112. Connell, "Personalities in the Popular Media," 73–74.

113. Gledhill, *Stardom*. For a more specific discussion of the ideological struggles surrounding Latinidad, see Beltrán, "The Hollywood Latina Body as Site of Social Struggle"; María Elena Cepeda, "Shakira as the Idealized, Transnational Citizen: A Case Study of *Colombianidad* in Transition," *Latino Studies* 1, no. 2 (July 2003).

114. Gina Pérez discusses the race and gender discrimination faced by Operation Bootstrap migrants during this era. See Gina M. Pérez, *The Near Northwest Side Story: Migration, Displacement, and Puerto Rican Families* (Berkeley: University of California Press, 2004).

115. Dyer, *Heavenly Bodies*.

116. "Jessica's the New Booty Queen," *in Touch*, September 4, 2006.

117. Mara Reinstein, "Jennifer's Pregnant," *Us Weekly*, October 22, 2007.

118. Erin Bried, "Doing It Right," *Self*, September, 2008; Charlotte Triggs, "J. Lo's Triathlon after Twins!" *People*, September 8, 2008.

119. Josef Adalian, "Lopez, Univisión in Unison on Drama," *Variety*, April 9, 2007 [accessed January 4, 2009]; available from http://www.variety.com/article/VR1117962769.html?categoryid=14&cs=1.

CHAPTER 3

1. Juana María Rodríguez, *Queer Latinidad: Identity Practices, Discursive Spaces* (New York: New York University Press, 2003), 11.

2. Gayatri Chakravorty Spivak, *In Other Worlds: Essays in Cultural Politics* (New York: Methuen, 1987).

3. Gareth Griffiths, "The Myth of Authenticity," in *The Post-Colonial Studies Reader*, ed. Bill Ashcroft, Gareth Griffiths, and Helen Tiffin, 237–241 (London, New York: Routledge, 1995).

4. For a discussion of the "authenticity" debates between and within Latina/o communities, see Coco Fusco, *English Is Broken Here: Notes on Cultural Fusion in the Americas* (New York: New Press, 1995).

5. A total of sixty-four stories published in U.S. Latina/o newspapers from 1997 through 2003 were collected using the terms *Hayek, Frida*, and *Hayek and Frida*. Of those, only news stories, features, and reviews dealing with the movie or Hayek's role in the making of the movie were analyzed. The resulting fifty-one stories included nine profiles of Hayek, eighteen *Frida* movie reviews, and twenty-four news stories about the production or reception of *Frida*. More than half the stories appeared in 2002, when seventeen reviews of the film were published.

6. All comments from Internet discussion boards are quoted as they appear on the Web sites.

7. The IMDb discussion thread was initiated by member xxxvidsring on July 21, 2003, with the last posting on December 28, 2004. During that time, 59 IMDb users posted 116 responses dealing with the film's representations of Mexican culture and broader issues of Mexican, Chicana/o, and Latina/o identity. The average number of postings per participant was two, with xxxvidsring posting the most responses at twenty-six. Twenty-three posters, including xxxvidsring, identified themselves as Mexican, Chicana/o, Mexican American, Latina/o, or Latin American. The remaining users did not identify themselves

explicitly by race or ethnicity. Although the identities of online participants are difficult to verify, at the very least they are people who are part of the public discourse about the movie, however limited their participation might be.

8. Hayden Herrera, *Frida, a Biography of Frida Kahlo*, 1st ed. (New York: Harper & Row, 1983). The biography is considered the canonical work on Kahlo. However, several scholars and popular critics challenged Herrera's construction of Kahlo's identity. See Rebecca Block and Lynda Hoffman-Jeep, "Fashioning National Identity: Frida Kahlo in 'Gringolandia,'" *Woman's Art Journal* 19, no. 2 (Autumn 1998); Irma Dosamentes-Beaudry, "Frida Kahlo: The Creation of a Cultural Icon," *The Arts in Psychotherapy* 29, no. 1 (2002); Sarah Kerr, "Viva Frida," *Vogue*, December, 2001.

9. Dosamentes-Beaudry, "Frida Kahlo: The Creation of a Cultural Icon"; Steven Volk, "Frida Kahlo Remaps the Nation," *Social Identities* 6, no. 2 (2000).

10. Julia Tuñón Pablos, *Women in Mexico: A Past Unveiled* (Austin: University of Texas, 1999); Volk, "Frida Kahlo Remaps the Nation."

11. Block and Hoffman-Jeep, "Fashioning National Identity"; Jean Franco, Mary Louise Pratt, and Kathleen E. Newman, eds., *Critical Passions: Selected Essays* (Durham, NC: Duke University Press, 1999); Margaret Lindauer, *Devouring Frida: The Art History and Popular Celebrity of Frida Kahlo* (Hanover, NH: Wesleyan University Press, 1999); Tuñón Pablos, *Women in Mexico*; Volk, "Frida Kahlo Remaps the Nation."

12. Lindauer, *Devouring Frida*; Volk, "Frida Kahlo Remaps the Nation."

13. Janis Bergman-Carton, "Strike a Pose: The Framing of Madonna and Frida Kahlo," *Texas Studies in Literature and Language* 35, no. 4 (Winter 1993); Seth Fein, "Film Reviews," *American Historical Review* 108, no. 4 (October 2003); Isabel Molina-Guzmán and Angharad Valdivia, "Brain, Brow or Bootie: Iconic Latinas in Contemporary Popular Culture," *Communication Review* 7, no. 2 (April–June 2004).

14. Norma Alarcón, Caren Kaplan, and Minoo Moallem, "Introduction: Between Woman and Nation," in *Between Woman and Nation: Nationalisms, Transnational Feminisms, and the State*, ed. Caren Kaplan, Norma Alarcón, and Minoo Moallem, 1–18 (Durham, NC: Duke University Press, 1999), 10.

15. Portions of this section were first published in Isabel Molina-Guzmán, "Mediating Frida: Negotiating Discourses of Latina/o Authenticity in Global Media Representations of Ethnic Identity," *Critical Studies in Media Communication* 23, no. 3 (August 2006); Isabel Molina-Guzmán, "Salma Hayek's *Frida*: Transnational Latina Bodies in Popular Culture," in *From Bananas to Buttocks: The Latina Body in Popular Film and Culture*, ed. Myra Mendible, 117–128 (Austin: University of Texas Press, 2007).

16. *Frida*, Box Office Mojo [accessed January 17, 2009]; available from http://www.boxofficemojo.com/movies/?page=intl&id=frida.htm.

17. Herrera received a writing credit for the movie, and a still from the movie now graces the most recent edition of the biography.

18. Toby Miller et al., *Global Hollywood* (London: British Film Institute, 2001).

19. Kevin Zimmerman, *Latin American Filmed Entertainment Market*. The Hollywood Reporter, February 21, 2005 [accessed August 20, 2007]; available from http://www.hollywoodreporter.com/hr/search/article_display.jsp?vnu_content_id=1000809514.

20. Arlene M. Dávila, *Latinos, Inc.: The Marketing and Making of a People* (Berkeley: University of California Press, 2001).

21. Michael Quintanilla, "Having Her Say," *Latina*, December, 2004, 120.

22. Christine Spines, "One from the Heart," *Premiere*, September, 2002, 40.

23. Ibid.

24. Quintanilla, "Having Her Say," 120.

25. Chris Holmlund, *Impossible Bodies: Femininity and Masculinity at the Movies* (London, New York: Routledge, 2002); Angharad Valdivia, *A Latina in the Land of Hollywood and Other Essays on Media Culture* (Tucson: University of Arizona Press, 2000).

26. Valdivia, *A Latina in the Land of Hollywood*.

27. Isis Sauceda, "Salma Le Dio La Bienvenida a 'Frida,'" *La Opinión*, October 16, 2002. The original text stated: "Como actriz, me gusta ser capaz de tener una voz y poder hablar de algo que me interesa. [Esta cinta] es una convicción. Una historia extraordinaria de una mujer extraordinaria. Valía la pena contar esta historia, que se desarrolla en un tiempo en que mi país era un lugar muy interesante. Aún lo es, pero es una parte de México con la cual la gente no está muy familiarizada. Así que me apasioné por contar la historia de los heroes con los que crecí, quise que el mundo supiera eso." For other examples of Hayek's use of language and authenticity, see the English-language articles Krista Smith, "An Irresistible Force," *Vanity Fair*, February, 2003; Spines, "One from the Heart"; Anne Stockwell, "The Velocity of Salma," *The Advocate*, December 10, 2002.

28. Julia Reynolds, "Las Dos Fridas: Hollywood's Long, Slow Race to Make the Definitive Frida Kahlo Film," *el Andar*, Summer 2001, 39.

29. Smith, "An Irresistible Force," 181.

30. René Rodríguez, "Imaginative Directing, Acting Illuminates Frida," *Hispanic Magazine*, October 2002, 38.

31. Griffiths, "The Myth of Authenticity."

32. Josefina López, personal interview, Paris, France, June 30, 2006.

33. Holmlund, *Impossible Bodies*.

34. Elana Levine, "Constructing a Market, Constructing an Ethnicity: U.S. Spanish-Language Media and the Formation of a Syncretic Latino/a Identity," *Studies in Latin American Popular Culture* 20 (2001): 45.

35. Dávila, *Latinos, Inc*; Marilyn Halter, *Shopping for Identity: The Marketing of Ethnicity* (New York: Schocken Books, 2000); Levine, "Constructing a Market, Constructing an Ethnicity"; América Rodríguez, *Making Latino News: Race, Language, Class* (Thousand Oaks, CA: Sage Publications, 1999).

36. Franco, Pratt, and Newman, eds., *Critical Passions*.

37. See Herrera, *Frida, a Biography of Frida Kahlo*; Anthony Lee, *Painting on the Left: Diego Rivera, Radical Politics, and San Francisco's Public Murals* (Berkeley: University of California Press, 1999); Tuñón Pablos, *Women in Mexico*.

38. Taymor's comments come from a 2001 question-and-answer session with Dezsö Magyar at the American Film Institute. This quote comes from a transcription by the author of the session, which is included as a special feature on the *Frida* DVD.

39. Herrera, *Frida, a Biography of Frida Kahlo*, 110.

40. René Rodríguez, "Salma: Living Free, Like Frida," *Hispanic Magazine*, October, 2002; "Salma Muestra Su Espíritu En Frida," *La Crónica de Hoy*, September 1, 2002.

41. See Herrera, *Frida, a Biography of Frida Kahlo*; Lee, *Painting on the Left*; Tuñón Pablos, *Women in Mexico*.

42. Taymor's quote comes from the 2001 question-and-answer session with Dezsö Magyar at the American Film Institute. It was included as a special feature on the *Frida* DVD.

43. Holmlund, *Impossible Bodies*.

44. Angharad Valdivia, "Community Building through Dance and Music: Salsa in the Midwest," in *Double Crossings: Entrecruzamientos*, ed. Mario Martín Flores and Carlos von Son, 153–176 (Fair Haven, NJ: Ediciones Nuevo Espacio, 2001).

45. Holmlund, *Impossible Bodies*.

46. Fein, "Film Reviews."

47. Franco, Pratt, and Newman, eds., *Critical Passions*, 43.

48. Serafín Méndez-Méndez and Diane Alverio, *Network Brownout 2002: The Portrayal of Latinos in Network Television News, 2001*. Washington, DC: National Association of Hispanic Journalists, 2002, 3.

49. Daniela Montalvo and Joseph Torres, *Network Brownout Report 2006: The Portrayal of Latinos & Latino Issues in Network Television News, 2005*. Washington, DC: National Association of Hispanic Journalists, 2006, 4.

50. Alison R. Hoffman and Chon A. Noriega, *Looking for Latino Regulars on Prime-Time Television: The Fall 2004 Season* (No. 4). Los Angeles: UCLA Chicano Studies Research Center (December 2004), 2.

51. Carl DiOrio, "SAG: Minority Actors See Gains," *The Hollywood Reporter*, October 30, 2007; Dave McNary, "WGA Issues Minority Report," *Daily Variety*, May 9, 2007; Carlina Rodríguez, *Remarks before FCC Public Hearing on Media Ownership*. Screen Actors Guild, 2007 [accessed January 28, 2008]; available from http://www.sag.org/files/documents/CRodriguezFCCTmny043007.pdf.

52. Eva Sanchis, "Salma Hayek Defiende Su Pelicula *Frida*," *El Diario La Prensa*, October 25, 2002.

53. Although the movie's negative reception in Mexico barely made the pages of U.S. Latina/o newspapers, it did seep into the Latina/o television news through such popular programs as *Noticiero Univisión* and *El Gordo y La Flaca*.

54. Viviana Rojas, "The Gender of Latinidad: Latinas Speak About Hispanic Television," *Communication Review* 7, no. 2 (April–June 2004).

55. ErikaP22, "Re: WRONG! Not another case of the 'prostitution of mexican culture," comment posted September 4, 2003, http://www.imdb.com/title/tt0120679/board/flat/2391685 (accessed February 14, 2005).

56. In *Making Latino News*, Rodríguez discusses the transnational imperative of most U.S. Latina/o news media to cater to U.S. Latina/o audiences with nostalgic and familiar connections to their countries of origin.

57. Rene Jordan, "Frida, De Julie Taymor El Color De La Pasión," *El Nuevo Herald*, November 7, 2002. All of the translations from Spanish to English are the author's. The original Spanish text read: "Este fue el proyecto que, por enorme suerte, se le malogró a Madonna. Después, Laura San Giacomo y Jennifer López se mencionaron como candidatas, pero a Hayek, com o mexicana, le iba de orgullo interpretar a su compatriota."

58. Sauceda, "Salma Le Dio La Bienvenida a 'Frida.'" In this *La Opinión* article, Hayek emphasizes her identification with Mexico by stressing the importance of "telling this story, which develops during a Mexican era in which my country was a very interesting place. Actually, it still is, but this is a part of Mexico that few people know about. So I was very passionate about telling the story of the heroes that I grew up with. I wanted the world to know."

59. Latina/o media are produced in English and Spanish for the primary consumption of Latina/o audiences.

60. César Huerta and Omar Cabrera, "Frida, Muy Mexicana," *Reforma*, August 1, 2002; "Salma Muestra Su Espíritu En Frida."

61. Néstor García Canclini, *Consumers and Citizens: Globalization and Multicultural Conflicts* (Minneapolis: University of Minnesota Press, 2001).

62. AlexThomas17, "Re: Ignorance of Mexican Culture," comment posted July 26, 2003, http://www.imdb.com/title/tt0120679/board/flat/2391685 (accessed February 14, 2005).

63. cheapdate, "Re: (how sad, cheapdate)," comment posted November 27, 2003, http://www.imdb.com/title/tt0120679/board/flat/2391685 (accessed February 14, 2005).

64. FLuMpKiNz, "Re: Ignorance of Mexican Culture," comment posted August 4, 2003, http://www.imdb.com/title/tt0120679/board/flat/2391685 (accessed February 14, 2005).

65. Kielbaso, "Re: Ignorance of Mexican Culture," comment posted August 6, 2003, http://www.imdb.com/title/tt0120679/board/flat/2391685 (accessed February 14, 2005).

66. Judd Tully, "The Kahlo Cult," *ARTnews* 93, no. 4 (April 1994). Olmedo, reportedly one of Rivera's last lovers, was named by him as the trustee of the Diego Rivera Foundation. The Frida Kahlo Museum is part of the Rivera Foundation. Olmedo died in 2005.

67. *Frida*, Box Office Mojo [accessed January 17, 2009]; available from http://www.boxofficemojo.com/movies/?page=intl&id=frida.htm.

68. *El Crimen Del Padre Amaro*, Box Office Mojo [accessed January 17, 2009]; available from http://www.boxofficemojo.com/movies/?page=intl&id=elcrimendelpadreamaro.htm; *Harry Potter and the Chamber of Secrets*, Box Office Mojo [accessed January 17, 2009]; available from http://www.boxofficemojo.com/movies/?page=intl&id=harrypotter2.htm; *The Lord of the Rings: The Two Towers*, Box Office Mojo [accessed January 17, 2009]; available from http://www.boxofficemojo.com/movies/?page=intl&id=twotowers.htm.

69. "Acusan a Salma De Racismo," *Reforma*, October 9, 2002; "Salma Hayek, Racista: Mexica Movement," *La Crónica de Hoy*, October 8, 2002. The Notimex wire service story was picked up by several other Mexico City newspapers.

70. "Salma Hayek, Racista: Mexica Movement."

71. Huerta and Cabrera, "Frida, Muy Mexicana." The original Spanish text read: "Frida es una pelicula gringa, no me importa, no es cine mexicano. Digo, no tiene nada que ver que esté Salma."

72. Omar Cabrera, "Dice Que Daña a Frida," *Reforma*, November 8, 2002; Guadalupe Loaeza, "Frida Made in USA," *Reforma*, November 7, 2002.

73. Solange García, "Con dudas sobre la fuerza con que Salma encarnó a Frida preparan en México la premier de la pelicula," *La Crónica de Hoy*, November 7, 2002. Con dudas sobre la fuerza con que Salma encarnó a Frida preparan en México la premier de la película (Novembre 7, 2002): The original Spanish text read: "Las primeras risas estallaron en la oscuridad, apenas unos minutos de iniciada la proyección. El motivo: el uso de palabras en espanol dentro un largomentraje filmado en ingles que hacia pensar en el famoso spanglis."

74. xxxvidsring, "Another case of the 'prostitution of mexican culture,'" comment posted July 21, 2003, http://www.imdb.com/title/tt0120679/board/flat/2391685 (accessed February 14, 2005).

75. Alma M. García, "Introduction," in *Chicana Feminist Thought: The Basic Historical Writings*, ed. Alma M. García, 1–20 (New York: Routledge, 1997).

76. xxxvidsring, "Re: Another case of the 'prostitution of mexican culture,'" comment posted August 3, 2003, http://www.imdb.com/title/tt0120679/board/flat/2391685 (accessed February 14, 2005).

77. Dosamentes-Beaudry, "Frida Kahlo: The Creation of a Cultural Icon"; Lindauer, *Devouring Frida*; Molina-Guzmán and Valdivia, "Brain, Brow or Bootie"; Volk, "Frida Kahlo Remaps the Nation."

78. Ella Shohat, "Introduction," in *Talking Visions: Multicultural Feminism in Transnational Age*, ed. Ella Shohat, 1–63 (Cambridge, MA: MIT Press, 1998), 24. The italics are in the original.

79. May Joseph, "Transatlantic Inscriptions: Desire, Diaspora, and Cultural Citizenship," in *Talking Visions: Multicultural Feminism in a Transnational Age*, ed. Ella Shohat, 357–359 (Cambridge, MA: MIT Press, 1998).

CHAPTER 4

1. Andrew Paxman and Felicia Levine, "Summit Spotlights Miami's Biz," *Daily Variety*, February 5, 1997.

2. Allison J. Waldman, "Hispanic Interests Move to Mainstream," *TelevisionWeek*, November 26, 2007.

3. Steve Clarke, "Rise of Telenovelas: U.S. Fare Gets Competition," *Variety*, February 16, 2006 [accessed March 5, 2008]; available from http://www.variety.com/article/VR1117938390.html?categoryid=14&cs=1.

4. Josef Adalian, "Nets Take a Novela Tack," *Variety*, February 6, 2006; Anna Marie De La Fuente, "Primetime Faves Fail to Translate En Español," *Variety*, October 10, 2005; Andrew Hindes, "WB Targets Untapped Demo with Its 'Selena,'" *Variety*, March 17, 1997; Paxman and Levine, "Summit Spotlights Miami's Biz."

5. John Tomlinson, "Globalisation and National Identity," in *Contemporary World Television*, ed. John Sinclair and Graeme Turner, 24–27 (London: BFI, 2004).

6. Timothy Havens, "'The Biggest Show in the World': Race and the Global Popularity of *The Cosby Show*," in *The Television Studies Reader*, ed. Robert Clyde Allen and Annette Hill, 442–456 (London and New York: Routledge, 2004).

7. Wayne Karrfalt, "A Novela Approach to Mainstream TV," *TelevisionWeek*, September 25, 2006.

8. O. Hugo Benavides, *Drugs, Thugs, and Divas: Telenovelas and Narco-Dramas in Latin America* (Austin: University of Texas Press, 2008), 212.

9. Arlene M. Dávila, *Latinos, Inc.: The Marketing and Making of a People* (Berkeley: University of California Press, 2001); Marilyn Halter, *Shopping for Identity: The Marketing of Ethnicity* (New York: Schocken Books, 2000).

10. Katy Bachman, *Univisión's KMEX Tops TV Stations Pack in '08*. Mediaweek, January 15, 2009 [accessed February 14, 2009]; available from http://www.mediaweek.com/mw/content_display/news/local-broadcast/e3i4b7a99706a1f6a0766e7969952d1dc13; James Hibberd, "Univisión Pitching Growth of Market," *TelevisionWeek*, May 14, 2007; Sergio Ibarra, *Univisión's KMEX-TV Dominates 18-49, Nielsen Says*. TVWeek, January 15, 2009

[accessed February 14, 2009]; available from http://www.tvweek.com/news/2009/01/uni-vision_affiliate_kmex_domin.php.

11. John Sinclair, "'The Hollywood of Latin America': Miami as Regional Center in Television Trade," *Television and New Media* 4, no. 3 (August 2003): 213.

12. Meg James, "Spanish TV Soap Opera Turns into Court Drama," *Los Angeles Times*, January 6, 2009; John Sinclair, *Latin American Television: A Global View* (Oxford: Oxford University Press, 1999).

13. Christopher Goodwin, "Latino TV Station Tops U.S. Ratings," *The Observer*, January 18, 2009.

14. Anna Marie De La Fuente, "'Ugly Betty' Grows into Swan around Globe," *Variety*, February 6, 2006.

15. Roland Soong, *The Phenomenon of Yo Soy Betty La Fea*. Zona Latina, July 1, 2001 [accessed February 4, 2009]; available from http://www.zonalatina.com/Zldata185.htm Soong cited IBOPE Media Information as his source.

16. Anna Marie De La Fuente, "Battle of the 'Betty' Beauties," *Variety*, October 9, 2006.

17. "'La Fea Más Bella' Scores Ratings Hit for Univisión," *USA Today*, June 27, 2007.

18. Maureen Ryan, *Silvio Horta on 'Ugly Betty': 'Write What You Know'*. chicagotribune. com, 2006 [accessed January 17, 2009]; available from http://featuresblogs.chicagotribune. com/entertainment_tv/2006/11/silvio_horta_on.html.

19. Adalian, "Nets Take a Novela Tack."

20. For a discussion of the global integration of television markets, see Edward S. Herman and Robert W. McChesney, *The Global Media: The New Missionaries of Corporate Capitalism* (London, Washington,DC: Cassell, 1997).

21. Kim Akass and Janet McCabe, *Not So Ugly: Local Production, Global Franchise, Discursive Femininities, and the Ugly Betty Phenomenon*, FlowTV, 2007 [accessed January 17, 2009]; available from http://flowtv.org/?p=74.

22. "2006–07 Primetime Wrap," *The Hollywood Reporter*, May 25, 2007; Charo Toledo, "Alphabet Spells Hope for Diverse America," *Daily Variety*, July 27, 2007; Waldman, "Hispanic Interests Move to Mainstream."

23. Jillian M. Báez, "Speaking of Jennifer Lopez: Discourses of Iconicity and Identity Formation among Latina Audiences," *Media Report to Women* 35, no. 1 (Winter 2007); Vicki Mayer, *Producing Dreams, Consuming Youth: Mexican Americans and Mass Media* (New Brunswick, NJ: Rutgers University Press, 2003); Viviana Rojas, "The Gender of Latinidad: Latinas Speak About Hispanic Television," *Communication Review* 7, no. 2 (April–June 2004).

24. Cristina Pieraccini and Douglass L. Alligood, *Color Television: Fifty Years of African American and Latino Images on Prime-Time Television* (Dubuque, IA: Kendall/Hunt, 2005).

25. Ibid.

26. "2006–07 Primetime Wrap"; Mary Elena Fernandez, "Stuck on 'Ugly': A Diverse Viewership Has Made 'Ugly Betty' the No. 1 New Show," *Los Angeles Times*, November 8, 2006.

27. William Booth, "Building 'Betty': How Did Silvio Horta Turn a Telenovela into Fall's Highest-Rated New Series? One Detail at a Time," *Washington Post*, October 22, 2006.

28. Ibid.

29. Kathy Lyford, 'Ugly Betty': 'We Always Want to Surprise Our Audience.' *Variety*, October 6, 2008 [accessed January 17, 2009]; available from http://weblogs.variety.com/season_pass/2008/10/q-what-did-dani.html.

30. Booth, "Building 'Betty.'"

31. Robert Bianco, "Likable 'Betty' Aided by a Lovable Lead," *USA Today*, September 28, 2006; Tim Goodman, "The Main Character May Not Be Pretty, but Her Show Is," *San Francisco Chronicle*, September 27, 2006; Virginia Heffernan, "A Plucky Guppy among the Barracudas," *New York Times*, September 28, 2006.

32. Chuck Barney, " 'Ugly Betty,' Premiering Thursday on ABC," *Contra Costa Times*, September 26, 2006; Bianco, "Likable 'Betty' Aided by a Lovable Lead"; David Bianculli, " 'Ugly Betty' Looks Pretty Good: Fun Redo of a Telenovela," *Daily News*, September 27, 2006; Mike Duffy, "ABC's 'Ugly Betty' Is Looking Good," *Detroit Free Press*, September 26, 2006; Matthew Gilbert, " 'Ugly Betty' Has Look of a Winner," *Boston Globe*, September 28, 2006; Goodman, "The Main Character May Not Be Pretty, but Her Show Is"; Heffernan, "A Plucky Guppy among the Barracudas"; Macarena Hernandez, "Beautiful 'Ugly': TV's New Betty Is Smart, Real and, Most Surprising, a Latina," *Dallas Morning News*, September 28, 2006; Cindy Rodríguez, " 'Ugly Betty' Brings a New Reality to TV," *Denver Post*, October 11, 2006; Jonathan Storm, "Betting on Betty," *The Philadelphia Inquirer*, September 28, 2006.

33. Tom Shales, "Look Homely, Angel: ABC's 'Ugly Betty' Is Plainly Lovable," *Washington Post*, September 28, 2006.

34. Maureen Ryan, *'Ugly Betty': Fall TV's Most Interesting Character.* chicagotribune.com, September 26, 2006 [accessed January 17, 2009]; available from http://featuresblogs.chicagotribune.com/entertainment_tv/2006/09/ugly_betty_fall.html.

35. Mike Parker, "Why Ugly Is the New Beautiful," *Sunday Express (London)*, January 7, 2007.

36. Goodman, "The Main Character May Not Be Pretty, but Her Show Is."

37. Rodríguez, "'Ugly Betty' Brings a New Reality to TV."

38. Frances R. Aparicio, "Jennifer as Selena: Rethinking Latinidad in Media and Popular Culture," *Latino Studies* 1, no. 1 (March 2003): 91.

39. Three reviews that pointed out the stilted use of stereotyped characters and stories in "Ugly Betty" are Bianco, "Likable 'Betty' Aided by a Lovable Lead"; Heffernan, "A Plucky Guppy among the Barracudas"; Rodríguez, "'Ugly Betty' Brings a New Reality to TV."

40. Rodríguez, "'Ugly Betty' Brings a New Reality to TV."

41. "Best of 2006: My Big Year," *TV Guide*, December 18–24, 2006, 14. For a discussion about Ferrera not fitting in, see Jenny Comita, "Hot Betty," *W Magazine*, May, 2007.

42. Comita, "Hot Betty," 167.

43. Ibid.

44. Ibid.

45. Joshua Gamson, *Claims to Fame: Celebrity in Contemporary America* (Berkeley: University of California Press, 1994).

46. All comments from blogs and Internet discussion boards are quoted as they appear on the Web sites, spelling and grammar left intact.

47. soapyee, "Is ugly betty ugly,ok,or beutiful??????," comment posted December 31, 2007, http://abc.go.com/primetime/uglybetty/index?pn=mb&cat=30895&tid=168604 (accessed March 5, 2008).

48. See whattheheckisthis222, "America Ferrera should stick with acting and stay out of politics," comment posted February 8, 2008, http://abc.go.com/primetime/uglybetty/index?pn=mb&cat=30895&tid=219254 (accessed March 5, 2008).

49. Transcription of the Golden Globe acceptance speech is by the author. The speech was highlighted in shows after the awards such as the January 15, 2007, broadcast of *Entertainment Tonight*, which identified Ferrera's acceptance speech as the highlight of the evening.

50. Olivia Ortiz, *An Open Letter to Ugly Betty's America Ferrera*. Women in Media and News, January 19, 2007 [accessed March 11, 2008]; available from http://www.wimnonline.org/WIMNsVoicesBlog/?p=397.

51. Lawrie Masterson, "Ugly Duckling Has Last Laugh," *The Sunday Mail (Australia)*, February 11, 2007.

52. Ibid.

53. Fernandez, "Stuck on 'Ugly.'"

54. Tom, "11 Ways I'm Like Our Favorite Ugly Betty Characters," comment posted February 27, 2008, http://www.uglybettynews.com/2008/02/27/11-ways-im-like-our-favorite-ugly-betty-characters/ (accessed February 2, 2009).

55. *Queens County Quick Facts*. U.S. Census Bureau, 2006 [accessed March 7, 2008]; available from http://quickfacts.census.gov/qfd/states/36/36081.html.

56. Paloma Dallas, "The Big Apple's Mexican Face," *Hispanic*, July–August, 2001.

57. Sut Jhally and Justin Lewis, *Enlightened Racism: The Cosby Show, Audiences, and the Myth of the American Dream* (Boulder, CO: Westview Press, 1992).

58. Herman Gray, *Watching Race: Television and the Struggle for 'Blackness'* (Minneapolis: University of Minnesota Press, 1995).

59. Havens, "'The Biggest Show in the World.'"

60. OLDROY43, "Racist Remark," comment posted October 4, 2007, http://abc.go.com/primetime/uglybetty/index?pn=mb&cat=30895&tid=14435 (accessed January 18, 2009). The original post didn't use the word *crackers* as Wilhelmina did on the show, only referring to her remark as "White _____."

61. Belladonna77, comment posted October 5, 2007, http://abc.go.com/primetime/uglybetty/index?pn=mb&cat=30895&tid=14435 (accessed January 21, 2009).

62. reality_blows, comment posted November 3, 2007, which started a discussion thread entitled "Gino Is An Offensive Token Character," on ABC's *Ugly Betty* message board, http://abc.go.com/primetime/uglybetty/index?pn=mb&cat=3089 (accessed March 2, 2008).

63. KrazyGlue2, comment posted November 4, 2007, in the "Gino Is An Offensive Token Character," discussion thread, http://abc.go.com/primetime/uglybetty/index?pn=mb&cat=3089 (accessed March 2, 2008).

64. See the discussion threads "Gio or Henry" started by carlybabes143 on February 7, 2008, http://abc.go.com/primetime/uglybetty/index?pn=mb&cat=30895&tid=217733 (accessed March 5, 2008); "Gio, Daniel, Henry" started by dazzled_green on January 17, 2008, http://abc.go.com/primetime/uglybetty/index?pn=mb&cat=30895&tid=189210 (accessed March 9, 2008); "Gio and Betty. Sorry, I just don't get it" started by Lost4GorhamAmI on January 27, 2008, http://abc.go.com/primetime/uglybetty/index?pn=mb&cat=30895&tid=198730 (accessed March 10, 2008); "Gio and Betty forever" started by lady30076 on January 5, 2008, http://abc.go.com/primetime/uglybetty/index?pn=mb&c

at=30895&tid=198462 (accessed March 10, 2008); "Is there any Gio love on this board?" started by wooster182 on January 16, 2008, http://abc.go.com/primetime/uglybetty/index?pn=mb&cat=30895&tid=188119 (accessed March 10, 2008).

65. justcozy, comment posted December 13, 2007, http://abc.go.com/primetime/uglybetty/index?pn=mb&cat=30895&tid=93342 (accessed March 5, 2008).

66. "Is anybody else still crying???" discussion thread started by lexis1818 on September 27, 2007, http://abc.go.com/primetime/uglybetty/index?pn=mb&cat=30895&tid=6833&tsn=1 (accessed March 30, 2008).

67. Michael Warner, "Introduction," in *Fear of a Queer Planet: Queer Politics and Social Theory*, ed. Michael Warner, vii–xxxi (Minnesota: University of Minnesota Press, 1994).

68. Fabio Cleto, ed., *Camp: Queer Aesthetics and the Performing Subject: A Reader* (Ann Arbor: University of Michigan Press, 1999).

69. Karrfalt, "A Novela Approach to Mainstream TV."

70. Michael Jensen, *'Ugly Betty' Is Freaking Fabulous (and Gay)*. After Elton, March 23, 2007 [accessed January 17, 2009]; available from http://www.afterelton.com/TV/2007/3/uglybetty.

71. Booth, "Building 'Betty.'"

72. Jonathan Bernstein, "Jonathan Bernstein's Aerial View of America," *The Guardian*, October 14, 2006.

73. Lyford, *'Ugly Betty': 'We Always Want to Surprise Our Audience.'*

74. For a report on the show's status in 2009, see Michael Ausiello, *Exclusive: 'Ugly Betty' Lives!* Entertainment Weekly, February 10, 2009 [accessed February 14, 2009]; available from http://ausiellofiles.ew.com/2009/02/exclusive-ugly.html; Scott Collins, "It's an Ugly Time for 'Betty,'" *Los Angeles Times*, January 27, 2009. For discussion of how to fix the show, see the *New York* magazine blog, "The Cut." *Fug Girls: Seven Ways to Revive Ugly Betty*. New York Magazine, January 29, 2009 [accessed February 12, 2009]; available from http://nymag.com/daily/fashion/2009/01/fug_girls_seven_ways_to_revive.html.

75. Richard T. Rodríguez, *Next of Kin: The Family in Chicano/a Cultural Politics* (Durham, NC: Duke University Press, 2009).

76. Jason Nelson, *There's Nothing a Little Mother's Love and Musical Theatre Can't Fix* Popnography, November 21, 2008 [accessed January 17, 2009]; available from http://www.popnography.com/2008/11/i-previously-me.html.

77. Mary Elena Fernandez, "Just the Way You Are: 'Ugly Betty's' Young Nephew Has Been Embraced by Those Who Don't 'Fit in,'" *Los Angeles Times*, January 31, 2007.

78. In 2008, Vanessa Williams received an award from the Human Rights Campaign. See Chris Johnson, *Vanessa Williams to Receive Ally for Equality Award at HRC New York Gala Dinner*. Human Rights Campaign, February 4, 2008 [accessed March 5, 2008]; available from http://www.hrcbackstory.org/2008/02/vanessa-willi-1.html. Also see Jeffrey Epstein, *Ladies' Night: We Hit West Hollywood's Gay Hotspots with Two of Ugly Betty's Beauties*. Out.com, April, 2007 [accessed March 5, 2008]; available from http://www.out.com/detail.asp?id=22358.

79. Jeffrey Epstein, *Pretty Ugly: Ugly Betty Was the Surprise Hit of Last Fall's Television Schedule* Out.com, April, 2007 [accessed March 5, 2008]; available from http://www.out.com/detail.asp?id=22276 The italics appear in the original.

80. Comita, "Hot Betty."

81. zazus001, comment posted January 31, 2008, http://abc.go.com/primetime/uglybetty/index?pn=mb&cat=30895&tid=203298 (accessed March 5, 2008).

82. Transcription of the January 15, 2007, Golden Globe acceptance speech is by the author.

83. jsolza, "Moving back in with the family?" comment posted February 6, 2009, http://abc.go.com/primetime/uglybetty/index?pn=mb&cat=30895&tid=560037 (accessed February 12, 2009).

CHAPTER 5

1. Isabel Molina-Guzmán and Angharad Valdivia, "Brain, Brow or Bootie: Iconic Latinas in Contemporary Popular Culture," *Communication Review* 7, no. 2 (April–June 2004).

2. *Prime Time for Latinos*, National Hispanic Foundation for the Arts (September 25, 2001).

3. The most recent exception on *Law and Order* is assistant district attorney Connie Rubirosa, a Latina secondary character played by Mexican-Irish American actor Alana De La Garza.

4. Jonathan Xavier Inda, "Biopower, Reproduction, and the Migrant Woman's Body," in *Decolonial Voices: Chicana and Chicano Cultural Studies in the 21st Century*, ed. Arturo J. Aldama and Naomi Helena Quiñonez, 98–112 (Bloomington: Indiana University Press, 2002).

5. Ella Shohat and Robert Stam, *Unthinking Eurocentrism: Multiculturalism and the Media* (New York: Routledge, 1994).

6. Arvind Rajagopal, "Communities Imagined and Unimagined: Contemporary Indian Variations on the Public Sphere," *Discourse* 21, no. 2 (Spring 1999).

7. Vivian Sobchack, "Postmodern Modes of Ethnicity," in *Unspeakable Images: Ethnicity in the American Cinema*, ed. Lester D. Friedman, 329–352 (Urbana: University of Illinois Press, 1991), 349.

8. Ella Shohat and Robert Stam, eds., *Multiculturalism, Postcoloniality, and Transnational Media* (New Brunswick, NJ: Rutgers University Press, 2003), 9.

9. Homi K. Bhabha, *The Location of Culture* (New York: Routledge, 2004).

10. Myra Mendible, "Introduction: Embodying Latinidad: An Overview," in *From Bananas to Buttocks: The Latina Body in Popular Film and Culture*, ed. Myra Mendible, 1–28 (Austin: University of Texas Press, 2007), 5.

11. Jorge Durand and Douglas S. Massey, "The Costs of Contradiction: U.S. Border Policy 1986–2000," *Latino Studies* 1, no. 2 (July 2003).

12. Lisa Lowe, "Work, Immigration, Gender: New Subjects of Cultural Politics," *Social Justice* 25, no. 3 (1998).

13. Jeffrey S. Passel and D'Vera Cohn, *Trends in Unauthorized Immigration: Undocumented Inflow Now Trails Legal Inflow*, Pew Hispanic Center (October 2, 2008).

14. Pierrette Hondagneu-Sotelo, *Doméstica: Immigrant Workers Cleaning and Caring in the Shadows of Affluence* (Berkeley: University of California Press, 2001); Alejandro Lazo, "Hispanic Immigrants Drop in U.S. Labor Force," *Washington Post*, December 16, 2008; Zaragosa Vargas, "Rank and File: Historical Perspectives on Latino/a Workers in the U.S.," in *The Latino Studies Reader: Culture, Economy, and Society*, ed. Antonia Darder and Rodolfo D. Torres, 243–256 (Malden, MA: Blackwell, 1998).

15. Gloria Anzaldúa, *Borderlands: The New Mestiza = La Frontera*, 1st ed. (San Francisco: Spinsters/Aunt Lute, 1987); Alejandro Lugo, "Reflections on Border Theory, Culture, and the Nation," in *Border Theory: The Limits of Cultural Politics*, ed. Scott Michaelsen and David E. Johnson, 43–67 (Minneapolis: University of Minnesota Press, 1997); José David Saldívar, *Border Matters: Remapping American Cultural Studies* (Berkeley: University of California Press, 1997).

16. Néstor García Canclini, *Hybrid Cultures: Strategies for Entering and Leaving Modernity* (Minneapolis: University of Minnesota Press, 1995).

17. Lisa M. Seghetti et al., *Border Security and the Southwest Border: Background, Legislation, and Issues.* Congressional Research Service (September 28, 2005).

18. Vargas, "Rank and File," 243.

19. Ibid., 252.

20. The Pew Hispanic Center report also illustrates that Latina/o immigrants are shifting their points of destination to the South and Midwest. See Jeffrey S. Passel, *Unauthorized Migrants: Numbers and Characteristics*, Washington, DC: Pew Hispanic Center (June 14, 2005).

21. Ibid.

22. Scott Baldauf, "U.S. Tries Spy Tactics to Stop Human Smugglers," *Christian Science Monitor*, August 30, 2000.

23. Passel, *Unauthorized Migrants*.

24. Ibid.

25. Saurav Sarkar, "The False Debate over 'Broken Borders,'" *Extra!* May/June, 2006.

26. Durand and Massey, "The Costs of Contradiction: U.S. Border Policy 1986–2000."

27. Claudia Smith, "Border Enforcement: Deadlier Than Ever and as Ineffective as Always," *Latino Studies* 2, no. 1 (April 2004).

28. Ibid., 112.

29. For a more detailed discussion of repatriation programs, see Seghetti et al., *Border Security and the Southwest Border*; Smith, "Border Enforcement: Deadlier Than Ever and as Ineffective as Always."

30. Seghetti et al., *Border Security and the Southwest Border*.

31. Durand and Massey, "The Costs of Contradiction: U.S. Border Policy 1986–2000"; Passel, *Unauthorized Migrants*.

32. Otto Santa Ana, *Brown Tide Rising: Metaphors of Latinos in Contemporary American Public Discourse*, 1st ed. (Austin: University of Texas Press, 2002).

33. See http://www.americanborderpatrol.com/.

34. Ana M. López, "Are All Latins from Manhattan?: Hollywood, Ethnography, and Cultural Colonialism," in *Unspeakable Images: Ethnicity and the American Cinema*, ed. Lester D. Friedman, 404–424 (Urbana: University of Illinois Press, 1991); Clara E. Rodríguez, *Heroes, Lovers, and Others: The Story of Latinos in Hollywood* (Washington, DC: Smithsonian Books, 2004), 82.

35. Maria Ruiz, "Border Narratives: HIV/AIDS, and Latina/o Health in the United States: A Cultural Analysis," *Feminist Media Studies* 2, no. 1 (March 2002).

36. BobDoughertyJr, "Re: Flor 5 years.cant speak a word of English," comment posted January 20, 2009, http://www.imdb.com/title/tt0371246/board/thread/127948165?d=128198 340&p=1#128198340 (accessed February 4, 2009).

37. See "why cant every latino learn english?" discussion thread started June 23, 2007, by duffman21215 with a one-word post, "porque?" http://www.imdb.com/title/tt0371246/board/thread/77713767?p=1 (accessed February 4, 2009).

38. For the purposes of this article, domestic work will encompass cleaning and caring labor conducted in public and private spaces.

39. L. S. Kim, "Invisible and Undocumented: The Latina Maid on Network Television," *Aztlán: A Journal of Chicano Studies* 24, no. 1 (Spring 1999): 109.

40. Arlie Russell Hochschild, "Love and Gold," in *Global Woman: Nannies, Maids, and Sex Workers in the New Economy*, ed. Barbara Ehrenreich and Arlie Russell Hochschild, 15–30 (New York: Metropolitan Books, 2003).

41. Hondagneu-Sotelo, *Doméstica*, 13.

42. Ibid., 15.

43. Prairie Miller, *Interview with Jennifer Lopez*. NY Rock, December, 2002 [accessed February 4, 2009]; available from http://www.nyrock.com/interviews/2002/lopez_int3.asp.

44. A. O. Scott, "Puttin' Down Mop, Puttin' on the Ritz," *New York Times*, December 13, 2002.

45. *Maid in Manhattan Synopsis*, Sony Pictures [accessed February 5, 2009]; available from http://www.sonypictures.com/homevideo/maidinmanhattan/title-navigation-2.html.

46. Roger Ebert, *Spanglish*. RogerEbert.com, December 17, 2004 [accessed February 4, 2009]; available from http://rogerebert.suntimes.com/apps/pbcs.dll/article?AID=/20041216/REVIEWS/41201005/1023.

47. See the discussion thread "Racism . . . the new product that Hollywood is selling," started with a posting by realreel on January 7, 2003, http://www.imdb.com/title/tt0252076/board/thread/526134 (accessed February 5, 2009).

48. Ibid.

49. Howlin Wolf, "Caucasian 'maid' falls in love with powerbroker and becomes manageress..," comment posted July 13, 2005, http://www.imdb.com/title/tt0252076/board/flat/526134?d=22388391&p=2#22388391 (accessed February 5, 2009).

50. pendong23, "Re: Racism . . . the new product that Hollywood is selling," comment posted June 22, 2005, http://www.imdb.com/title/tt0252076/board/thread/526134?d=21168910&p=1#21168910 (accessed February 5, 2009).

51. cpheonix, "Re: Racism . . . the new product that Hollywood is selling," comment posted June 24, 2005, http://www.imdb.com/title/tt0252076/board/thread/526134?d=21291683&p=1#21291683 (accessed February 5, 2009).

52. sparkling pink, "Re: Racism . . . the new product that Hollywood is selling," comment posted April 23, 2005, http://www.imdb.com/title/tt0252076/board/thread/526134?d=18298893&p=1#18298893 (accessed February 5, 2009).

53. Hondagneu-Sotelo, *Doméstica*, 146.

54. Ibid., 172.

55. Ibid., 13.

56. Ibid., 18.

57. Mary Romero, *Maid in the U.S.A*, 10th anniversary ed. (New York: Routledge, 2002).

58. Scott, "Puttin' Down Mop, Puttin' on the Ritz."

59. Hondagneu-Sotelo, *Doméstica*, 50.

60. For a discussion of the ways Latina immigrants are particularly targeted and policed by border patrol and health professionals, see Ruiz, "Border Narratives."

61. Sau-ling C. Wong, "Diverted Mothering: Representations of Caregivers of Color in the Age of 'Multiculturalism,'" in *Mothering: Ideology, Experience, and Agency*, ed. Evelyn Nakano Glenn, Grace Chang, and Linda Rennie Forcey, 67–91 (New York: Routledge, 1994), 69.

62. *A Day without a Mexican*, Box Office Mojo [accessed February 25, 2008]; available from http://www.boxofficemojo.com/movies/?id=daywithoutamexican.htm; *Fast Food Nation*, Box Office Mojo [accessed February 25, 2008]; available from http://www.boxofficemojo.com/movies/?id=fastfoodnation.htm; *Televisa Cine's 'A Day without a Mexican' Opens in 45 Additional Theaters Throughout the U.S.* Hispanic PR Wire, August 27, 2004 [accessed March 9, 2008]; available from http://hispanicprwire.com/news.php?cha=14&id=2831&l=in.

63. *Maid in Manhattan*, Box Office Mojo [accessed February 25, 2008]; available from http://www.boxofficemojo.com/movies/?id=maidinmanhattan.htm; *Spanglish*. Box Office Mojo [accessed February 25, 2008]; available from http://www.boxofficemojo.com/movies/?id=spanglish.htm.

CONCLUSION

1. For a sample of blogs critical of Jessica Alba's supposed denial of her Mexican heritage, see *Jessica 'Don't Call Me Latina' Alba*, New York Chique, May 16, 2008 [accessed February 15, 2009]; available from http://newyorkchique.blogspot.com/2008/05/jessica-dont-call-me-latina-alba.html; *Jessica Alba: Don't Call Me Latina!* Pop Culture Shock, July 2, 2007 [accessed February 15, 2009]; available from http://www.popcultureshock.com/blogs/jessica-alba-dont-call-me-latina/ and the "Jessica Alba 'Don't Call Me Latina' " discussion thread on The Purse Forum Web site, http://forum.purseblog.com/celebrity-section/jessica-alba-dont-call-me-latina-146055.html (accessed September 1, 2009). For a discussion of the inaccuracy of reports about Alba's denial of her Mexican heritage, see Mimi Valdés Ryan, *The Jessica Alba Controversy*, Latina, February 28, 2008 [accessed February 15, 2009]; available from http://www.latina.com/entertainment/jessica-alba-controversy?page=1.

2. Mimi Valdés Ryan, "Jessica Alba: 'I Want My Baby to Be Brown,'" *Latina*, March 2008.

3. Anne Barnard, "Latinos Recall Pattern of Attacks before Killing," *New York Times*, January 9, 2009.

4. Arjun Appadurai, "Disjuncture and Difference in the Global Cultural Economy," in *Theorizing Diaspora: A Reader*, ed. Jana Evans Braziel and Anita Mannur, 25–48 (Malden, MA: Blackwell, 2003), 33. The text from the epigraph at the beginning of this chapter also appears on page 33.

5. Magdalena Barrera, "Hottentot 2000: Jennifer Lopez and Her Butt," in *Sexualities in History: A Reader*, ed. Kim M. Phillips and Barry Reay, 407–420 (New York: Routledge, 2002); Martha Elizabeth Hodes, *Sex, Love, Race: Crossing Boundaries in North American History* (New York: New York University Press, 1999).

6. Mark Potter, *More Cubans Arriving with a 'Dusty' Foot*. MSNBC, October 1, 2007 [accessed April 8, 2008]; available from http://fieldnotes.msnbc.msn.com/archive/2007/10/01/388519.aspx.

7. Yvette's comment on the MSNBC blog was posted October 1, 2007, http://fieldnotes. msnbc.msn.com/archive/2007/10/01/388519.aspx (accessed September 1, 2009). As has been done throughout the book, Yvette's comment is quoted exactly as it appears on the Web site.

8. Vivian Sobchack, "Postmodern Modes of Ethnicity," in *Unspeakable Images: Ethnicity in the American Cinema*, ed. Lester D. Friedman, 329–352 (Urbana: University of Illinois Press, 1991).

9. For a discussion of the mother-daughter dynamics surrounding Latina domestic work, see Mary Romero, "Life as the Maid's Daughter: An Exploratory of the Everyday Boundaries of Race, Class and Gender," in *Challenging Fronteras: Structuring Latina and Latino Lives in the U.S.: An Anthology of Readings*, ed. Mary Romero, Pierrette Hondagneu-Sotelo, and Vilma Ortiz, 195–209 (New York: Routledge, 1997).

Bibliography

2000 Year in Review: TV's Leading News Topics, Reporters and Political Jokes. Washington, DC: Center for Media and Public Affairs (January/February 2001). Available from http://www.cmpa.com/files/media_monitor/01janfeb.pdf.

2002 National Survey of Latinos. Pew Hispanic Center (December 2002). Available from http://pewhispanic.org/files/reports/15.pdf.

"2006–07 Primetime Wrap." *Hollywood Reporter*, May 25, 2007.

"Acusan a Salma De Racismo." *Reforma*, October 9, 2002.

Average Total Paid and Verified Circulation for Top 100 ABC Magazines. Magazine Publishers of America, 2007 [accessed January 25, 2009]. Available from http://www.magazine.org/CONSUMER_MARKETING/CIRC_TRENDS/26643.aspx.

"Bad Blood over Club Fracas." *New York Post*, December 5, 2002.

Ben Affleck: I Should Never Have Got Engaged to Jennifer Lopez. fametastic, November 14, 2006 [accessed January 4, 2009]. Available from http://fametastic.co.uk/archive/20061114/3325/ben-affleck-i-should-never-have-got-engaged-to-jennifer-lopez/.

"Best of 2006: My Big Year." *TV Guide*, December 18–24, 2006, 14–16.

"Cuban Moms: 'Return Our Son!' Havana Mobilizes Thousands as Battle for Elián Drags On." *Miami Herald*, January 15, 2000.

Cubans in the United States. Washington, DC: Pew Hispanic Center (August 25, 2006). Available from http://pewhispanic.org/files/factsheets/23.pdf.

A Day without a Mexican. Box Office Mojo [accessed February 25, 2008]. Available from http://www.boxofficemojo.com/movies/?id=daywithoutamexican.htm.

El Cantante. Box Office Mojo [accessed January 1, 2009]. Available from http://www.boxofficemojo.com/movies/?id=elcantante.htm.

El Crimen Del Padre Amaro. Box Office Mojo [accessed January 17, 2009]. Available from http://www.boxofficemojo.com/movies/?page=intl&id=elcrimendelpadreamaro.htm.

"Elvira Arellano and the Law." *Chicago Tribune*, August 17, 2006.

Fast Food Nation. Box Office Mojo [accessed February 25, 2008]. Available from http://www.boxofficemojo.com/movies/?id=fastfoodnation.htm.

Frida. Box Office Mojo [accessed January 17, 2009]. Available from http://www.boxofficemojo.com/movies/?page=intl&id=frida.htm.

From News Highlights to Highlighting Hair. Associated Press, August 3, 2002 [accessed March 1, 2008]. Available from http://www.sptimes.com/2002/08/03/State/From_news_highlights_.shtml.

"Fug Girls: Seven Ways to Revive *Ugly Betty.*" *New York Magazine*, January 29, 2009 [accessed February 12, 2009]. Available from http://nymag.com/daily/fashion/2009/01/fug_girls_seven_ways_to_revive.html.

Gigli. Box Office Mojo [accessed January 2, 2009]. Available from http://www.boxofficemojo.com/movies/?id=gigli.htm.

"Haitians Continue to Protest for Equal Treatment under Immigration Policy." *Miami Times*, January 20, 2000.

Harry Potter and the Chamber of Secrets. Box Office Mojo [accessed January 17, 2009]. Available from http://www.boxofficemojo.com/movies/?page=intl&id=harrypotter2.htm.

Hispanic Fact Sheet. University of Georgia Business Outreach Services (January 2003). Available from http://www.sbdc.uga.edu/pdfs/hispanicfactsheet.pdf.

The Hispanic Population in the United States: 2004. U.S. Census 2004 [accessed July 22, 2007]. Available from http://www.census.gov/population/socdemo/hispanic/ASEC2004/2004CPS_tab1.2a.pdf.

"How Jennifer Won over Ben's Mom." *Star* magazine, May 25, 2005 [accessed April 9, 2008]. Available from http://www.starmagazine.com/news/670?print=1.

"*in Touch* Media Kit." *in Touch Weekly* 2008 [accessed January 26, 2009]. Available from http://www.bauerpublishing.com/ITW/ITW_mk/ITW-MK-EMAIL.pdf.

"Jen Shuts Brad Out." *in Touch*, March 13, 2006, 20–21.

"Jennifer Aniston's a True Friend Indeed." *Star*, June 17, 2003, 10.

Jennifer Lopez. Forbes.com, 2005 [accessed December 19, 2008]. Available from http://www.forbes.com/lists/2005/53/X5GN.html.

Jennifer Lopez. Forbes.com, 2007 [accessed December 19, 2008]. Available from http://www.forbes.com/2007/01/17/richest-women-entertainment-tech-media-cz_lg_richwomen07_0118womenstars_slide_10.html.

Jennifer Lopez Star Bio. Tribute Entertainment Media Group [accessed December 19, 2008]. Available from http://www.tribute.ca/people/JenniferLopez/1526.

Jessica "Don't Call Me Latina" Alba. New York Chique, May 16, 2008 [accessed February 15, 2009]. Available from http://newyorkchique.blogspot.com/2008/05/jessica-dont-call-me-latina-alba.html.

Jessica Alba: Don't Call Me Latina! Pop Culture Shock, July 2, 2007 [accessed February 15, 2009]. Available from http://www.popcultureshock.com/blogs/jessica-alba-dont-call-me-latina/.

"Jessica's the New Booty Queen." *in Touch*, September 4, 2006, 12.

J-Lo Confirms Affleck Engagement. BBC News, November 11, 2002 [accessed February 11, 2008]. Available from http://news.bbc.co.uk/1/hi/entertainment/showbiz/2439307.stm.

"'La Fea Más Bella' Scores Ratings Hit for Univisión." *USA Today*, June 27, 2007.

Legislation: Enforcement Only Will Not Fix Our Broken Immigration System. National Immigration Forum [accessed June 20, 2007]. Available from http://www.immigration-forum.org/DesktopDefault.aspx?tabid=777.

Lopez Announces Split from Affleck. CNN, January 23, 2004 [accessed February 11, 2008]. Available from http://www.cnn.com/2004/SHOWBIZ/01/22/affleck.lopez.ap/index.html.

The Lord of the Rings: The Two Towers. Box Office Mojo [accessed January 17, 2009]. Available from http://www.boxofficemojo.com/movies/?page=intl&id=twotowers.htm.

Maid in Manhattan. Box Office Mojo [accessed February 25, 2008]. Available from http://www.boxofficemojo.com/movies/?id=maidinmanhattan.htm.

Maid in Manhattan Synopsis. Sony Pictures [accessed February 5, 2009]. Available from http://www.sonypictures.com/homevideo/maidinmanhattan/title-navigation-2.html.

MSN Hotlist Presents: Top 100 Most Searched for Women. uk.msn.com [accessed March 25, 2008]. Available from http://hotlist.uk.msn.com/2007/top-100-women-2008.aspx.

"*National Enquirer* Media Kit." *National Enquirer* 2007 [accessed January 26, 2009]. Available from http://www.americanmediainc.com/mediakits/ne/pdf/ne_mediakit_all.pdf.

Overview of Race and Hispanic Origin. U.S. Census Bureau, March 2001 [accessed February 17, 2008]. Available from http://www.census.gov/prod/2001pubs/cenbr01-1.pdf.

"*People 2008* Rate Card." *People* 2008 [accessed January 26, 2009]. Available from ftp://ftp.timeinc.net/pub/people/mediakit/pdfs/ratecard.pdf.

Prime Time for Latinos. National Hispanic Foundation for the Arts (September 25, 2001). Available from http://www.hispanicarts.org/Media/REPORT2.pdf.

Queens County Quick Facts. U.S. Census Bureau, 2006 [accessed March 7, 2008]. Available from http://quickfacts.census.gov/qfd/states/36/36081.html.

"Salma Hayek, Racista: Mexica Movement." *La Crónica de Hoy*, October 8, 2002.

"Salma Muestra Su Espíritu En Frida." *La Crónica de Hoy*, September 1, 2002.

Selected Social Characteristics in the United States: 2005. U.S. Census Bureau, 2005 [accessed December 18, 2008]. Available from http://factfinder.census.gov/servlet/ADPTable?_bm=y&-context=adp&-qr_name=ACS_2005_EST_G00_DP2&-ds_name=ACS_2005_EST_G00_&-tree_id=305&-redoLog=true&-_caller=geoselect&-geo_id=04000US06&-format=&-_lang=en.

Selena. Box Office Mojo [accessed April 4, 2008]. Available from http://www.boxofficemojo.com/movies/?id=selena.htm.

Shall We Dance? Box Office Mojo [accessed February 13, 2008]. Available from http://www.boxofficemojo.com/movies/?id=shallwedance.htm.

"Should Elvira Arellano Be Deported or Allowed to Stay in the U.S.?" *Chicago Tribune*, August 18, 2006.

Spanglish. Box Office Mojo [accessed February 25, 2008]. Available from http://www.boxofficemojo.com/movies/?id=spanglish.htm.

Star: Why Star. Star 2008 [accessed January 26, 2009]. Available from http://www.americanmediainc.com/mediakits/star/pdfs/star_mediakit.pdf.

"Stepping Out Alone: Are J.Lo and Ben Putting the Brakes on Their Wedding?" *in Touch*, June 2, 2003, 14–17.

Us Weekly Demographics. SRDS Media Solutions 2008 [accessed December 19, 2008]. Available from http://www.srds.com/mediakits/us_weekly/demographics.html.

Adalian, Josef. "Nets Take a Novela Tack." *Variety*, February 6, 2006, 28–32.

———. "Lopez, Univisión in Unison on Drama." *Variety*, April 9, 2007 [accessed January 4, 2009]. Available from http://www.variety.com/article/VR1117962769.html?categoryid=14&cs=1.

Agresti, Aimee. "Brad & Angelina Are Adopting!" *Us Weekly*, July 18, 2005, 42–46.

Akass, Kim, and Janet McCabe. *Not So Ugly: Local Production, Global Franchise, Discursive Femininities, and the Ugly Betty Phenomenon.* FlowTV, 2007 [accessed January 17, 2009]. Available from http://flowtv.org/?p=74.

Alarcón, Norma, Caren Kaplan, and Minoo Moallem. "Introduction: Between Woman and Nation." In *Between Woman and Nation: Nationalisms, Transnational Feminisms, and the State*, edited by Caren Kaplan, Norma Alarcón, and Minoo Moallem, 1–18. Durham, NC: Duke University Press, 1999.

Almaguer, Tomás. "At the Crossroads of Race: Latino/a Studies and Race Making in the United States." In *Critical Latin American and Latino Studies*, edited by Juan Poblete, 206–222. Minneapolis: University of Minnesota Press, 2003.

Alvarez, Lizette. "Fear and Hope in Immigrant's Furtive Existence." *New York Times*, December 20, 2006.

———. "A Growing Stream of Illegal Immigrants Choose to Remain Despite the Risks." *New York Times*, December 20, 2006.

Anderson, Benedict. *Imagined Communities: Reflections on the Origin and Spread of Nationalism*. London: Verso, 1991.

Anzaldúa, Gloria. *Borderlands: The New Mestiza = La Frontera*. 1st ed. San Francisco: Spinsters/Aunt Lute, 1987.

Aparicio, Frances R. *Listening to Salsa: Gender, Latin Popular Music, and Puerto Rican Cultures*. Hanover, NH: University Press of New England, 1998.

———. "Reading the 'Latino' in Latino Studies: Toward Re-Imagining Our Academic Location." *Discourse* 21, no. 3 (Fall 1999): 3–18.

———. "Jennifer as Selena: Rethinking Latinidad in Media and Popular Culture." *Latino Studies* 1, no. 1 (March 2003): 90–105.

Aparicio, Frances R., and Susana Chávez-Silverman, eds. *Tropicalizations: Transcultural Representations of Latinidad*. Hanover, NH: Dartmouth College, University Press of New England, 1997.

Appadurai, Arjun. "Disjuncture and Difference in the Global Cultural Economy." In *Theorizing Diaspora: A Reader*, edited by Jana Evans Braziel and Anita Mannur, 25–48. Malden, MA: Blackwell, 2003.

Arthur, Lisa, Bruce Taylor Seeman, and Elaine De Valle. "5-Year-Old Survivor Clung to Inner Tube Two More Rafters Rescued, but 11 Other Cubans May Have Died at Sea." *Miami Herald*, November 26, 1999.

Astroff, Roberta J. "Capital's Cultural Study: Marketing Popular Ethnography of U.S. Latino Culture." In *Buy This Book: Studies in Advertising and Consumption*, edited by Mica Nava, 120–138. New York: Routledge, 1997.

Attkisson, Sharyl. "Five-Year-Old Cuban Boy Who Was Rescued Off the Coast of Florida Is Allowed to Remain in the United States." *CBS Evening News*, anchor John Roberts, November 26, 1999.

Ausiello, Michael. "Exclusive: 'Ugly Betty' Lives!" *Entertainment Weekly*, February 10, 2009 [accessed February 14, 2009]. Available from http://ausiellofiles.ew.com/2009/02/exclusive-ugly.html.

Avila, Oscar. "She Refuses to Go Silently." *Chicago Tribune*, November 19, 2005.

———. "Act of Faith, Defiance: Activist for Illinois' Illegal Immigrants Battles Deportation by Taking Shelter in a City Church." *Chicago Tribune*, August 16, 2006.

———. "Activist Steps into Debate Pulpit." *Chicago Tribune*, August 18, 2006.

———. "Hunger Strikers in Pilsen Seek Halt to Deportations." *Chicago Tribune*, May 25, 2006.

———. "Illegal Immigrant's Supporters, Foes in Made-for-TV Roles." *Chicago Tribune*, August 26, 2006.

———. "Boy Wages Fight for Mother: Critics Charge Immigrant's Son Being Exploited." *Chicago Tribune*, November 15, 2006.

Bachman, Katy. "Univisión's KMEX Tops TV Stations Pack in '08." *Mediaweek*, January 15, 2009 [accessed February 14, 2009]. Available from http://www.mediaweek.com/mw/content_display/news/local-broadcast/e3i4b7a99706a1f6a0766e7969952d1dc13.

Báez, Jillian M. "'En Mi Imperio': Competing Discourses of Agency in Ivy Queen's Reggaetón." *CENTRO* 18, no. 2 (Fall 2006): 62–81.

———. "Speaking of Jennifer Lopez: Discourses of Iconicity and Identity Formation among Latina Audiences." *Media Report to Women* 35, no. 1 (Winter 2007): 5–13.

Baker, Ken, and Jeremy Helligar. "Cris Judd: Life with & without J.Lo." *Us Weekly*, March 31, 2003, 38–43.

Baldauf, Scott. "U.S. Tries Spy Tactics to Stop Human Smugglers." *Christian Science Monitor*, August 30, 2000.

Banet-Weiser, Sarah. "Elián González and 'the Purpose of America': Nation, Family, and the Child-Citizen." *American Quarterly* 55, no. 2 (June 2003): 149–178.

Barnard, Anne. "Latinos Recall Pattern of Attacks before Killing." *New York Times*, January 9, 2009.

Barnes, Brooks. "Story Behind the Cover Story: Angelina Jolie and Her Image." *New York Times*, November 21, 2008.

Barney, Chuck. "'Ugly Betty,' Premiering Thursday on ABC." *Contra Costa Times*, September 26, 2006.

Barrera, Magdalena. "Hottentot 2000: Jennifer Lopez and Her Butt." In *Sexualities in History: A Reader*, edited by Kim M. Phillips and Barry Reay, 407–420. New York: Routledge, 2002.

Bartholet, Jeffrey, et al. "Grandma Diplomacy." *Newsweek*, January 31, 2000, 32–33.

Barvelo, Beatriz. "Con Sabor Latino: Jennifer Lopez, Enrique Iglesias, Ricky Martin y Carlos Santana Figuran En La Lista De Nominados De Los American Music Awards Que Se Celebrara El 17 De Enero." *La Opinión*, December 7, 1999.

Behar, Ruth. "Queer Times in Cuba." In *Bridges to Cuba = Puentes a Cuba*, edited by Ruth Behar, 394–415. Ann Arbor: University of Michigan Press, 1995.

Bell, Allan, and Peter Garrett, eds. *Approaches to Media Discourse*. Oxford: Blackwell, 1998.

Beltrán, Mary. "The Hollywood Latina Body as Site of Social Struggle: Media Constructions of Stardom and Jennifer Lopez's 'Cross-over Butt'." *Quarterly Review of Film and Video* 19, no. 1 (January–March 2002): 71–86.

Benavides, O. Hugo. *Drugs, Thugs, and Divas: Telenovelas and Narco-Dramas in Latin America*. Austin: University of Texas Press, 2008.

Bergman-Carton, Janis. "Strike a Pose: The Framing of Madonna and Frida Kahlo." *Texas Studies in Literature and Language* 35, no. 4 (Winter 1993): 440–452.

Bernstein, Jonathan. "Jonathan Bernstein's Aerial View of America." *The Guardian*, October 14, 2006.

Bhabha, Homi. *The Location of Culture*. London, New York: Routledge, 2004.

Bianco, Robert. "Likable 'Betty' Aided by a Lovable Lead." *USA Today*, September 28, 2006.

Bianculli, David. "'Ugly Betty' Looks Pretty Good: Fun Redo of a Telenovela." *Daily News*, September 27, 2006.

Bird, S. Elizabeth. *For Enquiring Minds: A Cultural Study of Supermarket Tabloids*. 1st ed. Knoxville: University of Tennessee Press, 1992.

Bird, S. Elizabeth, and Robert W. Dardenne. "Myth, Chronicle, and Story: Exploring the Narrative Qualities of News." In *Media, Myths, and Narratives: Television and the Press*, edited by James W. Carey, 67–86. Newbury Park, CA: Sage, 1988.

Blitzer, Wolf, et al. "Elián González Takes Center Stage in the Political Arena." *CNN Late Edition with Wolf Blitzer*, anchor Wolf Blitzer, April 9, 2000.

Block, Rebecca, and Lynda Hoffman-Jeep. "Fashioning National Identity: Frida Kahlo in 'Gringolandia.'" *Woman's Art Journal* 19, no. 2 (Autumn 1998): 8–12.

Bobo, Jacqueline. *Black Women as Cultural Readers*. New York: Columbia University Press, 1995.

bookofjoe. "J-Lo Fired by Louis Vuitton for Stealing." *Blogcritics* magazine, December 14, 2003 [accessed June 15, 2007]. Available from http://blogcritics.org/archives/2003/12/14/091910.php.

Booth, William. "Building 'Betty': How Did Silvio Horta Turn a Telenovela into Fall's Highest-Rated New Series? One Detail at a Time." *Washington Post*, October 22, 2006.

Bordo, Susan. *Unbearable Weight: Feminism, Western Culture, and the Body*. Berkeley: University of California Press, 1993.

Bragg, Rick. "Haitian Immigrants in U.S. Face a Wrenching Choice." *New York Times*, March 29, 2000.

Bratich, Jack Z, Jeremy Packer, and Cameron McCarthy. *Foucault, Cultural Studies, and Governmentality*. Albany: State University of New York Press, 2003.

Braziel, Jana Evans, and Anita Mannur. *Theorizing Diaspora: A Reader*. Malden, MA: Blackwell, 2003.

Bried, Erin. "Doing It Right." *Self*, September, 2008, 38–40.

Brinkley-Rogers, Paul, et al. "Case Provokes Harsh Feelings, Hope." *Miami Herald*, April 6, 2000.

Brown, Aaron. "Janet Reno Leaves Decision to Elián González's Father." *World News Tonight*, ABC, anchor Peter Jennings, January 12, 2000.

Cabrera, Omar. "Dice Que Daña a Frida." *Reforma*, November 8, 2002.

Cacho, Lisa Marie. "'The People of California Are Suffering': The Ideology of White Injury in Discourses of Immigration." *Cultural Values* 4, no. 4 (October 2000): 389–418.

Campbell, Richard. *60 Minutes and the News: A Mythology for Middle America*. Urbana: University of Illinois Press, 1991.

Castañeda, Mari. "The Importance of Spanish-Language and Latino Media." In *Latina/o Communication Studies Today*, edited by Angharad Valdivia, 51–68. New York: Peter Lang, 2008.

Castaño, Javier. "Los Boricuas Desafiaron La Lluvia Durante Su Desfile." *El Diario La Prensa*, June 15, 1998.

Cepeda, María Elena. "Shakira as the Idealized, Transnational Citizen: A Case Study of *Colombianidad* in Transition." *Latino Studies* 1, no. 2 (July 2003): 211–232.

Chardy, Alfonso. "Family Ties Spurred Rafters on Elián Trip." *Miami Herald*, June 23, 2000.

Claiborne, Ron. "Father of Elián González Says He'll Never Go to Miami." *World News Tonight*, ABC, anchor Peter Jennings, January 13, 2000.

———. "Elián González Meets Grandmothers on Neutral Ground." *World News Tonight*, ABC, anchor Peter Jennings, January 26, 2000.

———. "Miami Relatives of Elián González Won't Give Permission for Elián to Live with His Father While in Miami." *World News Tonight*, ABC, anchor Peter Jennings, March 31, 2000.

Clarke, Steve. "Rise of Telenovelas: U.S. Fare Gets Competition." *Variety*, February 16, 2006 [accessed March 5, 2008]. Available from http://www.variety.com/article/VR1117938390.html?categoryid=14&cs=1.

Cleto, Fabio, ed. *Camp: Queer Aesthetics and the Performing Subject: A Reader*. Ann Arbor: University of Michigan Press, 1999.

Cohen, Michael. "J.Lo and Ben Fall Out—Again!" *in Touch*, January 19, 2004, 20–22.

Coleman, Mark, et al. "J.Lo & Ben: Is It Finally Over?" *in Touch*, February 2, 2004, 14–17.

Colford, Paul D. "J.Lo: Cover Queen Singer's Life Saga Sells Mags." *New York Daily News*, December 30, 2004.

Collins, Scott. "It's an Ugly Time for 'Betty.'" *Los Angeles Times*, January 27, 2009.

Comita, Jenny. "Hot Betty." *W Magazine*, May 2007, 164–169.

Conboy, Martin. *The Press and Popular Culture*. Thousand Oaks, CA: Sage, 2002.

Connell, Ian. "Personalities in the Popular Media." In *Journalism and Popular Culture*, edited by Peter Dahlgren and Colin Sparks, 64–83. Newbury Park, CA: Sage, 1992.

Cooper, Anderson. "Jennifer Lopez and Ben Affleck Break Up." *Anderson Cooper 360 Degrees*, CNN, January 22, 2004.

Cornelius, Wayne A. "Ambivalent Reception: Mass Public Responses to the 'New' Latino Immigration to the United States." In *Latinos: Remaking America*, edited by Marcelo M. Suárez-Orozco and Mariela Páez, 165–189. Berkeley: University of California Press, 2002.

Dahlgren, Peter, and Colin Sparks, eds. *Journalism and Popular Culture*. Newbury Park, CA: Sage, 1992.

Dallas, Paloma. "The Big Apple's Mexican Face." *Hispanic*, July–August 2001.

Dam, Julie K. L., et al. "September Song: Jennifer Lopez and Cris Judd Tie the Knot, Then Do What They Do Best: Dance All Night." *People*, October 15, 2001, 110–116.

Davies, Frank. "Groups Call for Returning Elián to Father." *Miami Herald*, January 19, 2000.

Dávila, Arlene M. *Latinos, Inc.: The Marketing and Making of a People*. Berkeley: University of California Press, 2001.

De La Fuente, Anna Marie. "Primetime Faves Fail to Translate En Español." *Variety*, October 10, 2005, 18.

———. "'Ugly Betty' Grows into Swan around Globe." *Variety*, February 6, 2006, 28–32.

———. "Battle of the 'Betty' Beauties." *Variety*, October 9, 2006, 23.

Dean, Morton. "Tensions Rise between U.S. And Cuba over Six-Year-Old Boy." *World News Tonight*, ABC, anchor Peter Jennings, December 8, 1999.

DeSipio, Louis, and James Richard Henson. "Cuban Americans, Latinos, and the Print Media: Shaping Ethnic Identities." *Harvard International Journal of Press/Politics* 2, no. 3 (June 1, 1997): 52–70.

Diawara, Manthia. "Black Spectatorship: Problems of Identification and Resistance." In *Black American Cinema*, edited by Manthia Diawara, 211–220. New York: Routledge, 1993.

DiOrio, Carl. "SAG: Minority Actors See Gains." *Hollywood Reporter*, October 30, 2007.

Dosamentes-Beaudry, Irma. "Frida Kahlo: The Creation of a Cultural Icon." *The Arts in Psychotherapy* 29, no. 1 (2002): 3–12.

Duffy, Mike. "ABC's 'Ugly Betty' Is Looking Good." *Detroit Free Press*, September 26, 2006.

Dunkley, Gilbert. "On Stealing a Child, and Other Outrages." *Caribbean Today*, January 31, 2000, 9.

Durand, Jorge, and Douglas S. Massey. "The Costs of Contradiction: U.S. Border Policy 1986–2000." *Latino Studies* 1, no. 2 (July 2003): 233–252.

Durham, Aisha S., and Jillian M. Báez. "A Tail of Two Women: Exploring the Contours of Difference in Popular Culture." In *Curriculum and the Cultural Body*, edited by Stephanie Springgay and Debra Freedman, 131–147. New York: Peter Lang, 2007.

Dyer, Richard. *Heavenly Bodies: Film Stars and Society.* New York: St. Martin's Press, 1986.

Ebert, Roger. *Spanglish.* RogerEbert.com, December 17, 2004 [accessed February 4, 2009]. Available from http://rogerebert.suntimes.com/apps/pbcs.dll/article?AID=/20041216/REVIEWS/41201005/1023.

Egusquiza, Rick, et al. "Demi & Ashton's Hot New Romance." *Star*, June 17, 2003, 16–17, 20.

Epstein, Jeffrey. *Ladies' Night: We Hit West Hollywood's Gay Hotspots with Two of Ugly Betty's Beauties.* Out.com, April, 2007 [accessed March 5, 2008]. Available from http://www.out.com/detail.asp?id=22358.

———. *Pretty Ugly: Ugly Betty Was the Surprise Hit of Last Fall's Television Schedule* Out.com, April 2007 [accessed March 5, 2008]. Available from http://www.out.com/detail.asp?id=22276.

Fairclough, Norman. *Media Discourse.*New York: E. Arnold, 1995.

Farber, Jim. "Low Marks for Lopez: Diva's Disk Lacks 'Vida.'" *New York Daily News*, January 21, 2001.

———. "The High 'J.Lo' Country: Two No. 1s Jennifer Tops Music, Movie Charts." *New York Daily News*, February 1, 2001.

Fein, Seth. "Film Reviews." *American Historical Review* 108, no. 4 (October 2003): 1261–1263.

Fernandez, Mary Elena. "Stuck on 'Ugly': A Diverse Viewership Has Made 'Ugly Betty' the No. 1 New Show." *Los Angeles Times*, November 8, 2006.

———. "Just the Way You Are: 'Ugly Betty's' Young Nephew Has Been Embraced by Those Who Don't 'Fit in.'" *Los Angeles Times*, January 31, 2007.

Fiske, John. *Television Culture.* New York: Methuen, 1987.

Foucault, Michel. *Discipline and Punish: The Birth of the Prison.* 2nd Vintage Books ed. New York: Vintage Books, 1995.

Foucault, Michel, and Paul Rabinow. *The Foucault Reader.* 1st ed. New York: Pantheon Books, 1984.

Franco, Jean, Mary Louise Pratt, and Kathleen E. Newman, eds. *Critical Passions: Selected Essays.* Durham, NC: Duke University Press, 1999.

Fregoso, Rosa Linda. *The Bronze Screen: Chicana and Chicano Film Culture.* Minneapolis: University of Minnesota Press, 1993.

———. *MeXicana Encounters: The Making of Social Identities on the Borderlands.* Berkeley: University of California Press, 2003.

Fregoso, Rosa Linda, and Lourdes Portillo. *Lourdes Portillo: The Devil Never Sleeps and Other Films.* 1st ed. Austin: University of Texas Press, 2001.

Fusco, Coco. *English Is Broken Here: Notes on Cultural Fusion in the Americas.* New York: New Press, 1995.

Gamson, Joshua. *Claims to Fame: Celebrity in Contemporary America.* Berkeley: University of California Press, 1994.

Gannon, Sean. "Bed Rules for Ben & Jen." *Star* Magazine, October 11, 2005 [accessed December 19, 2008]. Available from http://www.starmagazine.com/news/5544.

García, Alma M. "Introduction." In *Chicana Feminist Thought: The Basic Historical Writings,* edited by Alma M. García, 1–20. New York: Routledge, 1997.

García Canclini, Néstor. *Hybrid Cultures: Strategies for Entering and Leaving Modernity.* Minneapolis: University of Minnesota Press, 1995.

———. *Consumers and Citizens: Globalization and Multicultural Conflicts.* Minneapolis: University of Minnesota Press, 2001.

García, María Cristina. "Exiles, Immigrants and Transnationals: The Cuban Communities in the United States." In *The Columbia History of Latinos in the United States since 1960,* edited by David Gutiérrez, 146–186. New York: Columbia University Press, 2004.

Garcia, Ruben J. "The Racial Politics of Proposition 187." In *The Latino/a Condition: A Critical Reader,* edited by Richard Delgado and Jean Stefancic, 118–124. New York: New York University Press, 1998.

García, Solange. "Salma Hayek Enfrenta Al Malinchismo Y Defiende a Frida." *La Crónica de Hoy,* November 9, 2002.

Gerbner, George, et al. "Growing up with Television: The Cultivation Perspective." In *Media Effects: Advances in Theory and Research,* edited by Jennings Bryant and Dolf Zillmann, 17–41. Hillsdale, NJ: Erlbaum, 1994.

Gilbert, Matthew. "'Ugly Betty' Has Look of a Winner." *Boston Globe,* September 28, 2006.

Gillespie, Mark. "Americans Support Resumption of Diplomatic Relations with Cuba." *Gallup Poll Monthly,* no. 416 (May 2000): 33.

Gledhill, Christine. *Stardom: Industry of Desire.* London: Routledge, 1991.

Gliatto, Tom, et al. "Under Pressure." *People,* August 18, 2003, 58–62.

Goodman, Tim. "The Main Character May Not Be Pretty, but Her Show Is." *San Francisco Chronicle,* September 27, 2006.

Goodstein, Ellen, Rick Egusquiza, and Patricia Towie. "Puffy's Sex Tape Wrecks J.Lo Marriage . . . Pals Say." *National Enquirer,* June 25, 2002, 4.

Goodwin, Christopher. "Latino TV Station Tops U.S. Ratings." *Observer,* January 18, 2009.

Gould, Martin. "J.Lo Lesbian Sex Shocker: Romp Caught on Tape." *Star,* February 5, 2002, 4.

Gray, Herman. *Watching Race: Television and the Struggle for 'Blackness.'* Minneapolis: University of Minnesota Press, 1995.

Grewal, Inderpal, and Caren Kaplan. *Scattered Hegemonies: Postmodernity and Transnational Feminist Practices.* Minneapolis: University of Minnesota Press, 1994.

Griffiths, Gareth. "The Myth of Authenticity." In *The Post-Colonial Studies Reader,* edited by Bill Ashcroft, Gareth Griffiths, and Helen Tiffin, 237–241. New York: Routledge, 1995.

Gross, Larry. "Out of the Mainstream: Sexual Minorities and the Mass Media." In *Gay People, Sex, and the Media,* edited by Michelle Andrea Wolf and Alfred P. Kielwasser, 19–46. New York: Haworth Press, 1991.

———. *Contested Closets: The Politics and Ethics of Outing.* Minneapolis: University of Minnesota Press, 1993.

Habell-Pallán, Michelle. *Loca Motion: The Travels of Chicana and Latina Popular Culture*. New York: New York University Press, 2005.

Habell-Pallán, Michelle, and Mary Romero, eds. *Latino/a Popular Culture*. New York: New York University Press, 2002.

Haberman, Lia. "J.Lo Fires and Hires." E! Online, June 17, 2003 [accessed December 19, 2008]. Available from http://www.moviefinder.com/uberblog/b45344_jlo_fires_hires.html.

Hall, Stuart, ed. *Representation: Cultural Representations and Signifying Practices*. Thousand Oaks, CA: Sage in association with the Open University, 1997.

Hall, Stuart, et al. *Policing the Crisis: Mugging, the State, and Law and Order*. New York: Holmes & Meier, 1978.

Halter, Marilyn. *Shopping for Identity: The Marketing of Ethnicity*. New York: Schocken Books, 2000.

Harris, Leon, Susan Candiotti, and Carol Lin. "Government Gives Elián González's Family until Noon to Accept Speedy Appeals Process." *CNN Early Edition*, March 27, 2000.

Havens, Timothy. "'The Biggest Show in the World': Race and the Global Popularity of *The Cosby Show*." In *The Television Studies Reader*, edited by Robert Clyde Allen and Annette Hill, 442–456. New York: Routledge, 2004.

Heffernan, Virginia. "A Plucky Guppy among the Barracudas." *New York Times*, September 28, 2006.

Herman, Edward S., and Robert W. McChesney. *The Global Media: The New Missionaries of Corporate Capitalism*. London: Cassell, 1997.

Hernandez, Macarena. "Beautiful 'Ugly': TV's New Betty Is Smart, Real and, Most Surprising, a Latina." *Dallas Morning News*, September 28, 2006.

Herrera, Hayden. *Frida, a Biography of Frida Kahlo*. 1st ed. New York: Harper & Row, 1983.

Hibberd, James. "Univisión Pitching Growth of Market." *TelevisionWeek*, May 14, 2007, 18.

Hicks, Connie. "Thousands of Protesters Marching in the Streets of Little Havana." *World News Now*, ABC, anchor Anderson Cooper, March 30, 2000.

Hindes, Andrew. "WB Targets Untapped Demo with Its 'Selena.'" *Variety*, March 17, 1997, 9.

Hochschild, Arlie Russell. "Love and Gold." In *Global Woman: Nannies, Maids, and Sex Workers in the New Economy*, edited by Barbara Ehrenreich and Arlie Russell Hochschild, 15–30. New York: Metropolitan Books, 2003.

Hodes, Martha Elizabeth, ed. *Sex, Love, Race: Crossing Boundaries in North American History*. New York: New York University Press, 1999.

Hoffman, Alison R., and Chon A. Noriega. *Looking for Latino Regulars on Prime-Time Television: The Fall 2004 Season* (No. 4). Los Angeles: UCLA Chicano Studies Research Center. (December, 2004). Available from http://www.chicano.ucla.edu/press/reports/documents/crr_04Dec2004_000.pdf.

Holmlund, Chris. *Impossible Bodies: Femininity and Masculinity at the Movies*. New York: Routledge, 2002.

Hondagneu-Sotelo, Pierrette. "The History of Mexican Undocumented Settlement in the United States." In *Challenging Fronteras: Structuring Latina and Latino Lives in the U.S.: An Anthology of Readings*, edited by Mary Romero, Pierrette Hondagneu-Sotelo, and Vilma Ortiz, 115–134. New York: Routledge, 1997.

———. *Doméstica: Immigrant Workers Cleaning and Caring in the Shadows of Affluence*. Berkeley: University of California Press, 2001.

hooks, bell. *Black Looks: Race and Representation*. Boston: South End Press, 1992.

Huerta, César, and Omar Cabrera. "Frida, Muy Mexicana." *Reforma*, August 1, 2002.

Ibarra, Sergio. "Univisión's KMEX-TV Dominates 18–49, Nielsen Says." *TVWeek*, January 15, 2009 [accessed February 14, 2009]. Available from http://www.tvweek.com/news/2009/01/univision_affiliate_kmex_domin.php.

Inda, Jonathan Xavier. "Biopower, Reproduction, and the Migrant Woman's Body." In *Decolonial Voices: Chicana and Chicano Cultural Studies in the 21st Century*, edited by Arturo J. Aldama and Naomi Helena Quiñonez, 98–112. Bloomington: Indiana University Press, 2002.

Jackson, Terry. "It's Time to Take Boy out of Spotlight." *Miami Herald*, December 9, 1999.

James, Meg. "Spanish TV Soap Opera Turns into Court Drama." *Los Angeles Times*, January 6, 2009.

———. "Televisa, Univisión Settle." *Los Angeles Times*, January 23, 2009.

Jamieson, Bob. "Elián González's Grandmothers Arrive in New York." *World News Tonight*, ABC, anchor Peter Jennings, January 21, 2000.

Jensen, Michael. "'Ugly Betty' Is Freaking Fabulous (and Gay)." *After Elton*, March 23, 2007 [accessed January 17, 2009]. Available from http://www.afterelton.com/TV/2007/3/uglybetty.

Jhally, Sut, and Justin Lewis. *Enlightened Racism: The Cosby Show, Audiences, and the Myth of the American Dream*. Boulder, CO: Westview Press, 1992.

Johnson, Chris. *Vanessa Williams to Receive Ally for Equality Award at HRC New York Gala Dinner*. Human Rights Campaign, February 4, 2008 [accessed March 5, 2008]. Available from http://www.hrcbackstory.org/2008/02/vanessa-willi-1.html.

Jordan, Rene. "Frida, De Julie Taymor El Color De La Pasión." *El Nuevo Herald*, November 7, 2002.

Joseph, May. "Transatlantic Inscriptions: Desire, Diaspora, and Cultural Citizenship." In *Talking Visions: Multicultural Feminism in a Transnational Age*, edited by Ella Shohat, 357–359. Cambridge, MA: MIT Press, 1998.

Kanellos, Nicolás. *Thirty Million Strong: Reclaiming the Hispanic Image in American Culture*. Golden, CO: Fulcrum Publishing, 1998.

Karrfalt, Wayne. "A Novela Approach to Mainstream TV." *Television Week*, September 25, 2006, 52.

Kerr, Sarah. "Viva Frida." *Vogue*, December 2001, 276–285, 340.

Kim, L. S. "Invisible and Undocumented: The Latina Maid on Network Television." *Aztlán: A Journal of Chicano Studies* 24, no. 1 (Spring 1999): 107–128.

Kramarae, Cheris, and Paula A. Treichler. *A Feminist Dictionary*. Boston: Pandora Press, 1985.

Kripalani, Jasmine, and Eunice Ponce. "Protests March to Different Beats." *Miami Herald*, January 30, 2000.

Laughlin, Meg. "Elián's Cousin in, out of Hospitals." *Miami Herald*, April 11, 2000.

Lazo, Alejandro. "Hispanic Immigrants Drop in U.S. Labor Force." *Washington Post*, December 16, 2008.

Lee, Anthony. *Painting on the Left: Diego Rivera, Radical Politics, and San Francisco's Public Murals*. Berkeley: University of California Press, 1999.

Leo, John. "Elián: The Opera." *U.S. News and World Report*, May 8, 2000, 12.

Levine, Elana. "Constructing a Market, Constructing an Ethnicity: U.S. Spanish-Language Media and the Formation of a Syncretic Latino/a Identity." *Studies in Latin American Popular Culture* 20 (2001): 33–50.

Lindauer, Margaret. *Devouring Frida: The Art History and Popular Celebrity of Frida Kahlo.* Hanover, NH: Wesleyan University Press, 1999.

Lipsky-Karasz, Elisa. "J.Lo & Ben vs. Gwyneth & Chris: With Exes Ben and Gwyn in the Arms of Others, Could Their Love Lives Be Less Alike?" *Us Weekly*, March 17, 2003, 62–63.

Loaeza, Guadalupe. "Frida Made in USA." *Reforma*, November 7, 2002.

López, Ana M. "Are All Latins from Manhattan?: Hollywood, Ethnography, and Cultural Colonialism." In *Unspeakable Images: Ethnicity and the American Cinema*, edited by Lester D. Friedman, 404–424. Urbana: University of Illinois Press, 1991.

Lowe, Lisa. "Work, Immigration, Gender: New Subjects of Cultural Politics." *Social Justice* 25, no. 3 (1998): 31–49.

Lowe, Lisa, and David Lloyd. *The Politics of Culture in the Shadow of Capital.* Durham, NC: Duke University Press, 1997.

Lugo, Alejandro. "Reflections on Border Theory, Culture, and the Nation." In *Border Theory: The Limits of Cultural Politics*, edited by Scott Michaelsen and David E. Johnson, 43–67. Minneapolis: University of Minnesota Press, 1997.

Lugones, María. *Pilgrimages = Peregrinajes: Theorizing Coalition against Multiple Oppressions.* Lanham, MD: Rowman & Littlefield, 2003.

Lyford, Kathy. "'Ugly Betty': 'We Always Want to Surprise Our Audience.'" *Variety*, October 6, 2008 [accessed January 17, 2009]. Available from http://weblogs.variety.com/season_pass/2008/10/q-what-did-dani.html.

Lynch, Marika. "Elián's Miami Relatives Say INS Is Tight-Lipped." *Miami Herald*, December 21, 1999.

MacPherson, Myra. "All in Elián's Family." *Salon*, April 8, 2000 [accessed December 18, 2008]. Available from http://archive.salon.com/news/feature/2000/04/08/family/.

Masterson, Lawrie. "Ugly Duckling Has Last Laugh." *The Sunday Mail (Australia)*, February 11, 2007.

Mayer, Vicki. *Producing Dreams, Consuming Youth: Mexican Americans and Mass Media.* New Brunswick, NJ: Rutgers University Press, 2003.

McCarthy, Cameron. *The Uses of Culture: Education and the Limits of Ethnic Affiliation.* New York: Routledge, 1998.

McCracken, Ellen. *New Latina Narrative: The Feminine Space of Postmodern Ethnicity.* Tucson: University of Arizona Press, 1999.

McHoul, A. W., and Wendy Grace. *A Foucault Primer: Discourse, Power, and the Subject.* New York: New York University Press, 1997.

McNary, Dave. "WGA Issues Minority Report." *Daily Variety*, May 9, 2007, 4.

Méndez-Méndez, Serafín, and Diane Alverio. *Network Brownout 2001: The Portrayal of Latinos in Network Television News, 2000.* Washington, DC: National Association of Hispanic Journalists. (2001). Available from http://www.nahj.org/pdf/brownout.pdf.

———. *Network Brownout 2002: The Portrayal of Latinos in Network Television News, 2001.* Washington, DC: National Association of Hispanic Journalists. (2002). Available from http://www.nahj.org/pdf/br2003.pdf.

Mendible, Myra. "Introduction: Embodying Latinidad: An Overview." In *From Bananas to Buttocks: The Latina Body in Popular Film and Culture*, edited by Myra Mendible, 1–28. Austin: University of Texas Press, 2007.

Michals, Bob, et al. "Julia Roberts Bombshell! She's Visiting Fertility Clinic." *Star*, December 31, 2002, 30–31.

Miller, Prairie. "Interview with Jennifer Lopez." *NY Rock*, December, 2002 [accessed February 4, 2009]. Available from http://www.nyrock.com/interviews/2002/lopez_int3.asp.

Miller, Toby, et al. *Global Hollywood*. London: British Film Institute, 2001.

Mirabal, Nancy Raquel. "'Ser De Aquí': Beyond the Cuban Exile Model." *Latino Studies* 1, no. 3 (2003): 366–382.

Molina-Guzmán, Isabel. "Gendering Latinidad through the Elián News Discourse About Cuban Women." *Latino Studies* 3, no. 2 (July 2005): 179–204.

———. "Latinas/os in Advertising." In *Oxford Encyclopedia of Latinas and Latinos in the United States*, edited by Suzanne Oboler and Deena J. González. New York: Oxford University Press, 2005.

———. "Competing Discourses of Community: Ideological Tensions between Local General-Market and Latino News Media." *Journalism: Theory, Practice and Criticism* 7, no. 3 (August 2006): 281–298.

———. "Mediating Frida: Negotiating Discourses of Latina/o Authenticity in Global Media Representations of Ethnic Identity." *Critical Studies in Media Communication* 23, no. 3 (August 2006): 232–251.

———. "Salma Hayek's Frida: Transnational Latina Bodies in Popular Culture." In *From Bananas to Buttocks: The Latina Body in Popular Film and Culture*, edited by Myra Mendible, 117–128. Austin: University of Texas Press, 2007.

Molina-Guzmán, Isabel, and Angharad Valdivia. "Brain, Brow or Bootie: Iconic Latinas in Contemporary Popular Culture." *Communication Review* 7, no. 2 (April–June 2004): 205–221.

Montalvo, Daniela, and Joseph Torres. *Network Brownout Report 2006: The Portrayal of Latinos and Latino Issues in Network Television News, 2005*. Washington, DC: National Association of Hispanic Journalists (2006). Available from http://www.nahj.org/resources/2006Brownout.pdf.

Montgomery, John. "Creep of the Week: Marisleysis Gonzalez." johnmonty.com, April 29, 2000 [accessed March 1, 2008]. Available from http://www.johnmonty.com/cotw/cwo00429.htm.

Moore, David W. "Public: Reunion of Elián with Father Should Have Occurred Earlier." *Gallup Poll Monthly*, no. 415 (April 2000): 29–32.

Moreno, Sylvia, and Lonnae O'Neal Parker. "The Voice of Dispassion for U.S. Cubans." *Washington Post*, April 28, 2000.

Navarro, Mireya. "Grandmothers Cite Family Values in Effort to Take Cuban Boy Home." *New York Times*, January 23, 2000.

———. "For Divided Family, Border Is Sorrowful Barrier." *New York Times*, December 21, 2006.

———. "Traditional Round Trip for Workers Is Becoming a One-Way Migration North." *New York Times*, December 21, 2006.

Negrón-Muntaner, Frances. "Jennifer's Butt." *Aztlán* 22, no. 2 (2000): 182–195.

————. *Boricua Pop: Puerto Ricans and the Latinization of American Culture.* New York: New York University Press, 2004.

Nelson, Jason. "There's Nothing a Little Mother's Love and Musical Theatre Can't Fix" *Popnography*, November 21, 2008 [accessed January 17, 2009]. Available from http://www.popnography.com/2008/11/i-previously-me.html.

Newman, Lucia. "Elian Gonzalez's Father Pleads for Son's Return." *CNN Worldview*, CNN, anchor Wolf Blitzer, January 27, 2000.

Newport, Frank. "Americans Say It Is in Elián González' Best Interests to Return to Cuba with His Father." *Gallup Poll Monthly*, no. 415 (April 2000): 26–28.

Noa, Ojani. "The Nasty Real J.Lo: Sex Crazed . . . Selfish . . . Cruel." *Star*, December 10, 2002, 17, 20–21.

Noriega, Chon A., ed. *Chicanos and Film: Essays on Chicano Representation and Resistance.* New York: Garland Publishing, 1992.

O'Brien, Pat. "Ben and Jen; Ben Affleck and Jennifer Lopez Discuss Their Lives, Careers and Upcoming Marriage." *Dateline NBC*, anchor Stone Phillips, July 17, 2003.

Oboler, Suzanne. *Ethnic Labels, Latino Lives: Identity and the Politics of (Re)presentation in the United States.* Minneapolis: University of Minnesota Press, 1995.

Olsen, Eric. "Ben 'Addict'—J Lo 'Freak.'" *Blogcritics Magazine*, December 5, 2002 [accessed January 28, 2009]. Available from http://blogcritics.org/archives/2002/12/05/123457.php.

————. "'Bennifer' History." *Blogcritics Magazine*, January 23, 2004 [accessed February 15, 2008]. Available from http://blogcritics.org/archives/2004/01/23/130126.php.

————. "About Blogcritics." *Blogcritics Magazine*, October 24, 2005 [accessed December 19, 2008]. Available from http://blogcritics.org/archives/2005/10/24/094437.php.

Omi, Michael, and Howard Winant. *Racial Formation in the United States: From the 1960s to the 1990s.* 2nd ed. New York: Routledge, 1994.

Ong, Aihwa. "Cultural Citizenship as Subject Making: Immigrants Negotiate Racial and Cultural Boundaries in the United States." In *Race, Identity, and Citizenship: A Reader*, edited by Rodolfo D. Torres, Luis F. Mirón, and Jonathan Xavier Inda, 262–294. Malden, MA: Blackwell, 1999.

Ortiz, Olivia. "An Open Letter to *Ugly Betty's* America Ferrera." *Women in Media and News*, January 19, 2007 [accessed March 11, 2008]. Available from http://www.wimnonline.org/WIMNsVoicesBlog/?p=397.

Osunsami, Steve. "Elián González Endures Spotlight and Adulation in Cuba and Miami." *World News Tonight*, ABC, anchor Carole Simpson, January 23, 2000.

Paredez, Deborah. "Remembering Selena, Re-membering Latinidad." *Theatre Journal* 54, no. 1 (March 2002): 63–84.

Parker, Mike. "Why Ugly Is the New Beautiful." *Sunday Express (London)*, January 7, 2007.

Parreñas Shimizu, Celine. *The Hypersexuality of Race: Performing Asian/American Women on Screen and Scene.* Durham, NC: Duke University Press, 2007.

Passel, Jeffrey S. *Unauthorized Migrants: Numbers and Characteristics.* Washington, DC: Pew Hispanic Center (June 14, 2005). Available from http://pewhispanic.org/files/reports/46.pdf.

Passel, Jeffrey S., and D'Vera Cohn. *Trends in Unauthorized Immigration: Undocumented Inflow Now Trails Legal Inflow.* Pew Hispanic Center (October 2, 2008). Available from http://pewhispanic.org/files/reports/94.pdf.

Patterson, Troy. "Rock Frock: Double Sided Tape Was This Fly Girl's Best Friend." *Entertainment Weekly*, December 19, 2000 [accessed December 19, 2008]. Available from http://www.ew.com/ew/article/0,,92259,00.html.

Paxman, Andrew, and Felicia Levine. "Summit Spotlights Miami's Biz." *Daily Variety*, February 5, 1997.

Pearce, Garth. "Livin' La Vida Lopez." *Sunday Times (London)*, April 1, 2001.

Pearson, Jennifer, Maggie Harbour, and Roger Hitts. "J.Lo & Ben Blowup! Valentine's Day Wedding Is Off." *Star*, December 31, 2002, 20–21.

Pedraza-Bailey, Silvia. "Cuba's Exile: Portrait of a Refugee Migration." *International Migration Review* 19, no. 1 (Spring 1985): 4–34.

Pérez Firmat, Gustavo. *Life on the Hyphen: The Cuban-American Way.* 1st ed. Austin: University of Texas Press, 1994.

Pérez, Gina M. *The Near Northwest Side Story: Migration, Displacement, and Puerto Rican Families.* Berkeley: University of California Press, 2004.

Pieraccini, Cristina, and Douglass L. Alligood. *Color Television: Fifty Years of African American and Latino Images on Prime-Time Television.* Dubuque, IA: Kendall/Hunt, 2005.

Pitts, Byron. "Tension Building in Miami as U.S. Immigration Decides the Fate of Elián González." *CBS Evening News*, March 29, 2000.

———. "Tensions Grow High in Custody Battle over Elián González." *CBS Evening News*, CBS, anchor Dan Rather, April 4, 2000.

Portes, Alejandro, and Leif Jensen. "The Enclave and the Entrants: Patterns of Ethnic Enterprise in Miami before and after Mariel." *American Sociological Review* 54 (December 1989): 929–949.

Portes, Alejandro, and Alex Stepick. "Unwelcome Immigrants: The Labor Market Experience of 1980 (Mariel) Cuban and Haitian Refugees in South Florida." *American Sociological Review* 50, no. 4 (August 1985): 493–514.

Potter, Mark. *More Cubans Arriving with a 'Dusty' Foot.* MSNBC, October 1, 2007 [accessed April 8, 2008]. Available from http://fieldnotes.msnbc.msn.com/archive/2007/10/01/388519.aspx.

Preston, Julia. "Low-Wage Workers from Mexico Dominate Latest Great Wave of Immigrants." *New York Times*, December 19, 2006.

———. "Making a Life in the U.S., but Feeling Mexico's Tug." *New York Times*, December 19, 2006.

Quintanilla, Michael. "Having Her Say." *Latina*, December, 2004, 119–120.

Rajagopal, Arvind. "Communities Imagined and Unimagined: Contemporary Indian Variations on the Public Sphere." *Discourse* 21, no. 2 (Spring 1999): 47–83.

Rakow, Lana, and Kimberly Kranich. "Women as Sign in Television News." *Journal of Communication* 41, no. 1 (1991): 8–23.

Ramírez Berg, Charles. *Latino Images in Film: Stereotypes, Subversion, Resistance.* Austin: University of Texas Press, 2002.

Rangel, Charles B. "Why Citizenship for Elián Is Wrong." *New York Amsterdam News*, February 3, 2000.

Rather, Dan. "Juan Miguel González Talks About Why He Wants His Son, Elián, Back." *60 Minutes II*, CBS, April 18, 2000.

Redding, Marie. "Too Haute to Handle: Six Designers Give Jennifer Lopez Tips on How to Dress for Oscar-Night Success." *New York Daily News*, March 16, 2000.

Reinstein, Mara. "Jennifer's Pregnant." *Us Weekly*, October 22, 2007, 62–67.

Reynolds, Julia. "Las Dos Fridas: Hollywood's Long, Slow Race to Make the Definitive Frida Kahlo Film." *el Andar* (Summer 2001): 38–41.

Rivero, Yeidy M. *Tuning Out Blackness: Race and Nation in the History of Puerto Rican Television*. Durham, NC: Duke University Press, 2005.

Rodríguez, América. *Making Latino News: Race, Language, Class*. Thousand Oaks, CA: Sage, 1999.

Rodríguez, Carlina. *Remarks before FCC Public Hearing on Media Ownership*. Screen Actors Guild, 2007 [accessed January 28, 2008]. Available from http://www.sag.org/files/documents/CRodriguezFCCTmny043007.pdf.

Rodríguez, Cindy. "'Ugly Betty' Brings a New Reality to TV." *Denver Post*, October 11, 2006.

Rodríguez, Clara E. *Changing Race: Latinos, the Census, and the History of Ethnicity in the United States*. New York: New York University Press, 2000.

———. *Heroes, Lovers, and Others: The Story of Latinos in Hollywood*. Washington, DC: Smithsonian Books, 2004.

Rodríguez, Juana María. *Queer Latinidad: Identity Practices, Discursive Spaces*. New York: New York University Press, 2003.

Rodríguez, René. "Imaginative Directing, Acting Illuminates Frida." *Hispanic Magazine*, October 2002, 38.

———. "Salma: Living Free, Like Frida." *Hispanic Magazine*, October 2002, 32–36.

Rodríguez, Richard T. "Imagine a Brown Queer: Inscribing Sexuality in Chicano/a-Latino/a Literary and Cultural Studies." *American Quarterly* 59, no. 2 (June 2007): 493–501.

———. *Next of Kin: The Family in Chicano/a Cultural Politics*. Durham, NC: Duke University Press, 2009.

Rojas, Viviana. "The Gender of Latinidad: Latinas Speak About Hispanic Television." *Communication Review* 7, no. 2 (April–June 2004): 125–153.

Romero, Mary. "Life as the Maid's Daughter: An Exploratory of the Everyday Boundaries of Race, Class and Gender." In *Challenging Fronteras: Structuring Latina and Latino Lives in the U.S.: An Anthology of Readings*, edited by Mary Romero, Pierrette Hondagneu-Sotelo, and Vilma Ortiz, 195–209. New York: Routledge, 1997.

———. *Maid in the U.S.A.* 10th anniversary ed. New York: Routledge, 2002.

Rosenberg, Carol. "Where Should Rafter Boy Live? S. Florida Split." *Miami Herald*, December 12, 1999.

———. "Tears Flow as Grandmas Meet Reno; They Ask for Elián's Return to Father." *Miami Herald*, January 23, 2000.

———. "Grandmas Find a Few D.C. Supporters." *Miami Herald*, January 26, 2000.

Rosenberg, Carol, and Elaine De Valle. "Boy May Be Sent Back: INS to Discuss Case with Elián's Father in Cuba." *Miami Herald*, December 8, 1999.

Ruiz, Maria. "Border Narratives: HIV/AIDS, and Latina/o Health in the United States: A Cultural Analysis." *Feminist Media Studies* 2, no. 1 (March 2002): 37–62.

Rumbaut, Rubén G. "Origins and Destinies: Immigration to the United States since World War II." *Sociological Forum* 9, no. 4 (December 1994): 583–621.

Ryan, Joal. "Lopez, Affleck: For Real! *E! Online*, November 11, 2002 [accessed December 19, 2008]. Available from http://www.eonline.com/uberblog/b44157_Lopez__Affleck__For_Real_.html.

Ryan, Maureen. "'Ugly Betty': Fall TV's Most Interesting Character." *Chicago Tribune*, September 26, 2006 [accessed January 17, 2009]. Available from http://featuresblogs.chicagotribune.com/entertainment_tv/2006/09/ugly_betty_fall.html.

———. "Silvio Horta on 'Ugly Betty': 'Write What You Know.'" *Chicago Tribune*, November 16, 2006 [accessed January 17, 2009]. Available from http://featuresblogs.chicagotribune.com/entertainment_tv/2006/11/silvio_horta_on.html.

Saldívar, José David. *Border Matters: Remapping American Cultural Studies*. Berkeley: University of California Press, 1997.

Samuels, Jeff, and Marcia Scott Harrison. "Ben & Jen Trying for a Baby!" *Star* Magazine, May 3, 2005 [accessed December 19, 2008]. Available from http://www.starmagazine.com/news/1262.

Sanchis, Eva. "Salma Hayek Defiende Su Pelicula *Frida*." *El Diario La Prensa*, October 25, 2002.

Santa Ana, Otto. *Brown Tide Rising: Metaphors of Latinos in Contemporary American Public Discourse*. 1st ed. Austin: University of Texas Press, 2002.

Santiago, Roberto. "Miami Cubans Lost, Big Time." *New York Daily News*, June 30, 2000.

Sarkar, Saurav. "The False Debate over 'Broken Borders.'" *Extra!* May/June 2006.

Sauceda, Isis. "Salma Le Dio La Bienvenida a 'Frida.'" *La Opinión*, October 16, 2002.

Sawyer, Diane. "Primetime Live J.Lo." *Primetime Live*, ABC, anchor Charles Gibson, November 13, 2002.

Schudson, Michael. *The Sociology of News*. New York: Norton, 2003.

Scott, A. O. "Puttin' Down Mop, Puttin' on the Ritz." *New York Times*, December 13, 2002.

Seghetti, Lisa M., et al. *Border Security and the Southwest Border: Background, Legislation, and Issues*. Congressional Research Service (September 28, 2005). Available from http://assets.opencrs.com/rpts/RL33106_20050928.pdf.

Shales, Tom. "Look Homely, Angel: ABC's 'Ugly Betty' Is Plainly Lovable." *Washington Post*, September 28, 2006.

Shohat, Ella. "Introduction." In *Talking Visions: Multicultural Feminism in Transnational Age*, edited by Ella Shohat, 1–63. Cambridge, MA: MIT Press, 1998.

———, ed. *Talking Visions: Multicultural Feminism in Transnational Age*. Cambridge, MA: MIT Press, 1998.

Shohat, Ella, and Robert Stam. *Unthinking Eurocentrism: Multiculturalism and the Media*. New York: Routledge, 1994.

Shohat, Ella, and Robert Stam, eds. *Multiculturalism, Postcoloniality, and Transnational Media*. New Brunswick, NJ: Rutgers University Press, 2003.

Sinclair, John. *Latin American Television: A Global View*. Oxford: Oxford University Press, 1999.

———. "'The Hollywood of Latin America': Miami as Regional Center in Television Trade." *Television and New Media* 4, no. 3 (August 2003): 211–229.

Smith, Claudia. "Border Enforcement: Deadlier Than Ever and as Ineffective as Always." *Latino Studies* 2, no. 1 (April 2004): 111–114.

Smith, Krista. "An Irresistible Force." *Vanity Fair*, February, 2003, 120–123, 181–183.

Smith, Russell Scott. "J. Lo—CEO." *Us Weekly*, June 10, 2002, 58–62.

Sobchack, Vivian. "Postmodern Modes of Ethnicity." In *Unspeakable Images: Ethnicity in the American Cinema*, edited by Lester D. Friedman, 329–352. Urbana: University of Illinois Press, 1991.

Soong, Roland. "The Phenomenon of Yo Soy Betty La Fea." *Zona Latina*, July 1, 2001 [accessed February 4, 2009]. Available from http://www.zonalatina.com/Zldata185.htm.

Spelman, Elizabeth V. "Woman as Body: Ancient and Contemporary Views." In *Feminist Theory and the Body: A Reader*, edited by Janet Price and Margrit Shildrick, 32–41. Edinburgh: Edinburgh University Press, 1999.

Spines, Christine. "One from the Heart." *Premiere*, September, 2002, 37–43, 85.

Spivak, Gayatri Chakravorty. *In Other Worlds: Essays in Cultural Politics*. New York: Methuen, 1987.

Stepick, Alex, et al. *This Land Is Our Land: Immigrants and Power in Miami*. Berkeley: University of California Press, 2003.

Stepick, Alex, and Carol Dutton Stepick. "Power and Identity: Miami Cubans." In *Latinos: Remaking America*, edited by Marcelo M. Suárez-Orozco and Mariela Páez, 75–92. Berkeley: University of California Press, 2002.

Sternbergh, Adam. "The Year in Ideas; Flirtation by Full-Page Ad." *New York Times*, December 15, 2002.

Stockwell, Anne. "The Velocity of Salma." *The Advocate*, December 10, 2002, 44–48, 50–53.

Storm, Jonathan. "Betting on Betty." *Philadelphia Inquirer*, September 28, 2006.

Stroup, Kate. "When Will He Marry Her?" *Us Weekly*, February 2, 2004, 42–45.

Tapia, Ruby C. "Un(di)ing Legacies: White Matters of Memory in Portraits of 'Our Princess.'" *Cultural Values* 5, no. 2 (April 2001): 261–287.

Tauber, Michelle, et al. "J. Lo Goes It Alone." *People*, June 24, 2002.

———. "Destiny's Darling." *People*, August 12, 2002, 75–76.

Thorburn, David. "Television as an Aesthetic Media." In *Media, Myths and Narratives: Television and the Press*, edited by James Carey, 48–66. Newbury Park, CA: Sage, 1988.

Toledo, Charo. "Alphabet Spells Hope for Diverse America." *Daily Variety*, July 27, 2007.

Tomlinson, John. "Globalisation and National Identity." In *Contemporary World Television*, edited by John Sinclair and Graeme Turner, 24–27. London: BFI, 2004.

Torres, María de los Angeles. *In the Land of Mirrors: Cuban Exile Politics in the United States*. Ann Arbor: University of Michigan Press, 1999.

———. *The Lost Apple: Operation Pedro Pan, Cuban Children in the U.S., and the Promise of a Better Future*. Boston: Beacon Press, 2003.

Torres, Rodolfo D., Luis F. Mirón, and Jonathan Xavier Inda. *Race, Identity, and Citizenship: A Reader*. Malden, MA: Blackwell, 1999.

Torres-Saillant, Silvio. "Inventing the Race: Latinos and the Ethnoracial Pentagon." *Latino Studies* 1, no. 1 (March 2003): 123–151.

Tracy, Kathleen. *Jennifer Lopez*. Toronto: ECW Press, 2000.

Triggs, Charlotte. "J. Lo's Triathlon after Twins!" *People*, September 8, 2008, 162.

Tuchman, Gaye. *Making News: A Study in the Construction of Reality*. New York: Free Press, 1978.

Tully, Judd. "The Kahlo Cult." *ARTnews* 93, no. 4 (April 1994): 126–133.

Tuñón Pablos, Julia. *Women in Mexico: A Past Unveiled*. Austin: University of Texas, 1999.

Valdés, M. Isabel. *Marketing to American Latinos: A Guide to the in-Culture Approach, Part II*. Ithaca, NY: Paramount Market Publishing, 2002.

Valdés Ryan, Mimi. "The Jessica Alba Controversy." *Latina*, February 28, 2008 [accessed February 15, 2009]. Available from http://www.latina.com/entertainment/jessica-alba-controversy?page=1.

———. "Jessica Alba: 'I Want My Baby to Be Brown.'" *Latina*, March, 2008.

Valdivia, Angharad. "Rosie Goes to Hollywood: The Politics of Representation." *Review of Education, Pedagogy, and Cultural Studies* 18, no. 2 (1996): 129–141.

———. *A Latina in the Land of Hollywood and Other Essays on Media Culture.* Tucson: University of Arizona Press, 2000.

———. "Community Building through Dance and Music: Salsa in the Midwest." In *Double Crossings: Entrecruzamientos*, edited by Mario Martín Flores and Carlos von Son, 153–176. Fair Haven, NJ: Ediciones Nuevo Espacio, 2001.

———. "Latinas as Radical Hybrid: Transnationally Gendered Traces in Mainstream Media." *Global Media Journal* 3, no. 4 (Spring 2004) [accessed August 24, 2007]. Available from http://lass.calumet.purdue.edu/cca/gmj/sp04/gmj-sp04-valdivia.htm

———. "Is Penélope to J.Lo as Culture Is to Nature? Eurocentric Approaches to 'Latin' Beauties." In *From Bananas to Buttocks: The Latina Body in Popular Film and Culture*, edited by Myra Mendible, 129–148. Austin: University of Texas Press, 2007.

———. *Latina/o Communication Studies Today.* New York: Peter Lang, 2008.

Vargas, Lucila. "Genderizing Latino News: An Analysis of a Local Newspaper's Coverage of Latino Current Affairs." *Critical Studies in Media Communication* 17, no. 3 (September 2000): 261–293.

Vargas, Zaragosa. "Rank and File: Historical Perspectives on Latino/a Workers in the U.S." In *The Latino Studies Reader: Culture, Economy, and Society*, edited by Antonia Darder and Rodolfo D. Torres, 243–256. Malden, MA: Blackwell, 1998.

Volk, Steven. "Frida Kahlo Remaps the Nation." *Social Identities* 6, no. 2 (2000): 165–188.

Wagener, Leon, Bob Smith, and J. D. Robinson. "J.Lo Reads Ben His Rights: Pre-Nup Lays Down the Law on Sex, Cash—Even Cheating." *Star*, December 10, 2002, 16–17.

Waldman, Allison J. "Hispanic Interests Move to Mainstream." *TelevisionWeek*, November 26, 2007, 15–18.

Warner, Michael. "Introduction." In *Fear of a Queer Planet: Queer Politics and Social Theory*, edited by Michael Warner, vii–xxxi. Minneapolis: University of Minnesota Press, 1994.

Weaver, Jay. "Rafter's Case Pits Family Emotion vs. Custody Law." *Miami Herald*, November 8, 1999.

Whitten, Norman E., and Arlene Torres. *Blackness in Latin America and the Caribbean: Social Dynamics and Cultural Transformations.* Bloomington: Indiana University Press, 1998.

Wickham, DeWayne. "Elian's 'Surrogate Mother' Should Get a Grip." *USA Today*, May 10, 2000 [accessed December 18, 2008]. Available from http://www.usatoday.com/news/opinion/columnists/wickham/wick091.htm.

Williams, Pete. "Battle over Elián González Heats Up." *NBC Nightly News*, anchor Tom Brokaw, March 27, 2000.

Wiltz, Teresa. "Booty Boon: Jennifer Lopez's Backside Makes an Impression on the Nation's Cultural Landscape." *Chicago Tribune*, October 15, 1998.

Wong, Sau-ling C. "Diverted Mothering: Representations of Caregivers of Color in the Age of 'Multiculturalism.'" In *Mothering: Ideology, Experience, and Agency*, edited by

Evelyn Nakano Glenn, Grace Chang, and Linda Rennie Forcey, 67–91. New York: Routledge, 1994.

Yanez, Luisa. "'She Loves Elian Very Much': A Woman Is Thrown into Spotlight for Her Devotion to a Cuban Cousin Who Floated in on an Inner Tube." *Sun Sentinel, Fort Lauderdale*, March 13, 2000.

You, Brenda, et al. "Ben Forces J.Lo Makeover: She's Fixin' Vixen Image." *Star*, July 1, 2003, 30–31.

Zacharias, Usha. "Trial by Fire: Gender, Power, and Citizenship in Narratives of the Nation." *Social Text* 19, no. 4 (Winter 2001): 29–51.

Zelizer, Barbie. "Achieving Journalistic Authority through Narrative." *Critical Studies in Mass Communication* 7, no. 1 (1990): 366–376.

———. *Taking Journalism Seriously: News and the Academy*. Thousand Oaks, CA: Sage, 2004.

Zimmerman, Kevin. "Latin American Filmed Entertainment Market." *The Hollywood Reporter*, February 21, 2005 [accessed August 20, 2007]. Available from http://www.hollywoodreporter.com/hr/search/article_display.jsp?vnu_content_id=1000809514.

Index

audience/audiences (*continued*)
    blog discussions on, 10, 19, 52–53, 65,
        78–81, 81–83, 84–86, 176
    discussion of *Ugly Betty*, 131–133,
        140–142
    generational differences in viewing
        habits, 124–125
    identity formation and, 15–16, 21
    IMDb discussions on depictions
        of domestic labor in *Maid in
        Manhattan,* 151–152, 168–171
    IMDb discussions on *Frida*, 106–107,
        109–111, 114–115, 202n5
    IMDb discussions on politics of
        language in *Spanglish,* 151–152,
        161–162
    letters to the editor in González case,
        17, 32, 37
    methodology, 16–17
    Mexican identity and, 87–88, 114–115
    online discussion boards on Lopez,
        78–81, 81–83
    sublimation of difference and, 122
    symbolic ruptures and, 9–10, 20
    tabloid news audiences, 55–57
    See also blogs; online discussion boards;
        Web site coverage; *individual case
        studies*
authenticity
    of actors as characters, 131
    commodification of identity and, 115–117
    emotional authenticity, 19, 130–134
    global markets and, 115–117, 121
    Hayek and, 87, 95–97, 107–108, 113,
        114–115, 204n27, 205n57, 205n58
    linguistic signifiers and, 16–17, 96, 113,
        206n71
    lo indigena, 114–115
    Mexican identity and, 87–88
    myth of authenticity, 87–88
    strategic essentialism and, 87
    symbolic colonization and, 88
    use of Spanglish/Spanish slang, 113,
        206n71
    See also signifying practices; *individual
        case studies*

Báez, Jillian M., 57, 83
Banderas, Antonio, 112, 113
Barrera, Magdalena, 61
Beltrán, Mary, 52, 57–58, 61, 198n57
Benavides, O. Hugo, 122
Berry, Halle, 84
Bhabha, Homi, 153–154
Biel, Jessica, 86
Bird, Elizabeth, 52, 53–54, 56
blackness
    brownness and, 5–6
    Combs and, 63–65
    ethnoracial identity and, 4–6, 10–11,
        13–14, 66, 73–74, 176–177
    Lopez and, 15, 18, 59, 62–65
    music videos and, 15, 63–64
    whiteness *vs.*, 5–6, 13–14, 15, 176
    See also brownness; racialization;
        individual case studies
blanqueamiento, 5
Blogcritics Magazine (Web site), 52–53,
    78–81, 81–83
blogs
    on Affleck, 79
    on Alba, 175, 215n1
    audience sense-making and, 4, 9–10, 21,
        65, 78, 122
    Blogcritics Magazine, 52–53, 78–81, 81–83
    on Cuban immigration, 179–180
    on Elián González case, 10, 44, 46
    on Lopez, 10, 19, 52–53, 65, 78–81,
        81–83, 84–86, 176
    on Marisleysis González, 10, 44
    symbolic ruptures and, 20
    tabloid journalism and, 17, 18, 20,
        78–81, 81–83, 84–86, 176
    on *Ugly Betty,* 19, 21, 131–134, 148
Border Protection, Antiterrorism, and
    Illegal Immigration Control Act of 2005,
    (H.R. 4437), 156–157, 191n38
border theories, 155–158
Bordertown (2006), 61
Bordo, Susan, 11–12
Bracero Program (1942-1964), 27
Bratich, Jack Z., Jeremy Packer, and
    Cameron McCarthy, 11

broadcast news
  use of term, 188n1
  Elián González case and, 17–18, 23–26,
    33–34, 35, 42–46
  on immigration, 157
  on Lopez, 59, 196n15
Brotons, Elisabet, 10, 25–26, 29–32, 33–34,
  34–37, 38–39, 48, 190n30
brownness
  blackness and, 5–6
  commodification of identity and, 5–6
  linguistic signifiers of, 94
  racial formations and, 4–6, 47–48
  signifying practices of, 94–95
  whiteness and, 5–6
  See also blackness; racial flexibility;
    racialization; individual case studies
Brownout Report (2006), 106, 156–157

Cardenas, José, 47
celebrity tabloid discourse, 51, 52–53,
  84–86, 179
Central American Free Trade Agreement
  (CAFTA), 154
Chicano/a identity
  use of term, 184n6
  Kahlo and, 90–91
  Latino/a terminology and, 187n61
cinematic discourse, 91–92, 153–154,
  159–161
class
  Balseros and, 27–28, 33, 192n49
  Bracero program, 27
  class mobility, 165
  Mariel boatlift and, 27–28, 192n49
  meritocracy and, 31, 79, 120, 142, 166,
    170
  signifying practices of, 46, 56, 66, 75,
    82, 84–85, 115, 136–137, 138, 140,
    144–146, 166
  whiteness and, 85
  See also Hayek, Salma; Lopez, Jennifer;
    Maid in Manhattan; Spanglish
Clinton-Castro agreement (1994), 29
Cold War, the, 26–28, 34, 37, 47–48
commodification of identity

advertising revenues and, 1, 3, 5–6, 19,
  60, 125
authenticity and, 115–117
brownness and, 5–6
ethnoracial identity and, 6–7, 15, 16–17
genderization and, 5–6, 11, 19
global markets and, 2–3, 6–7, 7–9, 19,
  87–88, 111
identity formation and, 6–7, 115–116
Lopez and, 57–58, 60–62, 85–86
panethnic identity and, 5–6
signifiers of Latinidad and, 5–7, 57–58,
  60, 87–88, 115–117
Cosby Show (television show), 8, 138–139,
  150
critical reviews
  on Frida, 90, 105, 111–113
  on Ugly Betty, 122, 127–128, 130, 146
Cruz, Penélope, 11, 13, 95, 187n61
Cuba/Cubans
  Balsero exile, 192n49
  blogs on Cuban immigration, 179–180
  Cuban exceptionalism, 26–28, 34, 37,
    47–48
  Cubanidad, 18
  Cuban identity formation, 34, 36–39, 54,
    179–180
  Cuban immigration vs. Mexican
    immigration, 27
  El Nuevo Herald and, 18, 25, 26, 30, 40,
    88, 107, 188n1
  ethnoracial identity and, 4–5, 17–18, 25
  Mariel boatlift (1980), 27–28, 192n49
  media representations of, 28, 189n15
  racial transformation of, 4–5
  symbolic colonization and, 179–180
  symbolic status of women, 24–25
  victimization discourse of exile
    community (U.S.), 33
  whiteness and, 4–5, 17–18, 25
  See also Elián González case study;
    immigration, Cuban
Cuban Adjustment Act (1995), 29

Damon, Matt, 73
Dávila, Arlene M., 3, 5, 9, 93

Dawson, Rosario, 13, 59, 176, 180
Day Without a Mexican (2004), 173–174
De La Garza, Alana, 212n3
del Rio, Dolores, 159–160, 161
DeSipio, Louis and James Henson, 28, 189n15
Desperado (1995), 92, 93
Diawara, Manthia, 198n57
Diaz, Cameron, 4, 11, 51
Diego Rivera Foundation, 206n66
docile bodies, 11, 12–13, 15, 18, 32–33, 85, 158, 179. *See also* symbolic colonization
domestic Latina labor
  use of term, 214n38
  anti-immigration discourse and, 152, 163–165, 171–172
  class and, 165
  globalization and, 155–156, 163–164
  global trade agreements and, 154
  linguistic signifiers of, 94
  maternalization of, 163, 172–174
  nation-building and, 12–13
  racialization and, 163–165
  romantic cinematic discourse and, 20, 158–162, 163–165, 171–172
  whiteness and, 162, 173, 174
  See also *Maid in Manhattan*; *Spanglish*
Dusk Til Dawn (1996), 92
Dyer, Richard, 51, 85

Ebert, Roger, 168
El Cantante (2006), 61
Elián González case study
  overview of, 17–18, 24–25, 44
  African American news media on, 18, 36–37
  Arrelano case *vs.*, 31–32
  blogs on, 46
  broadcast news on, 17–18, 23–26, 33–34, 35, 42–46
  citizenship and, 18, 34, 36–37, 179–180
  class and, 46
  Cuban American National Foundation and, 47
  Cuban identity formation and, 34, 36–39, 54, 179–180

  Cuban women and, 37–39
  Elisabet Brotons and, 10, 25–26, 29–32, 33–34, 34–37, 38–39, 48, 190n30
  emotionality and, 25, 42–46
  ethnic media and, 25, 30, 36
  ethnoracial identity and, 17–18, 31–32, 34, 36–37, 180–181
  exceptionalist discourses and, 17–18, 26–28, 32–34, 37, 45, 54, 180
  exile privilege and, 27–28, 39–40
  femininity and, 25–26, 31, 42–46, 48–49
  genderization and, 41, 46
  Hagel on, 38
  immigration and, 34, 36–37, 179–180, 180–181
  irrationality and, 4–5, 25, 46
  letters to the editor, 17, 32, 37
  March of the Mothers, 39
  marginalized immigrants status and, 18
  Marisleysis González and, 4–5, 10, 14, 42–46, 46–49
  masculinity and fatherhood, 39–40
  motherhood/maternalization and, 29–32, 33
  mural depiction of, 33–34, 35
  national identity and, 33–34, 36–37, 42–46, 180–181
  news columns/editorials on, 25, 37, 40
  news coverage of, 17–18, 23–26, 42–46, 48–49
  paternal rights and, 39–41
  racialized brownness and, 47, 179–180
  religious imagery in, 33–34
  Reno on, 39–40, 41, 45
  self-sacrificing discourse and, 29–32, 33
  sexualization and, 44, 46
  symbolic colonization and, 17–18, 47–48, 178
  symbolic ruptures, 10, 180
  Virgin Mary appearance, 192n47
  white ethnic privilege and, 18, 36–37
  whiteness and, 4–5, 17–18, 34, 37, 46, 47–48
  womanhood and, 37–39
  women and immigration news coverage, 29–32, 32–34, 34–37

elite news
    use of term, 195n12
    mainstream news *vs.* tabloid journalism,
        53–54
    media discourse and, 13–14
El Norte (1983), 168
El Nuevo Herald (newspaper), 18, 25, 26, 30,
    40, 88, 107–108, 188n1
entertainment news
    Maid in Manhattan and, 161, 168
    on *Spanglish,* 168
    on *Ugly Betty,* 19, 127–129, 131, 133
    See also tabloid journalism
ethnicity
    authenticity and, 87–88, 109, 116–117
    commodification of, 57, 61, 87–88, 89, 146
    ethnic *vs.* racial signifiers of Latinidad,
        4–7, 11
    gendering of, 10–14
    Hollywood cinematic discourse and, 153
    panethnicity as global product, 19
    signifiers of Latinidad, 4
    See also authenticity; commodification
        of identity; racialization
ethnic news
    use of term, 188n1
    Elián González case coverage, 25, 30, 36
    on *Frida,* 88–89, 106–108
    symbolic colonization and, 18
ethnoracial identity
    use of term, 4–7
    blackness and, 4–6, 10–11, 13–14, 66,
        73–74, 176–177
    brownness and, 4–7
    citizenship and, 15
    commodification of, 6–7, 15, 16–17
    deracialized liberalism, 121
    docile bodies and, 11, 12–13, 15, 179
    femininity and, 10–14
    hybridity and, 15–17, 109, 110, 111,
        114, 180
    hypersexuality and, 65
    identity formation and, 180–181
    immigration and, 34, 36–37
    impact of political status on media
        representation, 28, 189n15

Latina *vs.* Latin, 95–96
    Latinidad and, 9
    liberalism and, 120
    masculinity and, 7
    meritocracy and, 79, 120
    miscegenation and, 4
    nation-building and, 15
    racial formation and, 4–7, 140, 149–150
    racialization and, 4–7
    sexuality and, 13–14
    symbolic colonization and, 8–9
    symbolic ruptures and, 8–9, 109–111,
        180
    whiteness and, 4–6, 10–11, 13–14, 15,
        18, 81–82.
    See also racial formations; racialization
Euro-Spanish identity
    use of term, 184n6
exceptionalist discourses, 17–18, 26–28,
    32–34, 37, 45, 54, 180

Fast Food Nation (2006), 173–174
femininity
    ethnoracial ambiguity and, 7
    gendering/genderization and, 10
    motherhood and, 10, 28, 73, 100, 134, 146
    racialization and, 135–136
    sexuality and, 63, 71, 161
    signifying practices of, 12–14, 42–46,
        79–80, 142, 144
feminization
    global trade agreements and, 154
    Latina labor and, 20
    Latinidad and, 10
    symbolic colonization and, 10–14
    transnational migration and, 20, 29,
        155, 172
Ferrera, America
    emotional authenticity of, 19, 130–134
    ethnic self-identification, 127
    ethnoracial ambiguity of, 14
    Golden Globe acceptance speech, 132–
        133, 210n49
    Real Women Have Curves (2002), 132
    resistance to identification as Latina, 60
    See also *Ugly Betty*

Hayek, Salma (*continued*)
    resistance to identification as Latina, 60
    self-identification, 60, 95–97
    Spanish-language speaking ability and,
        93, 204n27, 205n58
    strategic essentialism and, 87–88
    Ugly Betty and, 95
    whiteness and, 93
    Wild Wild West, 93
    See also *Frida*
Hayes Code, 159
Hayworth, Rita, 180
Heroes (television show), 176
Herrera, Hayden, 89–90, 89–91, 99–100,
    203n8, 203n17
Hispanic
    use of term, 183n1, 187n61
Hondagneu-Sotelo, Pierrette, 163–164, 172
Honduras/Hondurans, 14, 36, 119, 127,
    130, 133
hooks, bell, 198n57
Horta, Arianna, 29–30
Horta, Silvio
    as producer of *Ugly Betty*, 119, 122, 125,
        126, 127, 149
    queer sensibility and, 122, 143, 144, 147
H.R. 4437 (Border Protection,
    Antiterrorism, and Illegal Immigration
    Control Act of 2005), 156–157, 191n38
Huerta, César and Omar Cabrera, 113,
    206n71
hybridity
    audience reception and, 109–111, 114,
        122, 180
    border theories and, 155–158
    ethnoracial identity and, 109, 110, 111,
        114, 180
    immigration and, 155
    as liminality, 109–111, 114
    panethnic identity *vs.*, 180
    racial ambiguity and, 14, 109, 110, 111,
        114
    racial fixity *vs.*, 15, 70, 80, 85, 114
    symbolic colonization and, 109–111, 114
    symbolic ruptures and, 14–17
    See also *individual case studies*

hypervisibilty, 7, 19, 77, 83, 109, 110, 111,
    114, 171, 180

identity formation
    audience reception and, 15–16, 21
    commodification of identity, 6–7, 115–116
    Cuba/Cubans, 34, 36–39, 54, 179–180
    ethnoracial identity and, 57–58, 115–
        117, 180–181
    interlatino relationships and, 3–4
    Latinidad and, 15–16, 21
    oppositional identity formation, 3, 15–16
    racial flexibility and, 180–181
    symbolic ruptures and, 15–16
    See also racial formations; *individual*
        case studies
imagined nation, 12–13, 14, 18, 45–48, 55,
    83, 95, 174, 179–180
immigration
    Border Protection, Antiterrorism, and
        Illegal Immigration Control Act,
        191n38
    border theories and, 155–158
    Brownout Report, 156–157
    child refugees and, 36
    coverage of undocumented immigrants,
        155–158
    Cuban exceptionalism and, 17–18,
        26–28, 32–34, 37, 45, 54, 180
    domestic labor and, 152
    globalization and, 26–28, 85, 112, 137,
        155–156, 155–158, 163–164, 177
    global trade agreements and, 154
    hate-crime violence and, 177–178
    Immigration and Nationality Act
        amendments (1965), 31–32, 189n19
    news coverage of, 156–157
    perceived racial identity and, 36
    racialization and, 4–5, 34, 36–37
    romantic cinematic discourse and, 20,
        158–162, 163–165, 171–172
    symbolic ruptures and, 155–158
    violence against women and, 157–158
    violence against women migrants,
        157–158
    women and, 158

Judd and, 65, 66–67, 68, 71–72
as Latina, 57–58, 60
in *Maid in Manhattan,* 165, 170–171
marketability of, 18, 58
meritocracy and, 79, 120
motherhood and, 85, 86
music career, 59, 62–63
Noa and, 71
Oprah interview, 67–68
in *Out of Sight,* 58, 59, 60–61, 64–65
popularity of, 197n36
Puerto Rican/Nuyorican authenticity
    and, 18, 58, 59, 62
racial ambiguity and, 15, 18
racial binaries and, 80
racial fixity and, 15, 70, 80, 85
racial flexibility and, 21, 53, 58–59
resentment discourse and, 79–80, 82–83
in *Selena,* 57–58, 130
self-identification with roles, 165
sex tape scandal, 199n64
sexual identity and, 18, 62–63
sexuality and, 65, 66–73
sexuality/sexualization/sexual identity
    of, 13–14, 62–63, 67, 69, 71–73
in *Shall We Dance?,* 59, 61, 197n35
Spanish-speaking ability and, 58, 61
surveillance and, 66, 70–71, 85, 179
symbolic colonization and, 18, 75, 84
symbolic ruptures and, 10, 61–62, 180
Versace dress, 62–63
in *Wedding Planner,* 15, 58, 59, 64–65
white gaze and, 65–66, 70
whiteness and, 15, 53, 58–59, 64, 73–74,
    80, 84–85, 179
López, Josefina, 97
Lowe, Lisa and David Lloyd, 187n57
Lugo, Alejandro, 155
Lugones, María, 6, 16

Madonna, 91, 97, 108, 114, 205n57
Maid in Manhattan (2002)
    case study overview, 20, 151–152
    plot overview, 165, 166, 169
    American dream discourse and,
        170–171
    anti-immigration discourse and, 20,
        158–162
    assimilation and, 165–166
    audience reception of, 20, 151–152,
        168–171
    class and, 165, 166, 170, 171–172, 181
    domestic labor and, 20
    economic discourses and, 20
    entertainment news and, 161, 168
    ethnic ambiguity in, 165–166
    femininity and, 20
    genderization of, 20
    IMDb discussions, 151–152, 168–171
    liberalism and, 170
    linguistic signifiers in, 165
    maternalization and, 172–173
    meritocracy discourse and, 170–171
    motherhood and, 166
    racialization in, 171–172
    romantic cinematic discourse and, 20,
        158–162, 163–165, 171–172
    Spanglish vs., 166
    symbolic colonization and, 178
    symbolic ruptures and, 155, 171–174,
        180
    transnational migration and, 20
    whiteness and, 172–173
mainstream media
    use of term, 1–3, 188n1
    alternative media *vs.,* 186n31
    celebrity tabloid discourse, 51, 52–53,
        84–86, 179
    Latina/o visibility and, 23–24, 105–106,
        178–181
    news media, 196n15
    strategic essentialism and, 87
    white gaze, the, 65–66, 70
    See also elite news; entertainment
        news; ethnic news; tabloid
        journalism
Making Latino News (Rodríguez), 98,
    205n56
Maldonado Miracle (2003), 95
malinchismo, 112
Mariel boatlift, 27–28, 192n49. *See also*
    Elián González case study

About the Author

ISABEL MOLINA-GUZMÁN is a cultural critic, educator, and former journalist. She currently teaches and conducts research on Latina/o media and culture at the University of Illinois at Urbana-Champaign.